Also by Nat Hentoff

A POLITICAL LIFE

A Political Life

The Education of John V. Lindsay

Nat Hentoff

Alfred A. Knopf, New York 1969

THIS IS A BORZOI BOOK
PUBLISHED BY ALFRED A. KNOPF, INC.

First Edition
Copyright © 1967, 1969 by Namar Productions, Ltd.
All rights reserved under International and Pan-American
Copyright Conventions. Published in the United States
by Alfred A. Knopf, Inc., New York, and simultaneously
in Canada by Random House of Canada Limited, Toronto.
Distributed by Random House, Inc., New York.
Library of Congress Catalog Card Number: 78–88743

Sections of this book, in somewhat different and briefer
form, first appeared in *The New Yorker* as "The Mayor,"
"Your City as Much as Mine," and "The Worst Alternative Is Doing
Nothing." I am grateful to *The New Yorker* for
permission to use the material here and to William Shawn
for his confidence and encouragement.

Manufactured in the United States of America

for Maurice Sendak

"Be it life or death, we crave only reality. If we are really dying, let us hear the rattle in our throats and feel cold in the extremities; if we are alive, let us go about our business."

THOREAU

Contents

A POLITICAL
LIFE

Prologue

We had seen them many times before, my father and I, but whenever a rally was called by the tribunes of the people, we were there. Our tribunes were Democrats. Our allegiance to the party was as natural and unchanging as our Sundays with The Shadow, Jack Benny, and Eddie Cantor. In the 1930's, if you were a Jew in Roxbury, you were a Democrat. From kids in knickers like me to the ancient, bearded men in Segal's Cafeteria, sipping steaming tea through lumps of sugar clenched in their teeth, we belonged in and to the Democratic Party.

Nationally, the reason was cast in bronze, a figure on top of the radio in my family's living room—the President, standing straight, no sign of leg braces, holding on to a ship's wheel almost as big as he. At the center of the wheel was a clock; below it: ROOSEVELT AT THE WHEEL OF A NEW DEAL. We had won the ikon at a carnival stand in Revere Beach. The clock soon stopped working, but Roosevelt remained on top of the radio until he died, and for some time after. A graven image, yes, but it wasn't that we worshipped him. It was simply right that he be there, like the photographs of my grandparents, and the picture of my mother and father on the day of their marriage. Roosevelt was our President, and always would be. The President of the Jews and, we acknowledged tangentially, of the Irish and the Italians and the Poles and those colored people who seemed to name so many of their children after him.

We certainly knew he was not the President of those infinitely remote patricians, the Yankees, on the other side of the city. Those white Anglo-Saxon Protestants to whom we and the Irish and the Italians and the Poles and the colored were of such low caste as to barely exist at all in their consciousness. We Jews, of course, had our own codes of caste, placing ourselves far above all the other non-Yankees; but the one quasi-egalitarian satisfaction we shared with those others who, like ourselves, would never ever be invited inside a home in Louisburg Square was our delight that the damn Yankees hated *our* President. To be sure, he was a patrician too; but he had become a traitor to his class and so he was an honorary Jew as, we supposed, he was also an honorary Irishman, Italian, Pole, and Negro.

In Boston we were in our ghetto, but through Roosevelt and the Democratic Party, we felt ourselves part of the country. Most of us. I exaggerated when I said all Jews in Roxbury were Democrats. There were Communists and some Trotskyites. They kept trying to tell us that ours was a politics of illusion, that our enemy was everyone in power and beyond them, capitalism. But to the majority of us, these diligently self-encapsulated sectarians were willful, stubborn exiles, quirkily refusing to be part of that warm, contentious family that was the Democratic Party. And every four years, Ward 12, Roxbury, and the adjoining Jewish Ward 14, Dorchester, reaffirmed our place in the family by casting overwhelming votes for Roosevelt.

For us, election night was the politics of joy. Call it illusion, but it was always a marvelous celebration. And that was why, like my friends, I was *political* from elementary school on. Politics was pleasure. Politics was beating the Republicans time after time. Politics was beating those aloof bastards who would be appalled at the prospect of their daughters marrying one of us. (How does one meet those daughters?, we occasionally speculated, and some of us later found out.)

In state and city and ward elections, we were Democrats not only because the party's candidates were family, but also because our contenders were so much more lively than the pale Republicans. The civil wars in the state and local Democratic Party were savage, the rhetoric slashing, the feuds vicious. But it was a hell of a show. We knew that a sizable percentage of our party's candidates were thieves and liars, but they performed at the rallies in our neighborhood with such gusto, such delight in battle that politics was often better entertainment than the movies. And when James Michael Curley came, it was like watching Koussevitzky conduct or Lefty Grove pitch or Clark Gable make love. James Michael Curley would slowly, surely ascend the platform, ignore sullen enemies who had been trying to ambush him for years, and turn his shrewdly benign countenance upon us. As often as we'd heard him, we would become silent in expectation, suddenly starving for the rolling, resonant oratory which would remind us, who did not need to be reminded, that the snapping, snarling intra-party bickering was only the natural life style of free Democrats who, when the time came, and it was almost upon us, would unite against the bankers, the desiccated aristocrats, the Beacon Hill and State Street Protestants who had not yet fully learned that all doors must now be opened for the newer Americans, the more virile Americans whose time had come to take power and spread it widely.

There was a story, perhaps apocryphal, but so many swore they were there that we all believed it had happened. It was a night in Ward 14 at the G & G Delicatessen, the Jewish Agora, where all Democratic politicians, from Roosevelt down, traditionally came to show themselves to their people, to acknowledge Jewish Power. On that night, so it was said, James Michael Curley, then mayor of Boston, standing on a platform outside the G & G, looked at the thousands of people filling the sidewalk, Blue Hill Avenue, the side streets, and raised his hand. There had been reports, as there had always been reports, of graft in the city administration; and the Republicans were once more sounding alarms, calling the citizenry to bring back decent, ethical government. "Yes," James Michael Curley's organ tones filled the air. (For those in Beacon Hill, we said, it must sound like the start of a thunderstorm.) "Yes, some of us are *gonifs,* but look at how much we give back to the people!" There was laughter (we knew he knew we knew there were thieves in City Hall), and applause at the candor (in Yiddish besides), and affection for the style of the man. "Better a *gonif* who's a *mensch,*" I heard an old man behind me, "than a dried-up anti-Semite who gives all the money to the banks."

The Yankees hated Curley, and he returned their hatred exultantly. "The State Street wrecking crew," he would call the Wasp bankers who were invariably—but not always implacably—resistant to his plans for the betterment, as he put it, of the city. They were not always implacable because he had the counter-power of politics and would and did use whatever pressures he could master without hesitation, without mercy.

I realize, these long years after, that Curley never did "better" the city—except by the drama of his resilient presence. Even then, we were somewhat wary of his good works. Did the contractors use the materials they were supposed to or did their high political operating expenses lead them to economize on the job? After all, who cared? That is, who checked? James Michael Curley built a tunnel under water and we used it every Sunday on our family drives. And every Sunday, my father or I would say, as we moved into the tunnel, "What do you suppose the odds are today that we'll make it?" And laughed.

We enjoyed Curley. He was not precisely Spencer Tracy in *The Last Hurrah,* but he did indeed exemplify that now vanished way of politics. And well vanished it is. For while Curley—and such far less amusing political bosses as Hague in Jersey City and Kelley in Chicago—were reigning over their coalition of ethnic tribes, the cities were rotting. The legacy of the old way is our disastrous school systems, lumpish mass transit, decaying housing. And the black resistance.

By the time I was in college in the early 1940's, I had become decidedly ambivalent about my boyhood political enthusiasms. The bronze Roosevelt clock was a curio of innocence—mine and the country's. "War saved the New Deal," a fallen Communist turned Socialist said to me of Roosevelt. James Michael Curley had gotten much older and was more often cranky than picaresque. "That crippled son-of-a-bitch," he said of Roosevelt during an intra-party skirmish. In the postwar years, I was chronically skeptical of politicians, even one so beguiling as John F. Kennedy. He was my congressman, and a poor one. My last political act as a citizen of Massachusetts was to vote against him when he ran for the Senate. I was no partisan of Henry Cabot Lodge—a dumb Yankee—but I saw no reason to promote a man just because he was wittier and much richer than his opponent.

In 1953, I moved to New York. And with Democrats as my mayors, I watched this city rot. Politics had long since ceased being pleasure—in the city or in the nation. There were stirrings of the old sense of communal possibility, of belonging, during the Presidential campaigns of Adlai Stevenson—less the second time than the first— but then, not too surprisingly, he ended his career as a liar for his country at the United Nations.

In 1960, I had voted for John Kennedy, but it was essentially a vote against Richard Nixon. During the next three years, I could not help but recognize the effect Kennedy's style had on the young, but I was not persuaded. I don't mean only the Bay of Pigs. I mean especially the later confrontation with Khrushchev over Cuba that might have incinerated us all. And the lateness of Kennedy in beginning to understand the civil-rights movement. And the insensitivity—there's a euphemism—of the Kennedy Administra-

tion to civil liberties. And Vietnam. And the continued disintegration of the cities. A man of grace and spirit, John
Kennedy, but not my man.

There had been no diminution in my interest in politics
during these years, but wholly unlike when I was a youth in
Boston, I was now an outsider. The men in politics to whom
I was most drawn were the mavericks—Wayne Morse, for
example, in the Senate, and, starting in 1959, John Lindsay,
a freshman congressman from my district in New York,
the Seventeenth. He first intrigued me because he was so
stubbornly concerned with civil liberties—a rarity among
politicians, a rarity among us all. He also had no political
machine, and he seemed extraordinarily hung up on ethics.
That he was a Republican put me off somewhat, because I
still had a vestigial pact with my father and James Michael
Curley that no Republican could be trusted to give a damn
for anything but the "State Street wrecking crew" and their
allies in the Wasp centers of economic power throughout
the country. And Lindsay was a Wasp. I have known few of
that tribe, and have seldom felt comfortable with any of
them. My friends through the years have been Jews and
blacks. Wasps are another country for me, a country I never
felt sufficiently curious about—let alone welcome in—to
penetrate.

Yet I was curious about Lindsay. He had hardly been
elected to his first term in Congress before there was some
talk about him as a Presidential possibility in a decade or
two. And yet, during that first term, he was very much an
irregular within his party. I wondered why he was a Republican at all. Why was he in politics? What was he after?
If he was what he seemed—an authentic independent—how
long could he last?

I began doing research for a *New Yorker* profile of this
odd politician in 1960. The profile of Lindsay as a congressman was never printed because he was elected mayor of
New York City in 1965. In those five years, I had learned

enough about him to want to know more—particularly to find out if he could politically survive those infinite circles of civic Hell that are the City of New York in the 1960's.

The larger part of this book is about Lindsay as mayor, because the years since 1965 have been the most maddening, challenging, and revealing of his political career. Also I wanted—through Lindsay—to explore the most difficult office in the country, next to the Presidency. All mayors of big cities are under siege, having many more problems than resources, but the complexities—moral as well as economic and political—endemic to being mayor of New York are so enormous that an examination of Lindsay's on-the-line education in trying to cope with them may help clarify basic urban dilemmas throughout the country.

My approach has been—in the main section of the book —to write of a city administration in process. That is, an act of continuous reporting which hopefully will give a sense of the changing rhythms and textures of Lindsay's experience as mayor as he keeps learning how much he still has to learn in order to govern with direction. That section begins with Lindsay beginning, and continues through the crises that are normative to living in, let alone being mayor of, the City of New York. Lindsay and the city are at the center of the narrative, but there are many other voices, in and out of his administration—supporters, detractors, and those who are skeptical that the city can do more than just barely survive. A final chapter includes my assessment of Lindsay as the most visible and vulnerable of mayors in this decade—along with a projection of what his self-education as an urbanist may mean for other cities and for his own future in politics.

But to place Lindsay as mayor in perspective, I felt it necessary to start with what I consider to be the essence of his years in Congress and of those earlier experiences which were part of shaping the man who was to become the one hundred and third mayor of New York.

When I was very young, I thought that if I were ever to write nonfiction about politics, my subject would be just such a vivid daguerreotype as the man who considered himself the model for *The Last Hurrah*. I never did write a book about James Michael Curley, but I discovered a differently arresting—and for me, more significant—drama in John Lindsay's struggle to be both effective and ethical, to remain stubbornly self-directed while also being responsive to a constituency that grew as hugely in contentiousness and in conflicting needs as it did in numbers.

Neither rogue nor radical, he is of that tradition which he described in his Yale thesis on the life and times of Oliver Cromwell: "Two fundamental demands . . . were common to all Puritan sects—the demand for liberty of conscience and the demand for reform. . . . 'Reform of the universities. . . . Reform of the cities . . . the countries . . . the ordinances . . . ,' thundered a Puritan preacher before parliament and indeed he reflected the thought of the entire Puritan movement which, finding expression through parliament, more and more threatened a king whose very position of kingship scorned the independence that Puritanism championed."

Lindsay has had nothing so simple as a single king to do battle against. From the hierarchy of the House of Representatives to the "power brokers," as he describes them, in the City of New York, his opposition has been more mundane, but for all of that—and because of that—exceedingly difficult to dislodge. Perhaps the alternatives are different than he sees them—reform or stultification. Perhaps reform is not enough. That preacher before parliament he quoted went beyond reform—"Every plant which my Heavenly Father hath not rooted shall be rooted up!" he also thundered. But Lindsay believes, less so on some days than on others, that real change can come and that power can be redistributed through the politics of democracy. It is a common-

place belief. What makes Lindsay uncommon is the tenacious-
ness with which he acts on that belief.

Some of the young—those, for example, who would
agree with the basic societal analysis of Herbert Marcuse—
consider Lindsay at best ingenuous. He is, they would say,
both an example of and a largely unwitting practitioner of
"repressive tolerance." By remaining part of the present institutional system, while trying to humanize it, he reinforces
it. And so, if he is not precisely "the enemy," he is irrelevant.

For others—those of the young in his administration
and those who crowd college auditoriums to hear him—Lindsay offers some basis for belief that he represents more than
a style, more than rhetoric. I emphasize the relationship between Lindsay and the young because he bases so much of
his hope for change on them—an act many of his age, and
those older, may well consider ingenuous. "If there is one
thing that sets much of this generation apart from earlier,
activist ones," he told students at Columbia in December
1968, "it is the insistence on personal worth—the refusal to
subordinate humanity to dogma. The demand to replace corporate bureaucracy with community participation; the values
of the single human spirit."

He was also, I think, delineating his own intentions as
a man in politics. And that is what this book is about—those
intentions and the degree to which they have been fulfilled,
so far.

The Apprenticeship:
The Years Before
City Hall

I Since the primary focus of this book is on John Lindsay as mayor of the City of New York, I shall not provide a comprehensive account of his time in Congress. Despite its hortatory title, Daniel E. Button's *Lindsay: A Man for Tomorrow* (Random House, 1965) is an accurate summary of Lindsay's record as a congressman, and I would recommend the book for those interested in the details of that part of his career.

My focus in this distillation of Lindsay's political apprenticeship is on what the pre-City Hall years revealed of the man's character, preoccupations, and methods of operation.

I remember that in 1960, when I started looking into whether I wanted to write about Congressman Lindsay, I was first intrigued by the fact that he had made himself argumentatively visible in the House just nineteen days after he had taken his seat in the first session of the Eighty-sixth Congress in late January of the year before. Noah Mason, a portly, stentorian, white-haired Republican from Illinois, had been lashing the Warren Court. A member of the House since 1937, Mason's immovable conservatism had long since established him as one of the respected elders of his party. In his speech that day, Mason had accused the Supreme Court of "brazenly" substituting "Socialist doctrines" for cherished American traditions. "How can our citizens," Mason boomed in conclusion, "respect present-day decisions of that Court?"

Several Southern Democrats, including Howard Smith of Virginia and John Davis of Georgia, rose to commend Mason. Lindsay sat, waiting for someone on either side of the

aisle to defend the Court. Finally he nervously asked for recognition. "The only reason I was recognized," Lindsay told
me later, "is that nobody knew who the hell I was. They expected more praise for Mason."

With considerable emotion, though in the public-statue
language he was later, as mayor, to use with labor leaders,
Lindsay spoke for the Court:

> I will defend as long as I have voice in my body the jurisdic-
> tion of the Supreme Court in every area involving the per-
> sonal rights and liberties of our people, including the area
> of internal security. I would oppose any effort to cut down
> the jurisdiction of the Supreme Court when there is a dis-
> agreement because of the result in one particular case. . . .
> In my view, historians will write that this Supreme Court is
> one of the great courts of our country. . . . I subscribe to
> the theory that the Constitution is a living and growing
> document. Therefore I should like to say that as much as
> I respect the remarks of my distinguished senior, I am con-
> strained to disagree with him.

When Lindsay finished, there was spontaneous applause
—a rarity in the House—mostly from the Democratic side
of the aisle. The following Sunday, the St. Louis *Post-Dis-
patch* ran a rather prescient editorial, "An Old Rule Well
Broken":

> A seldom-broken rule of Congress is that a freshman member
> of the House does not challenge publicly a statement by a
> senior member, particularly by a senior member of the
> freshman's own party. First-term Republican member John
> V. Lindsay of Manhattan has broken the rule, greatly to his
> credit. . . . Congressman Lindsay's answer is in the best of
> constitutional traditions. This is the first time that the
> country as a whole has heard his name. If his defense of the
> Supreme Court is a sample of his thinking and his courage,
> the country will hear from him again.

The rule-breaker went on, during the next seven years,
to challenge prestigious members of both parties in the
House, particularly on civil-liberties and civil-rights issues.
In February 1959, for instance, the new congressman op-

posed an Eisenhower Administration bill that would have broadened the authority of the State Department to refuse passports on the basis of confidential information. "I start with the premise," Lindsay began his testimony before both the House Foreign Affairs and the Senate Foreign Relations committees, "that we are dealing here with a Constitutional right." He also pointed out that "the authority to use confidential information in the administrative process, under imprecise standards, coupled with the power to delegate the authority to subordinates, can result in a breeding ground of arbitrariness." The bill was not passed.

In September of the same year, Lindsay was the only congressman to speak and vote against a bill introduced by Representative Kathryn Granahan of Pennsylvania which would have allowed the Postmaster General an extension from twenty to forty-five days in which he would have the power to decide whether to impound allegedly obscene mail if he considered it in "the public interest" to do so. The measure, moreover, shifted the burden of proof to the mailer. Any appeal from the Postmaster General's decision would have to prove that he had been "arbitrary and capricious."

Lindsay had just arrived on the floor when the bill came up for debate at exactly noon, the House's official starting time, without any advance notice. At small tables at each entrance to the floor, copies of each day's bills are stacked, and Lindsay picked up the Granahan bill. "I couldn't believe my eyes," he told a friend later. "They were trying to sneak by a bill that seemed to me thoroughly unconstitutional. That's why I never miss a session and try to get to the House on time every day. In this case, the American Civil Liberties Union has fallen down on its job. They hadn't warned me of the bill. The only tip I had that something funny might be coming up was from a reporter on *The New York Times*." After reading the measure, Lindsay rose and said angrily that using "the public interest" as a standard meant that "we are breaking new ground. It is too loose and it raises constitutional questions. Must we burn down the whole barn to catch the rat? I wish the Postmaster General would worry a little more about delivering the mail and a little less about what is in it."

His colleagues were unimpressed by his dissent. John W. McCormack, the sempiternal Majority Leader, spoke fervently in support of the bill, lauding Mrs. Granahan's devotion to safeguarding public morality. The measure passed with Lindsay yelling the sole "Nay!" at the top of his lungs. The Washington *Post* took approving notice of his stand and the *Village Voice,* a Greenwich Village newspaper in his district, rather grandly proclaimed him "the Congressman from the Constitution." But Lindsay, characteristically stubborn, was far from satisfied. Still angry, he went back to his office and instructed Robert Blum (then his legislative assistant and later a member of his administration as counsel to the Mayor) to alert New York's senators, Jacob Javits and Kenneth Keating, to the fact that the Granahan bill would be coming to the Senate.

Lindsay then decided, as became his custom, to search for an expert on the subject in the relevant executive department of the government. "You can always find somebody," Lindsay used to lecture his staff, "who has quietly worked out a bill in his specialty for his own satisfaction, if for no other reason." Lindsay's assistants did find such a man in the Post Office Department, and on the basis of his recommendations, Lindsay constructed a new obscenity bill. In the Senate meanwhile, the late Senator Estes Kefauver had misgivings about the Granahan measure. When he found out about Lindsay's substitute measure, he got part of it incorporated into his own bill, which passed the Senate and was later approved by the House. The measure in its final form gave the courts the power to review any decision on obscenity by the Postmaster General; such decisions had accordingly to rest on more than a simple declaration that a piece of mail was not in "the public interest."

In March 1961, Lindsay again assumed his not always successful role as guardian of the free flow of the mail, moving into combat with the late Representative Francis Walter of Pennsylvania, chairman of the House Un-American Activities Committee, who had proposed a bill resuming federal interception of mail from Communist countries. The bill passed the House, with only two votes in opposition, those of Lindsay and William Fitts Ryan, Democratic congressman from New York's Twentieth District.

A few days before, the two New York mavericks had also cast the sole votes against another Walter bill that barred from employment "in any capacity aboard any merchant vessel of the United States or within any waterfront facility" anyone who had refused to answer questions about allegedly subversive activities before a congressional committee or an agency of the executive branch. *The New York Times* lauded Ryan and Lindsay for their courage and good sense in voting against what the *Times* described as "this clearly discriminatory and probably unconstitutional bill." In a moment of despair, however, the *Times* mourned that "if this one could pass all but unanimously, anything can."

In May 1962, the formidable Representaive Walter, with the support of the Kennedy Administration and the House leadership, introduced an Industrial Security Bill that provided procedures for denying workers access to classified material involved in certain government contracts. In many cases, such a denial would be equivalent to dismissing the alleged security risk. The bill covered some five million of those employed in private industry and in universities on defense contracts or corollary research. Under the Walter bill, the accused would not have been able to confront and cross-examine those who submitted information against them. There was also no provision for appeals to the courts.

Walter first tried to get his bill passed by placing it on the "consent calendar," a procedure by which a measure is adopted by the House automatically if no member objects.

It is usually used for comparatively noncontroversial bills. Lindsay did object, and he was the only congressman to stand up and block passage. Under the rules of the House, the next time Walter introduced the bill on the consent calendar, three or more members of the House would have had to oppose it for the bill to be stopped. Walter tried again in August, and by then, Lindsay had three allies—Democrats Ryan of New York, James Roosevelt of California, and Henry Reuss of Wisconsin.

On September 19, the indomitable Walter brought the same bill before the House under suspension of the rules—a device which limits debate to twenty minutes on each side, prohibits amendments, and requires for passage the support of two thirds of the members present and voting. Lindsay and several colleagues worked to collect negative votes. The House did vote for the Industrial Security Bill 247–132, but the tally was six votes short of a two-thirds majority. It was the first time, Lindsay noted with considerable satisfaction, that the Un-American Activities Committee had ever been defeated in a floor fight.

The history of that Industrial Security Bill, Lindsay felt, demonstrated not only the appallingly frequent insensitivity of Congress to civil liberties, but also illustrated the pressures applied by what the late President Eisenhower had termed "the military-industrial complex." After Pentagon officials had testified for the Walter measure, Lindsay later told Murray Kempton, then of the *New Republic,* "every Congressman got a letter from the largest association of defense contractors urging him to vote for the Industrial Security Bill. And this would have been the first law ever written in the United States which would have given the government the power to fire people in private industry!"

Another example of Pentagon power which Lindsay described to Kempton concerned an occasion when "we were debating the raise in the debt limit from $306 billion to $308 billion. One congressman took the floor to report that

the chairmen of the boards of mighty corporations had called
to ask him to vote to raise the debt. The chairmen in turn
freely admitted that the Pentagon had called and told them
that, if the debt limit wasn't increased, they wouldn't get
paid."

As for his battle to keep the mails unobstructed, Lindsay
and Representative William Ryan were the only congressmen to vote in January 1962 against a Republican-sponsored
amendment to a bill raising postal rates. The amendment to
which the two representatives objected would have empowered the Attorney General to ban from the mail "matter
determined by the Attorney General of the United States to
be Communist political propaganda sponsored directly or indirectly by any Communist controlled government." No
hearings had been held before the amendment reached the
floor.

"You'd be surprised," Lindsay told me, "at how many
of the younger congressmen came up to me after that amendment passed the House and said they agreed with my vote.
It's a shame how quickly new men adjust to the accommoda-
tions that take place in this joint. Besides, some had been
afraid to stick their necks out for fear they'd be criticized for
being 'soft' on Communism. Others simply hadn't thought
the problem through. In this madhouse, your mind gets
crowded with so many things. There actually were congressmen who had paid practically no attention to the amendment. They were too involved with studying the new postal
rates. As for the majority of the House, I suppose they felt
the major goal was to get the postal rates through, and if
the amendment was the only way to do it without a lot of
trouble, why be a hero?"

Lindsay's wife, Mary, was harsher than he in her reaction to the vote. "Where were the liberal congressmen from
New York? They'll go down the line on a bill when there's
a crowd of them, but when do you see any of them stand up
alone or with only a few other representatives?"

There were other civil-liberties battles, some won, some lost. Also in 1962, the Kennedy Administration, in one of a number of moves during those years which convinced Lindsay that neither John Kennedy nor Robert Kennedy were particularly concerned with civil liberties, had proposed a bill which would have made it a crime to "obstruct or impede" the Federal Bureau of Investigation, the Narcotics Bureau, or the Internal Revenue Bureau during any "lawful inquiry or investigation" of certain interstate high crimes, including murder, kidnapping, narcotics traffic, and extortion.

The proposal came before the Judiciary Committee, of which Lindsay was a member. He offered a substitute that changed the language of the bill, making it a crime "wilfully to injure or threaten or attempt to injure any person or property" as a retaliation against the furnishing of information to those federal agencies during their investigations of the specified crimes.

The heavily Democratic Judiciary Committee adopted Lindsay's measure by a vote of 17 to 15, and he was delighted. I was in his office when he came out of the committee meeting, and an assistant asked him why he was so gleeful.

"The Administration bill was dangerously broad," Lindsay said. " 'Impede' could cover any kind of conduct. A 'lawful inquiry' could be anything a federal agency might say is lawful. If we hadn't altered that bill, a lawyer or any citizen could have been indicted for entirely proper conduct in questioning a non-judicial federal investigation. My substitute ties the offense solely to bodily harm or threat of bodily harm to a person who has cooperated with the government in the investigation of those crimes. What I did was to narrow considerably possible government interference with the exercise of perfectly reasonable rights. Now do you see?"

The assistant nodded. "It's too complex though. That substitute won't win you any elections."

Lindsay grinned. "No, but it's satisfying to be in a position to get it through. There are a lot more kicks in this job than just piling up the votes."

II And there were often times when kicks were absent. As when Lindsay lost in the House to Attorney General Robert Kennedy in the latter's 1963 expansion of the 1918 Sedition Act which had originally prohibited anyone to "utter, print, write or publish any disloyal, profane, scurrilous or abusive language about the form of government of the United States, of the Constitution of the United States, or the uniform of the Army or Navy of the United States, or any language intended to . . . encourage resistance to the United States or to promote the cause of its enemies." That noxious statute was now to cover Americans anywhere in the world. The abuses to free speech in the act, Lindsay said on the floor of the House, "are so great that even a Congressman possibly could be cited and prosecuted for verbal attacks on United States policies and action." The House was unimpressed and passed the measure broadening the bill.

Of all his defeats in Congress, however, I expect Lindsay was most personally galled by an incident in June 1961. It illustrates with particular clarity the essential problem he had in the House—as an irregular, he was not trusted by his own party leadership nor could he trust them. And as a Republican, he certainly could not count on any Democratic organizational support.

That June, Democratic Congressman Albert Rains of Tennessee, chairman of the House Subcommittee on Housing, presented a multimillion-dollar housing bill which had the backing of the Kennedy Administration. Lindsay broke with the majority of his party to vote for it, but he wasn't entirely satisfied with the measure. Among the amendments he proposed was one which would have prevented federal funds from being used for any public housing project initiated under the bill that permitted discrimination against its occupants.

In the course of the debate on this anti-discrimination amendment to the 1961 bill, Lindsay, although he had consistently advocated similar clauses in previous housing measures and was on record as supporting federal housing in general, was accused of trying to sabotage the bill by deliberately riling up the South. Hurt, Lindsay rose, and said, with a mixture of anger and anguish, that he had often walked up the aisle with Democrats on housing measures:

> At times, I assure my friends on the Democratic side, it was not easy, because there is some disagreement on my side of the aisle on the public housing question. Having done so, now let me say this: that I will vote for programs when I think that they are important to the health and future of this country. But at the same time I will expect that you on the majority side will stand up and be counted on a matter of principle regardless of the special provincial pressures you might be under.
>
> Why should we provide Federal funds to perpetuate practices of discrimination in one-third of the country and, indeed, in many other areas of the country? And do not let anybody suggest for one moment that this amendment to the public housing section of the bill will kill the whole bill, because it will not. In the first place, it is limited to one section of the bill. In the second place the distinguished chairman of the committee, the author of the bill, is too much of a statesman and has pride in his bill; in the third place, the leadership would not allow it at this stage of the game. . . .
>
> This housing bill will pass, and you know it as well as I do. I will vote for the bill and I am willing to take the abuse that I may possibly have to take from my side of the aisle for voting for it. All I ask is that you on the majority side stop this unholy coalition when it comes to matters

involving individual rights. The President of the United States on three occasions in the campaign stated that in January he would have a civil rights bill before the Congress. January came, February, March, April, and May. No civil rights bill. And then, when the distinguished Chairman of the House Committee on Judiciary, the gentleman from New York [Mr. Celler] introduced a bill, the administration went out of its way to disassociate itself from the bill. So, when they suggest to you that there is Executive power here to do what I seek to do by legislation, think twice, because we have had broken promises down the line since January on this question. I need not talk further. I have walked up the aisle with you. Now let us see you walk up the aisle with me.

Lindsay sat down, but was soon on his feet again, demanding to be recognized after Congressman Abraham Multer of Brooklyn, a Democratic Party hack who has since been rewarded with a judgeship, had said scornfully of Lindsay:

This amendment is completely unnecessary in this bill. The gentleman who offered it knows he does not need it in the State of New York nor in the city of New York where we have local statutes against discrimination and they are across the board. Why does he offer it to this bill, and why only to the public housing provision? Perhaps he would like to see the bill carry with it; I doubt it.

"The gentleman," Lindsay rejoined furiously, "should take time to examine my voting record on housing." Later that afternoon, after the debate and the voting on the amendment were over, Lindsay rushed across the aisle, confronted Multer, and said fiercely, "You'd better be damn careful you know what you're talking about before you make that kind of statement about me again." Multer, shocked at this Puritan reaction to the normally loose standards of polemics on the House floor, tried to appease Lindsay, assuring him he had meant no personal offense. He promised to soften his remarks by changing them as they would appear in the *Congressional Record*. Lindsay was not mollified.

Lindsay's uncharacteristic public loss of temper had resulted from the mounting strain of having gone against his own party on nearly all the teller votes concerning the housing bill during the previous two days. Now, he was actually close to tears in frustration at having had his motives questioned by what he subsequently described as "one of those Tuesday-to-Thursday Tammany guys whom I've often seen vote with their Southern brethren on teller votes—on which they're not recorded by name—in order not to rock the boat on some later legislation for which the South reciprocates their support. Their A.D.A. record stays clean, and they go laughing up the aisle as if this were some kind of game. Nor would they think of crossing their leadership on such issues as limiting the free flow of mail. They're regulars all right. Not one of them would stand up alone."

Lindsay had received support from one New York congressman, the anti-Tammany Reform Democrat, William Fitts Ryan. In the debate, Ryan told the House the Lindsay amendment was "an issue of principle. . . . I am also very much concerned that this housing bill pass, and I believe it will."

A voice vote was taken, and Lindsay's amendment appeared to have been decisively defeated. Lindsay demanded a teller count. The procedure on teller votes is for the members of the House to file down the center aisle past tellers who count those for and those against the measure. Lindsay acted as teller for those supporting his amendment. Counting opposite him was Albert Rains of Tennessee, chairman of the Subcommittee on Housing and author of the Administration's housing measure.

During the vote, William Dawson, a Negro congressman from Chicago, stopped the line, and paused in front of Lindsay. Dawson is a rigid organization man, but he was concerned about discrimination in housing. He put his hand on Lindsay's shoulder and said softly, "I'm voting against you, not because I don't trust *you*, but because of what I see over there." Lindsay looked to where Dawson was pointing and saw Charles Halleck, the then Republican Minority leader, grinning broadly. Dawson was afraid that Halleck's glee meant the Republican leadership did, in effect, believe it could defeat the housing bill with Southern support if the Lindsay amendment carried. Dawson felt he could take no chances. The amendment was again rejected, 178 to 132.

"Until that moment," Lindsay said during the melancholy evening following the vote, "Halleck had presented his usual granite face to me. It was a hell of a time for me to bring him pleasure. The least he could have done was to contain himself or leave the floor. The whole situation was very depressing. But that's part of the training—the highs and lows—of being here. In time, a lot of congressmen develop a thick skin, and they don't let this sort of thing affect them deeply. But when you get to that point, you lose something too, which is why it may be right to run amateurs for public office from time to time—men like Willkie and Eisenhower. They haven't become that toughened."

"How's your skin by now?" a member of Lindsay's staff asked him.

Lindsay grimaced. "Thin as paper."

Lindsay soon recovered and continued to walk up the aisle with the Democrats during the Eighty-seventh Congress whenever their position coincided with his. In the long and bitter debate two months later on the Administration's Foreign Aid Bill, when the bill came close to being emasculated by the usual coalition of Southern Democrats and conservative Republicans, Lindsay was of considerable help to the Democratic leadership. His own amendments, however, were regularly defeated for lack of Democratic support. Finally, he strode over to Dr. Thomas Morgan, Democratic chairman of the House Foreign Affairs Committee, and said sharply, "Doc, if you don't accept the next amendment I offer, I'm not going to vote for your damn bill." Startled, Morgan agreed, and the House eventually passed a Lindsay amendment to the Foreign Aid Bill requiring that "to the

maximum extent practicable, officers and employees perform-
ing functions under this Act abroad shall be assigned to
countries and positions for which they have special competence, such as appropriate language and practical experience." In arguing for the amendment, Lindsay had cited
figures proving that only a small fraction of American officials administering the aid program abroad had any proficiency in either the primary or secondary languages of the
countries in which they were working. It was a small victory
for the Congressman, but something he could call his own.

III In talking with colleagues of Lindsay's on both
sides of the aisle during those years, I got the impression that many of them—even conservatives—rather
wished they could help this irregular from New York get more
than such marginal satisfaction in terms of legislation. He
was respected as well as liked by most of his colleagues and
by many of the long-term professionals in government agencies. James V. Bennett, then director of the United States
Bureau of Prisons, and a Democrat, told me, for example,
"This man is one of the hardest-working congressmen I've
ever seen. I've been around Washington for nearly forty
years, and I have some notion of how congressmen can duck
their office. But there are a few, like John, who never miss
a committee meeting or fail to do their homework."

Lindsay's usual schedule, after reading the papers and
the *Congressional Record*, was to get to his office by at least
nine—and often earlier. And throughout the day, he would
keep trying to grasp whatever bits of time he could to absorb
information. Although much of his day was spent on the
floor, in committee, seeing constituents, and answering mail,

he remained in touch with developments in and outside of Washington by what he described to me at the time as "the damnedest Scotch-tape method. I maintain a whole string of contacts in and out of the government and I do as much reading as I can cram in."

A number of times, I watched the cramming during moments of the day when he came to a brief stop at his desk in the New House Office Building. Surrounded by a map of his district, drawings by his children and even bolder paintings by his artist constituents who were invited to exhibit their work in both his New York and Washington offices, Lindsay used to skim through newspapers, reports, letters, magazines, and books with impressive power of concentration. I also remember the stacks of books on his bedside table in his Washington home, most of them history and biography. And maps were a constant study aid. As a problem grew or exploded in a particular country—it was Angola during one week I was in Washington—Lindsay would buy a map of the area, gum it on the wall, and as he talked on the phone or at spare moments in between appointments, he would stare at the map until he had it memorized.

Although jealous of his time, Lindsay, from the start of his career in Congress, was always, however, easily accessible to visiting constituents and to lobbyists of all kinds. "He listened to anyone who came," Robert Blum recalls. "But they all soon realized that he always made up his own mind." The lobbyists in particular also quickly learned that Lindsay was scouringly conscientious about observing ethical proprieties. As the late Stanley Isaacs, an implacably independent Republican and a long-time New York City councilman whom Lindsay deeply admired, said of the Congressman, "John is one of the very few men in whom I can say I have complete confidence. I just cannot conceive of his ever doing anything wrong in matters of conscience and morality. It's just impossible."

Soon after the new congressman had arrived in Washington, for example, the lobbyist for a major railroad sent all the freshmen congressmen a dozen Old-Fashioned glasses. Lindsay opened the package, frowned, and told a secretary, "This is the place to stop this sort of thing right now. Send them back." A few days later, the lobbyist met Lindsay at the Mayflower Hotel. "You know," he told the Congressman aggrievedly, "you were the only one to send those glasses back." Within a short time, Lindsay had also hurt the feelings of an old friend, a Washington lawyer, who had sent him a pair of bookends, a gift on which the congressman's name had been engraved. Lindsay returned them too.

When the pressure became direct and specific, Lindsay invariably stiffened even more. "If there was anything I wanted in Congress," his brother, David, told me during those years, "John would be the last person I'd go to."

Because of the reputation he soon acquired, however, for being willing to listen to all sides of a question—provided the advocate did not bear gifts—Lindsay's Washington office was usually clogged. When his workload became too heavy, he would invariably assemble a batch of papers and take refuge in the House. "It's easier for the girls to say I'm on the floor," he would explain. But even in the House, he was pursued.

During his first term, for instance, Lindsay was followed constantly by labor lobbyists who were trying to persuade him to vote against the Landrum-Griffin bill. Under the measure, which set up safeguards against abuse of power by union officials, union members were provided such civil liberties—enforceable in court—as free speech at union meetings. All union finances, moreover, had to be fully disclosed, and new standards were set for trusteeships and fair elections. Although many labor leaders have since conceded that the bill has worked out fairly well, nearly all were against it at the time of its appearance on the floor. One lobbyist rushed up to Lindsay as the Congressman was entering the House on the third day of debate on the measure. "If you vote against us," he threatened, "we'll certainly remember it." Lindsay smiled thinly, and thanked him for the warning.

The Landrum-Griffin bill did cause Lindsay to engage in considerable inner debate. At his request, a friend in the Department of Labor prepared a thirty-page study of the measure, and Lindsay supervised several weeks of research by his own staff. He finally decided to vote for the bill because, he explained to his constituents in his newsletter, "One of the first duties of government is the safeguarding of individual rights and freedoms in the context of organized power groups, whether such groups stem from management or labor or from government itself."

Lindsay would frequently agonize over a bill. "He *lives* with these things," I was told by Anthony Morella, a former Lindsay legislative assistant who left the Congressman's staff in 1962 to become Assistant Professor of Law at American University in Washington. In the process of making up his mind, Lindsay constantly asked questions, and not only of those who were likely to agree with him. I talked with a frequent target of those questions. He was a Democrat, a political science professor then working on Senator William Fulbright's staff through a fellowship sponsored by the Political Science Association. The professor, an astute, customarily sardonic observer of Washington's inhabitants, told me that he was startled, on first meeting Lindsay, to discover that "underneath all that charm, the guy is exceptionally bright. And curious. He's really curious. When he asks a question, he really cares what the answer is. A lot of these egomaniacs here ask one rhetorical question after another."

Lindsay cultivated disagreement with other intellectuals in Washington in addition to the professor. When he was trying to decide about an especially thorny bill, Lindsay would deliberately invite to dinner or to an evening's discussion at his home in Cathedral Park, near Washington Cathedral, those associates and outside experts who, he knew, were strongly opposed to his own tentative conclusions.

"But," Anthony Morella emphasized, "after the experts were questioned and the research done, he'd agonize some more on his own. And he didn't take the tensions out on his staff. He kept them inside." At such times, Lindsay used to become so abstracted that, as one assistant put it, "he doesn't hear a word you say and you learn to leave him alone until he's made up his mind."

During bouts of indecision, Lindsay was apt to sit at his desk for long periods, his head in his hands, pulling mechanically at his hair or twirling a pencil. Once he did make up his mind, however, he entered battle for or against a bill with vehemence. But, as firmly as he would then defend his decisions, he remained quite sensitive to the reactions of his constituents. He would brood over negative letters on positions he had taken, and usually answered even the most abusive. "He tries to read all his mail," Morella once told a constituent, "but if you want to be really sure of reaching him, write him a nasty letter." (Lindsay's mail used to average 2,000 to 2,500 letters a week, considerably above the normal amount of mail received by a congressman from a large city.)

"Also in the mail are reports on key bills from study committees he's set up in his district," Morella told me in the middle of one legislative session. "Those he reads carefully, but with all the reading and studying, it's never enough. No one man can cover all legislative issues in depth any more. It's frustrating for John, and the deeper he gets into a bill, the more frustrated he is that he can't spend even more time on it. Some of the men on the Hill give up after a while and concentrate only on their specialties. But John gets friends, staff members, experts, volunteers, the college interns in political science who work in his office—anyone with capacity—to do the research he can't do.

"The men of most stature in Congress," Morella continued, "are those who make the maximum use of the people around them, and John has an exceptional ability to find

out what people are best at. He then draws them into helping him by convincing them that they can thereby actually
affect the course of legislation. Those interns, for example,
work in the Washington and New York offices for several
months under plans set up by various colleges and universities. John never asks an intern what his politics are, but
as soon as he feels the intern has reliable work habits, he
makes him produce. And not just stuffing envelopes. In Washington, interns have done research and worked on amendments. In New York, they man the phones, service some of
the constituents, and also occasionally do research."

One intern in Lindsay's Washington office, Robert Kimball, later became a Carnegie Teaching Fellow in American
History at Yale, and after that, Lindsay's legislative assistant
in Washington. Kimball recalled that when he was an intern,
"even the ill-conceived opinions of a novice like myself
seemed to matter to John. He is an exceptionally fine listener.
His office was always open to me, and overwhelmed with work
as he was, he often would take time to explain things to me.
John's qualities as an educator, incidentally, are very high."

One of the themes on which Lindsay persistently tried
to educate his volunteer workers and his constituency at large
was the unreliability of statistical appraisals of congressmen
on the basis of their voting records alone—whether the analysis is done by conservative or liberal groups. During his
second term, Lindsay, one Saturday morning, was outlining
the main issues in the House at the time for a group of his
volunteer workers. One of them, a young lawyer, stood up
and said, "Some time ago, Americans for Democratic Action
gave you a sixty per cent rating. That disturbed me a trifle."

Lindsay looked at him quizzically, and grinned. "Did
you think it was too high or too low?"

"Too high," said the disturbed Republican.

"Now look," Lindsay answered with evident impatience,
"I've been through this business of percentages so damn
often. In 1961, Americans for Constitutional Action, a very

conservative outfit, also gave me a sixty per cent rating. When
you combine the two, it looks as if I'm practicing black
magic. But when you get to the bottom of it, you find both
organizations pick different areas in which they're interested
in order to decide whether you've been 'right' or 'wrong.'
Besides, the wrong vote is sometimes picked as the basis for
judgment. I've been charged with a negative mark for voting
to recommit a bill to committee in order to strengthen it,
but my vote for the final passage of the bill was not considered in the tally. I don't like this approach to assessing congressmen at all. It's unbelievably inadequate. How can you
fully appraise a legislator's performance by picking on just
a few of his votes? The press, even the great *New York Times,*
can be just as bad. The papers seldom include an analysis
of why a congressman voted as he did, particularly on a complex bill which has had attached to it many amendments and
substitutes. Sometimes, on a final vote, you declare yourself
for a bill, parts of which you're against, because otherwise
there'd be no legislation at all in that area. On other occasions, it's conceivable that a congressman has voted against
a bill whose overall purpose he supports because it was too
inadequate in too many respects and would have done more
harm than good."

No matter what rating he received from the various
statisticians of doctrinal purity, Lindsay as congressman won
the continued respect of a somewhat more influential body
of assayers, the Washington press corps. As early as the spring
of 1960, when *Newsweek* magazine asked fifty reporters to
rate congressmen, Lindsay was selected the best freshman
Republican congressman and was listed second only to Chester Bowles as the most impressive new representative of either
party in the Eighty-sixth Congress. Lindsay, moreover, rated
ninth among all congressmen, regardless of length of service.
His standing remained high during the rest of his years in
the House, and by the beginning of Lindsay's fourth term,
in 1965, Robert J. Donovan, a veteran Washington corre-

spondent, was writing of Lindsay as "the least tarnished of Republican presidential possibilities." A long shot, by all means, but all the more unusual a congressman—a minority within a minority—to even be considered a Presidential possibility, however remote.

IV   At home, meanwhile, the Congressman was reveal-
ing an accelerating ability to attract votes from sizable numbers of Democrats and independents as well as Republicans. In 1960, as an illustration of Lindsay's bipartisan appeal, while John F. Kennedy was carrying the city by over 791,000 votes—the worst Republican defeat in local Presidential balloting since 1936—Lindsay overwhelmed his liberal, articulate, if rather stuffy, Democratic, opponent, William vanden Heuvel, by a plurality of 27,432 —taking 59.8 per cent of the ballots. A further measure of the breadth of Lindsay's support that year was a two-dollar cash contribution by Norman Thomas. Two years later, Lindsay's opponent was the late Martin Dworkis, an amiable professor at New York University's Graduate School of Public Administration. The incumbent won by 98,129 to 45,566 although the majority of registered voters in the Seventeenth District were Democrats. In 1964, Lindsay, as a Republican not supporting Barry Goldwater, defeated Eleanor Clark French by 91,000 votes—taking a startling 71 per cent of the ballots. As New York political writer, Oliver Pilat, pointed out, "This was a higher proportion of the vote than virtually any other major Republican candidate in the country received that year."

But Lindsay's ability to win so much support from non-

Republicans did not impress the Republican leadership in the House. It was further proof, along with his individualistic voting record, of his unreliability. He was not marked for promotion. It was not forgotten, for example, that in 1961, Lindsay had been one of twenty-two Republican congressmen who supported the Kennedy Administration's barely successful drive to enlarge the House Rules Committee from twelve to fifteen members. It is the Rules Committee that primarily determines which bills are to be sent to the floor for a vote, and in what order. The committee, under the chairmanship of Howard Smith of Virginia, an expert delayer, had long been controlled by a coalition of conservative Republicans and Southern Democrats. Bills disapproved by the coalition often languished in the committee, and thereby, the rest of the House was deprived of a chance to vote on them.

The Republican Policy Committee opposed any enlargement of the Rules Committee because obviously the party leadership was content with its conservative cast. Lindsay tried to lead a revolt among the younger Republican congressmen, pointing out insistently that in addition to the patently undemocratic nature of the prevailing system, it was poor political strategy for the Republican minority in the House to be so closely identified with the posture of obstruction represented by the Rules Committee's history. "The coalition has never been *quid pro quo,* in any case," Lindsay would tell potential recruits. "The Southern Democrats vote with the Republicans only when it's in their interest and meanwhile this alliance has created an image of the Republican party that hurts us both in the Northern big cities and in the South where it has made it difficult for real Republican opposition to grow. If the Rules Committee is not enlarged, moreover, we let the Democrats continue to make us the whipping boy when their legislation doesn't get through. They can always blame the Republicans on the Rules Committee."

The expansion of the committee was finally voted early in 1961 by 217 to 212. As House Republican leaders glumly noted, the pro-Administration ballots of Lindsay and two other New York Republicans, Paul Fino of the Bronx and Seymour Halpern of Queens, made the difference.

At home, the New York Young Republican Club promptly censured Lindsay, Halpern, and Fino, and praised the "courageous stand" of the 148 House Republicans who had followed their leader, Charles Halleck. Characteristically, Lindsay asked for a chance to be heard before the club, and he invited all his constituents who had written him in criticism of his stand to attend the session.

In the week before his scheduled confrontation with the Young Republicans, Lindsay underlined in press releases and interviews that less than five per cent of the club's membership had been present at the meeting which resulted in his censure. He further tried to put his opponents on the defensive by pointing out: "I'm going to remind my club that my district elected *me* to Congress, not Howard Smith or Clarence Brown of the Rules Committee. To allow twelve or six men to exercise the power of life or death over legislation, the consideration of which is important to the Seventeenth District of the country, is inconsistent with the democratic process."

On February 24, 1961, Lindsay faced one hundred and sixty Republicans, most of them dourly accusatory, at a meeting held in the Women's National Republican Club on West Fifty-first Street. Behind him on the platform was a row of flags, including an American flag to his left and one from the Confederacy to his right. After he was introduced, four young men tried to set off a standing ovation but failed. Lindsay forcefully explained his position in the context of a brief, lucid history of the Rules Committee and its functions. He accused the Republican Policy Committee of having again "put its head in the sand," and added defiantly, "My vote to expand the Rules Committee was the easiest one I ever cast."

His tempo and volume increased until he ended by almost shouting, "We're the party of Lincoln! What on earth are we afraid of?"

Most of the questioning was hostile, but Lindsay did not give any ground. "If you think opposition means blockade," he snapped at one young conservative, "you and I have a sharp difference in opinion." An hour and a half after Lindsay left the meeting, a motion was introduced to affirm the Young Republican Club's censure of him. Passage required two thirds of those present, and the motion failed, 38 to 31. Lindsay had picked up some support, but those who agreed with him were still in the minority.

In March of that year, Lindsay clashed with the Young Republican Club again. He had refused to sign a manifesto circulated by the Committee of One Million which pledged unremitting opposition to the admission of Communist China to the United Nations and to recognition of its government by the United States. Previously, 388 members of Congress, including 55 senators, had signed. Lindsay's position was that although he was not at the time in favor of seating Communist China in the UN, "this may not be our government's position three or four years from now and we do not know what our position in the United Nations may be then. Why create for ourselves a situation of rigid inflexibility? What purpose does it serve?" It would be a serious mistake, Lindsay continued, if Congress should discover it had taken a stand which would later make any president's handling of foreign affairs more difficult.

The directors of the Young Republican Club adopted a resolution unanimously lauding the congressmen who *had* signed the pledge while noting coldly that Lindsay had been the only New York Republican member of the House who had not signed. His party's leadership in the House made the same notation.

I was present on Capitol Hill in early February of the next year to witness for myself the chasm between Lindsay and the congressional chieftains of his party. John Kennedy was trying—unsuccessfully, as it turned out—to create a Department of Urban Affairs. The Republican Party was opposed, but since Lindsay had been urging—before Kennedy was elected—the establishment of just such a cabinet post to meet the spiraling needs of the cities, he ignored party discipline and appeared as the first witness before the House Government Operations Committee in support of the Kennedy bill.

The Republicans on the Government Operations Committee glowered at Lindsay as he briskly gave his testimony before hurrying away to a meeting of the Judiciary Committee. Later that day, on the floor of the House, Lindsay saw Clarence J. Brown, Jr., of Ohio, a Republican member of the Government Operations Committee, in a whispered conference with Charles Halleck, the House Minority Leader. They looked grimly in his direction. Lindsay sighed. "I know what that's all about. It's bad enough that I'm for the bill, but to have the *first* witness in its favor a Republican—" Lindsay stopped, and laughed. "Well, if you're going to oppose your party on a specific issue, you might as well go all the way. It doesn't make any sense to hedge. I might as well be hung for a sheep as for a lamb." His smile faded. "I may *never* get on the Foreign Affairs Committee."

It was a Foreign Affairs Committee assignment that Lindsay most coveted during his seven years in Congress. He never made it. His intense interest in foreign affairs was acknowledged only tangentially by his being named for four consecutive years as an official delegate from the House of Representatives to the annual conferences in Europe of the NATO Parliamentarians—legislators from the NATO countries. There were satisfactions in the assignment. He became executive secretary—"rapporteur"—of the Parliamentarians' political committee and in 1964 was elected its chairman, a gratifying victory because Lindsay was known as a principal advocate of the creation of an Atlantic Parliamentary Assembly to broaden and deepen the ties between NATO countries. But for a congressman who wanted to exercise a degree of real power in shaping American foreign policy, these speculative seminars were hardly substitutes for a seat on the House Foreign Affairs Committee.

The only time Lindsay came close to getting that seat was in January 1963. He was being considered for a vacancy on the committee but his party irregularity did him in. During a meeting of the Republican Conference (an off-the-record caucus), Lindsay felt compelled to argue against the Republican hierarchy on the question of again expanding the House Rules Committee. Since this was a new session of Congress, there had to be another vote on the issue. Lindsay repeated his reasons for having supported expansion in 1961, and in the process, he demolished—if logic were to be the criterion of the debate—the position of the House Republican elders. After Lindsay had finished, Leslie Arends of Illinois, the House Minority Whip and a friend of Lindsay, walked over to him and said with mingled respect and regret, "John, in all my life, I never saw a man talk himself off the Foreign Affairs Committee so fast."

In addition to his stand for a larger Rules Committee, Lindsay differed from the majority of Republicans in the House in his consistent support of foreign aid and liberal trade programs as well as in his attempts to stress the potential of the United Nations. Domestically, Lindsay came closer to justifying his somewhat tenuous franchise in the Republican Party—but not all that close. He was distrustful, on the one hand, of overly centralized government power. A frequent motif in his speeches during those years was: "The Republican party must demonstrate that a concentration of central power through a government-dominated industrial-military complex is just as limiting to steady economic growth and to individual freedoms as are all other undue power concentrations." On the other hand, however, Lindsay was aware that decentralization of power would be meaningless without funds to make it work—funds of a quantity that could only come from Washington.

"Hell," Lindsay would point out to his more conservative constituents, "welfare is written right into the Constitution." And he continued to exacerbate conservative Republicans in Congress by supporting federal aid to education, extensive public housing plans, broadened social security coverage, the financing of medical care for the aged, and the establishment of a Department of Urban Affairs. "Of course, you've got to preserve the prerogatives and responsibilities of local government," I once heard him tell a basilisk Republican from Ohio, "but damn it, where's the *money* going to come from?"

Later I heard the gentleman from Ohio grumble to a colleague, "I don't consider that fellow a Republican at all." Actually, the state of Lindsay's Republicanism during the congressional years never seemed to satisfy any wing of his party. In 1963, I was instructed by Senator Jacob Javits concerning Lindsay's deficiencies as a maverick: "John hasn't cut loose from the party as often and as definitely as I did when I was in the House. He has to develop more in the area of combat, become more of an evangelist," Javits continued sternly. "So far, I would say of him that he's like a smoldering fire. It could go out, or it could burst into flame." (A rather intriguing assessment, I thought, from the carefully non-evangelistic senior Senator from New York.)

About the same time, I spoke to the then House Minority Charles Halleck in his spacious office in the Capitol Building. Leaning back in a black leather armchair, Halleck began slowly and softly: "Well, John is an able, brilliant legislator." There was a pause. I asked if the Minority Leader occasionally wished Lindsay's vote were more dependable. Suddenly Halleck sat up straight, and roared, "Goddamn it! I'm the Republican leader. Of course I want to win. And there are times when Lindsay stands almost alone out there against us."

Halleck regained control of himself, and added, "We've got members who think he's a complete renegade. I don't subscribe to that. Anyway,"—Halleck began to smile and then pursed his lips—"I've seen people come here and swing to the right or to the left, and eventually swing back again. Lindsay may be a regular yet."

V Nelson Rockefeller—at the time—was of a different persuasion. He had small expectations of Lindsay becoming a "regular." Nor did the Governor—at the time—think it would be advisable for Lindsay to become more responsive to the dictates of the party's congressional leadership.

"One of the most important things I've learned in politics," the Governor told me early in 1963, "is that voters react to you intuitively. And they're not nearly so easy to fool as some of the professionals think. After a while, they can tell pretty accurately what kind of a man you are, even if they've never looked at your voting record. And that's the important thing John has going for him—they can *feel* his independence."

Rockefeller himself had occasion to feel Lindsay's independence a few months later, in June of 1963. Under a provision of the new City Charter, ten additional city councilmen-at-large were to be elected that year. Each party was allowed to name only one candidate for the two councilmen-at-large seats in each of the five boroughs. No voter, moreover, could pick more than one candidate. As a result, a Republican nomination for any of the five seats was almost equivalent to victory in the general elections. For months, Richard Lewisohn, leader of the Ninth Assembly District, had been considered the Republican candidate for council-man-at-large for Manhattan. He had Lindsay's firm support, and Governor Rockefeller had declared that he would take no position in the contest. Suddenly, the regular Republican organization in Manhattan, under the insistence of Rocke-feller, switched to Richard S. Aldrich, a cousin of the Governor. Lindsay stood by Lewisohn (who later became for a time Commissioner of the Department of Commerce and Industrial Development under Lindsay as mayor of New York). But to the surprise of other Republican politicians in the city, Lindsay did not try to euphemize the split with Rockefeller in his public statements. He did not evade questions from the press as to how he felt about the concerted pressure to substitute Aldrich for Lewisohn.

In a statement to Oliver Pilat, then political writer for the New York *Post,* Lindsay charged that Vincent Albano, Republican leader of New York County, had told him that he would be considered an "insurgent" if he continued to back Lewisohn. Angry, Governor Rockefeller called a press conference to deny that he had ever ordered Albano to "de-liver" the nomination for Aldrich. At a meeting of the New York County Republican Committee, Aldrich defeated Lew-isohn by 2,057 votes to 311. Lewisohn, although he had a sizable chance to defeat Aldrich in the primaries by basing his campaign on "bossism," later withdrew from the election in order not to embarrass Rockefeller's chances for the Presidential nomination.

Several political observers speculated that Lindsay's open defiance of the Republican organization had signaled an early start on a possible Lindsay campaign for governor in 1966. "John's reaction," a close associate of his told me, "wasn't at all devious. It had nothing to do with his political plans. He felt a friend of his was being pushed around, and so he said what he thought about it. His refusal to go along may have been unpolitic, but it was a characteristic Lindsay reaction."

I doubt that Rockefeller was surprised, however irritated. He could not have forgotten the attempt in 1961 to include Lindsay on the Republican ticket in the New York mayoralty campaign that year. Before New York State Attorney General Louis Lefkowitz had been nominated, there were rumors that Lindsay was being considered to head the ticket. He didn't want to run but wondered if he would be able to refuse a direct request from Rockefeller. "After all," he told me at the time, "as of now, I'm tied, willy-nilly, to his future. If he really puts the pressure on, as Dewey used to, I'll be in a difficult position."

Rockefeller summoned Lindsay to dinner early that spring in what Lindsay calls Rockefeller's "Eagle's Nest," the top floor of the Governor's triplex apartment at 810 Fifth Avenue. (Later, after having been mayor of New York for a couple years, as his relationship with the Governor became increasingly strained, Lindsay changed the name to "Berchtesgaden.") In the small circular dining room with its sweeping view of Central Park, Lindsay waited uncomfortably for Rockefeller to begin. The Congressman had prepared a list of reasons why he should not run for mayor, but to his great relief, Rockefeller throughout the dinner gave *his* reasons why Lindsay would be unwise to try for the post. Rockefeller's main argument was that a private poll had indicated Lefkowitz would draw more votes than Lindsay. Lindsay disagreed with the poll, but he preferred to remain silent. "I was able to leave the impression," he said later, "that I had been big enough to sacrifice my ambitions for the party."

A few weeks after the dinner with Rockefeller, however, Lindsay had more difficulty in resisting an unexpected act of pressure. He was about to give a talk one evening at the Republican Club in the Ninth Assembly District, on the East Side, when he was told the Governor was on the phone and urgently wanted to speak to him. Lindsay rushed off the platform.

"John," the Governor began cheerfully, "I want you to

run for controller. Would you come over immediately to meet with us?"

"Us?" Lindsay asked suspiciously.

"Yes, the rest of the ticket is here along with Javits and a few others."

Lindsay immediately decided that he did not want to face mass persuasion that evening. "I'm giving a speech," he told the Governor.

"Well, can you come up immediately afterwards?"

"Nelson, it's going to be a long speech."

"That's all right. We'll be here all night."

Lindsay breathed deeply, and said firmly into the telephone, "This isn't right or fair. I'm not going to walk in on that mob."

"All right," said the Governor, "we'll go into another room first, and we'll talk about it."

"Nothing doing," said Lindsay. "I know damn well what's happening. Javits and Lefkowitz are desperate to find a Wasp for the ticket. Nelson, I'll be glad to have eggs with you in the morning, but I'm not coming over tonight."

After a long pause, the Governor agreed.

Lindsay delivered his speech and went home, troubled. The ticket was indeed not balanced in the traditional New York style of both parties since it did not include a Wasp. The next morning, Lindsay telephoned ahead to make certain he was not about to walk into an ambush.

"Nelson, is it you and me alone? If not, I'm not coming."

He met—alone—with the Governor. "John," Rockefeller told Lindsay solicitously, "you're trapped in this congressional post. You need to get more varied experience." Rockefeller continued in this vein for about a quarter of an hour. Finally, Lindsay shook his head negatively. "Nelson, you're not making a good case. I won't do it."

Throughout the breakfast with the Governor, Lindsay had the strong impression that "Rockefeller didn't have his heart in the pitch. He was simply following through after a monstrous clubbing he'd taken from the guys the night before. When he was sure I was going to decline, he let up immediately."

Two weeks later, Rockefeller again invited Lindsay to dinner, and this time he asked him to become campaign chairman for the Lefkowitz ticket. The Congressman agreed on one condition. He made it clear that he was willing to take on the job of chairman but not the more time-consuming role of campaign manager. The manager is involved in day-to-day details of publicity and finance while the chairman helps set more general strategy. "I don't intend," Lindsay told the Governor, "to let this interfere at all with my duties in Congress."

During the mayoralty campaign, Lindsay attended all sessions of the House and all meetings of the committees and subcommittees to which he had been assigned. He flew to New York several evenings each week in the course of the campaign, and spent all his weekends at the Republican headquarters in the Commodore Hotel. In two months, he lost ten pounds, but he had not missed a single vote on the House floor.

In the middle of the campaign, a friend of Lindsay accompanied him to Commodore headquarters. Before going into the suite reserved for the regular Republican organization, they walked into a room set apart for volunteer workers who were folding fliers and stuffing them into envelopes. Lindsay greeted everyone, signed a few autographs for some of the younger campaign workers, and teased a couple of matrons about their alleged proficiency in doing the twist. When Lindsay left, his friend stayed on for a moment. "Do you know," said one of the volunteers, "that John comes in here all the time, but we've yet to have a visit from anyone on the ticket?"

Soon after assuming the role of campaign manager, Lindsay was given a speech to deliver by one of Lefkowitz's press aides. He read it, and handed it back. "No," Lindsay said flatly. "This attack on Wagner may be accurate, but I don't like the tone. It's too damn destructive. I won't put out that statement, I'll write it myself." After this and similar instances, word got back to Lindsay that some of the party regulars were complaining he was uncooperative. "It figures," he said, "but I'm not having words put in my mouth. Anyway, they did get themselves a Wasp *somewhere* in the picture."

After Robert Wagner's victory, Lindsay and a few friends were analyzing the overwhelming Republican defeat. "No," he answered one of them, "I don't think I could have beaten Wagner. Javits could have, but I'd have done better than Louie. I'd have come closer than 400,000 votes."

Six months after the election, I asked Governor Rockefeller how strongly he had actually felt about Lindsay running as controller on the Lefkowitz ticket. "I still think John would have strengthened the ticket," said the Governor. "And I did and still do believe that eventually he's got to get out of that 'silk stocking' district. I don't mean anything derogatory about the district, but I expect he wants higher office eventually, and for that he'll need a broader base of experience. There's one of those old Chinese sayings, 'The longest journey starts with the first step.' Running for controller could have been one of those small steps on the way. But I don't know for sure. You never can tell in politics. Things can look one way today and quite another way tomorrow."

The Governor reflected on what he had just said and smiled rather ruefully. "How old is John?"

"Forty," I said.

Rockefeller grinned. "He's still young in my eyes. And he may find that although a straight line is the shortest distance between two points, it's not always possible to take it. In life, as well as in politics, you sometimes discover you've made progress by following a zigzag route. I guess that'll be John's way, independent as he is."

In Washington, a few months later, I remembered Rockefeller's comment when I saw Representative Thomas Curtis of Missouri. Politically, Curtis is somewhere between Lindsay and the unswervably right wing of the Republican party. At the time, he was a man of considerable power in Congress—senior Republican on the Joint Economic Committee of the House and Senate and a ranking member of the House Ways and Means Committee. I asked Curtis if he felt Lindsay was too independent to go much farther in politics as Republican.

"There's a difference," Curtis said, "between independence and willful, gratuitous rebelliousness. John makes a noise when he feels an important principle is at stake. He doesn't keep sounding off all the time to make himself look like the only righteous man in Congress. I think he'll go farther, though maybe not in the House. It's too bad for the party that the leadership doesn't pay attention to what he says more often. We'd wind up taking a more intelligent position on many issues. But the party aside, John has a lot of strength, and he's going to grow. That's as much as I can predict. But I'll tell you one thing—the man has a lot more courage than most of his colleagues, on either side. He's been able to resist that instinctive gregariousness of the House which party leaders use to keep the boys in line. It's hard to step out and disagree, and the longer you're here and the better you know your colleagues, the harder it gets. But John does just that, and yet he does it without making himself a loner."

The next day I had lunch with Lindsay in the House Dining Room, and told him what Curtis had said. "Well"—Lindsay drummed his fingers on the table—"you can't be a complete loner in politics. If you're a loner in this game all your life, there'll come a time when you're destroyed. It's all a matter of pressures and counter-pressures. So long as you know where you stand, you organize as much weight on your side as you can and then you apply all the pressure you can

—without stirring up unnecessary antagonism. If I did go around being contentiously righteous all the time, what would I accomplish? As it is, I'm often in a lonely position. I always have to be on my guard when I'm on my own side of the floor. When I've even gone against my party on a teller vote—you know, when no record is made of individual members' decisions—I get the kind of look which makes me think that maybe I ought to change my shirt. Or I hear the whispers behind my back, 'There goes Lindsay again.' But the best way to handle that sort of thing is to meet it head on, to develop a kidding bravado. They respect you more if you banter with them. I like it if I get ragged. It shows that at least they're fond enough of me to tease me. After all, I have to work with these guys, which doesn't mean I have to go along with them when it's not the right thing to do."

Leaving the restaurant, we walked to the principal floor of the Capitol, and stood for a moment in the rotunda. Lindsay pointed at a group of tourists roaming around Statuary Hall to his left. "Look at them," he said. "Look at the expressions on their faces. They're really moved. When I walk by here, I always wish Congress were a better place than it is. The trouble is we have to make up these deliberative bodies with human beings, and the members don't always stand up to the white marble. We even have a couple of drunks. The ranking minority member of one committee is hardly ever sober after three o'clock, and there's a woman on the Democratic side who occasionally has to be helped off the floor. I don't mean to alarm you unnecessarily. I'd say a comfortable majority of the congressmen are very decent people who want to do right, but many have inadequacies of one kind or another. Maybe thirty per cent of the House consists of reasonably conscientious men who generally know what they're doing."

"That's a rather frighteningly small figure," I said.

"Yes," Lindsay said, "but you've got to remember that Congress is a microcosm of the people it represents. And the way we work does involve interminable trial and error, but we somehow manage to progress as a society. It's like what Dr. Johnson said of the dog walking on his hind legs: 'It is perhaps not done well, but the amazing thing is that it is done at all.' "

VI   "The members don't always stand up to the white marble." The phrase was very much in character for Lindsay. In private, he is often irreverent and wryly self-skewering, but he fundamentally remains serious about the responsibilities of the public life. As Oliver Pilat noted in *Lindsay's Campaign* (Beacon Press)—a classic political diary of the 1959 New York mayoralty race—"In speeches he refers openly and without apology to his conscience. His decisive adjectives on public issues are frequently 'right' and 'wrong,' 'good' and 'bad.' "

He was brought up that way. His father, George Lindsay, was a vigorous, independent man, much concerned with probity—private and public. Politics were often discussed at the family dinner table and George Lindsay, as Pilat wrote, "played a role in convincing his four sons and daughter that the bad guys of Tammany Hall must be met periodically in electoral combat and reduced to penitence by the good guys of reform."

George N. Lindsay, who died in 1961 at the age of seventy-three, was born in New York on East Eighty-fourth Street, the child of an immigrant father from the Isle of Wight and an Irish mother. At fifteen, George Lindsay went to work as a runner for a Wall Street brokerage firm. He rose to various executive positions in the investment banking field, eventually helping found and becoming president and board chairman of the Swiss American Corporation, a wholly owned subsidiary of Crédit Suisse. By the time John and David Lindsay were born, on November 24, 1921, in the family apartment at Riverside Drive and Ninety-eighth Street, the Lindsays were affluent. (At his death, George Lindsay left $700,000, in addition to suburban acreage on Long Island to be divided among four sons and a daughter.)

"But my father never forgot," John Lindsay told me, "that he had been very poor as a child and as a young man. And he never let us forget it. He was very proud of the position he had reached and prouder still that among the men he dealt with, a man's word was all that was necessary. He used to say that he never needed a lawyer in his transactions but that he had acquired an LL.B, attending night classes at New York University from 1907 to 1910, so that he could compete with the college boys."

George Lindsay was a conservative, but had not been rigid in his Republicanism. In 1928, for instance, he had voted for Al Smith because he was convinced the economy needed firmer controls. Despite his habitual concern with stemming the forces of Tammany evil, he would have preferred all his sons to follow him in banking, and at first he was not pleased when John Lindsay began a political career. In time, however, he took pride in his son's achievements, and three years before his death, George Lindsay changed his voting registration for the first time in a quarter century from Oyster Bay to Manhattan, so that he could vote in the Seventeenth District where his son was about to challenge the regular Republican candidate in a congressional primary.

In 1916, George Lindsay had married Eleanor Vliet, daughter of a successful contractor. The Vliets, of Dutch descent, had lived in New Jersey since Colonial times. Eleanor Vliet, a graduate of Wellesley, had been an actress before her marriage, mostly in road companies; the apex of her career was a leading role in *Little Women*. John Lindsay speaks of her with pride and affection. "She had a great deal of spirit. In her time, after all, 'good girls' didn't go on stage, but that's what she wanted to do, and she did it. She was a brilliant, forceful woman, but also very gracious and unaffected."

It was a close family, but—so far as the three older boys were concerned—intensely competitive. Oliver Pilat writes of the constant intramural testing throughout boyhood among John, his fraternal twin, David, and George, his elder brother by two years. "All three were cut from the same mold, tall for their age, rangy, blue-eyed, quick of mind and body, and intensely energetic. . . . With his advantage in age, George offered a constant target of excellence for the twins. He seems to have been more contemplative in youth and maturity than the others. Whereas David often acted in an impulsive way, John exhibited a steady temperament. Certain open qualities seem to have made him the general favorite in the family. In no namby-pamby sense he emerged as the good brother. Robert (Rod), four years younger than the twins, never played much of a role in the fraternal competition. He was shorter, less athletic, more social than the others. If he needed protection, he turned to John. Whereas George, John, and David became naval officers and lawyers, Rod served in the merchant marine and then moved into his father's occupation of banking."

The brothers attended private, prestigious schools. John started at the Buckley School, around the corner from his home, and went on to St. Paul's in Concord, New Hampshire, where he was president of the sixth form (the senior class) in 1940. He was also a School Camp Councilor, a member of the Missionary and of the Cadmean Literary Societies, played football, and rowed on the St. Paul's crew. A boyhood friend, Allen Klots, who became an editor at Dodd, Mead & Company, recalls that "John was always exceptionally popular. He wasn't aggressive and so I didn't consciously think of him as a 'leader' until I realized as we grew older that he usually was the president of something and that people just looked to him to take charge."

When Lindsay went on to Yale, the pattern of popularity and multiple activities continued. He was stroke of the freshman crew, participated in intramural football, belonged to the fencing club, and was active in the Elizabethan Literary Society and the Yale Political Forum. He was also tapped for Scroll and Key, one of the two most exclusive senior secret societies at Yale. (David Lindsay was at least as active, and moreover, attained membership in Skull and Bones, a cut above Scroll and Key, as well as in Phi Beta Kappa—an academic honor that eluded his fraternal twin.)

William MacComber, currently Assistant Secretary of State for Congressional Relations in the Nixon Administration, was a roommate of John Lindsay at Yale and he remembers that for all his extracurricular interests, Lindsay was a serious student. "He also," MacComber adds, "had a great attraction for a considerable portion of the feminine population of the Eastern seaboard." A year ahead of Lindsay at Yale was Francis Thorne, a composer, who became and has remained a close friend. "John," says Thorne, "was a person you immediately heard about. I was told he was somebody special and to keep an eye on him. I wondered at first what all the shouting was about, but as I got to know him, the one quality he had that struck me most forcibly was that you could always trust what he said."

Lindsay and his friends engaged in many all-night political and philosophical discussions, and MacComber feels that "John hasn't changed very much since then. The only real difference is that in those days, his liberalism was an instinct and it now has been translated into concrete viewpoints on a wide range of specific issues. I doubt if his subsequent career has been a surprise to any of his college classmates. His intelligence and attractiveness as a leader were all fairly apparent even in those days. He was also tough when he needed to be, and this quality, together with an aggressiveness which was less apparent then, has certainly been useful in his political life."

Lindsay's major at Yale was English history. He had begun immersing himself in general European history while at St. Paul's, and history still accounts for a large percentage of his reading for pleasure. He wrote his senior thesis on Oliver Cromwell. "I was fascinated by him," says Lindsay, "because of his constant internal clashes. Although he gave the appearance of being absolutely convinced he was right, he was always bumping into himself. The experience has not been entirely unfamiliar to me as a congressman and then as mayor."

Lindsay had taken an accelerated program at Yale, and was graduated by himself in March 1943. His R.O.T.C. credits qualified him as a commissioned officer, and he reported to the Navy in Norfolk, Virginia, on May 1. For three years, he served as a gunnery officer on the destroyer U.S.S. *Swanson.* He took part in the invasion of Sicily and saw considerable action in the Pacific with the Seventh Fleet and Carrier Task Group 38.4. By the time he was discharged from the Navy in March 1946, Lindsay was a lieutenant, senior grade, and had acquired five battle stars.

"The war," Lindsay feels, "had a lot to do with my eventual decision to go into public service. I lost a barrel of friends. One of my roommates was killed, and one of my closest friends was among the initial casualties at Guadalcanal. Twenty per cent of my class at St. Paul's was wiped out. I felt something had to be done to make sure it wouldn't happen again, and politics finally seemed to me to be the way to get most fully involved instead of sitting in a business or profession.

"Then, too, the idea of service had already been knocked into me at St. Paul's. It was a private school, but there was certainly no coddling. The life was rather Spartan. We'd take a freezing cold shower in the morning, and then run through the snow to get breakfast. All that was supposed to mold our character so that we'd amount to something and contribute to society. Kids are impressionable, and I guess I absorbed the gospel of responsibility that was preached there. By the time I'd finished Yale, I had had all the 'advantages' and what the hell was all that money for if I didn't do more with my education than just make a good living?"

Lindsay elaborated on the "gospel of responsibility" in a New York *Post* interview in 1958 during his first campaign for Congress: "I don't care if it does sound corny, but if you're able to get that kind of education, you not only have the opportunity to capitalize on it, but I say you've got to *justify* it. I think we can learn something from the British. Over there, higher education has much more of a purpose. There's less education in a vacuum. You *do* something with your education. And if you fit the bill, you go into politics."

This determination to justify his background had not, however, entirely crystallized at the time of Lindsay's discharge from the Navy. "I was on terminal leave and had a big roll of cash," he recalls, "and so I went ski-bumming. I was still thrashing around, not knowing quite what to do. I followed the snow trail until May, and then I came back to New York and had two months of experience in the training program of the First National Bank. I hated it. I expect my father was disappointed that I didn't take to banking, but I quickly became certain that the next step for me was law school."

Before his first term at Yale Law School, Lindsay was briefly introduced to practical politics. The congressman from the Seventeenth District at the time was Joseph Clark Baldwin, a short, dapper, sharp-edged man whom Lindsay had heard speak at St. Paul's on the value of politics as a career. "Baldwin was one of many speakers we had," says Lindsay, "but he had done an especially good job, and I'd remembered what he'd said. That experience, by the way, is one reason why I never turn down an invitation to speak at a school if I can help it."

When Lindsay returned from the war, he discovered that Baldwin, whom he describes as a "Stanley Isaacs type of Republican," was in trouble with the regular Republican organization. The late Tom Curran, county chairman, had dropped Baldwin and selected Frederic R. Coudert, Jr., a state assemblyman and leader of the Ninth Assembly District as the official candidate. Baldwin ran as an insurgent. Lindsay volunteered to help, and started pushing doorbells. Before the campaign was over, Lindsay had to leave for Yale, and he was dismayed to learn afterwards that after a bitter campaign, Baldwin had been overwhelmingly defeated.

"I've always regretted," Lindsay says, "that Joe Baldwin didn't live long enough to know that in my first campaign for public office, I ran as an insurgent against the organization, and beat it."

Lindsay enjoyed the challenge of Yale Law School. "The tradition there," he emphasizes, "was to teach you to question everything. They'd probe at your ideas and try to argue you off the track. There weren't more than five Republicans in my whole class so that the experience of being constantly forced to justify my ideas was extremely valuable—particularly in view of the district I came to represent, and the city I've tried to govern."

In 1948, Lindsay received his LL.B. degree from Yale, and was admitted to the New York State Bar the next year. Also in 1949, Lindsay married. His wife, Mary Anne Harrison—or "Mare," as she is called by her family and friends —was born in Richmond, Virginia, grew up in Greenwich, Connecticut, was graduated from Vassar, and had taught at the Buckley School, which Lindsay attended. Her father was head of the trust department of the Hanover Bank. The only professional political tradition in the family stemmed from a distant relationship to Presidents William Henry and

Benjamin Harrison. "Not very sterling political credentials," Mrs. Lindsay has pointed out.

The Lindsays set up their first home in an apartment in Stuyvesant Town. John Lindsay had joined the law firm of Webster, Sheffield and Horan, of which he later became a partner, but was devoting what time he could spare from his practice to politics. Following the advice of Joseph Clark Baldwin, he had joined the New York Young Republican Club, and by 1949, was a member of its board of governors. He helped in whatever local campaigns were under way, and made a special effort to get speaking assignments, particularly service on sound trucks. "One reason," he admits, "is that I wanted to be a trial lawyer, and I thought street-corner speaking would be good experience. And I suppose it was the ham in me which attracted me to trial law to begin with. I could have made more money in some other branch of the law, but I do like an audience."

Both Lindsay and his wife worked in support of Oren Root, in his losing battle in 1949 against Robert Wagner for the presidency of the Borough of Manhattan. "They made quite a team," recalls Joan Hamlin, secretary to Stanley Isaacs when he was City Council Minority Leader, and later in charge of Lindsay's New York office during part of his congressional years. "Mare was pregnant, but she was just as energetic as John. She rushed up and down the stairs of Stuyvesant Town, ringing doorbells, and she held several house parties. Their enthusiasm was contagious. John had begun to indicate his talent for mobilizing young Republicans."

In 1950, John Lindsay and his brother David were among the founders of Youth for Eisenhower, a movement that soon spread through the country. In the summer of 1951, Lindsay, by then vice-president of the New York Republican Club, and his wife went to Paris, where Lindsay saw General Eisenhower to urge him to run for President in 1952. The General heard him out, smiled, and remained silent on the subject of politics. Subsequently, Hugh Scott of Pennsylvania, then a Representative, made a similar pilgrimage. When he returned, Scott asked Republicans on Capitol Hill, "Who is this guy Lindsay? Eisenhower told me to get in touch with him when I get back." "I guess," Lindsay recalls, "I really did help put a flea in Eisenhower's ear. The big guns of the party didn't start in on him until some months later."

Lindsay maintained an active interest in politics after the Republican victory in 1952. He had been elected president of the Young Republican Club in 1952, and was made chairman of its board of advisers in 1953. He continued to practice law in New York until 1955, when he was appointed Executive Assistant to Attorney General Herbert Brownell.

In his two years in Washington, Lindsay acquired experience and contacts which were to be of considerable use to him later as a legislator. In the Justice Department, he acted as liaison between the department and the White House as well as between Brownell and the heads of divisions within the Justice Department itself. In addition, he was involved in the drafting of civil-rights and immigration legislation. During the Hungarian revolt, Lindsay, as Brownell's representative, twice traveled to Austria and Germany to expedite the admission of Hungarian refugees to America.

"He was a refreshingly candid official," Herman Edelsberg, director of the Washington office of the Anti-Defamation League of B'nai Brith and a skillful lobbyist in the civil-liberties field, told me later. "In security cases, Lindsay fought for civil liberties and common sense; and he pressed the Administration to offer a drastic amendment of the racist 'national origins quota system' in the McCarran-Walter Immigration Act."

Brownell was quickly impressed with Lindsay's ability as a lawyer and his capacity to make clear, logical recommendations after having assimilated complex issues ranging from reviews of patent applications to appeals for pardons. Lindsay's work brought him into frequent contact with James V. Bennett, who had been director of the Bureau of Prisons since 1937. "He handled legal problems arising from this bureau," Bennett has recalled, "with a degree of understanding, compassion, and awareness of the realities of life that was admirable and a delight to all people who are, shall I say, of a liberal turn of mind. I could appeal to him to help push through the pardon application of a prisoner who I thought had been unjustly dealt with or who was deserving of release for any number of reasons. He was unusually compassionate in dealing with the men and women who had a serious illness or a malignancy and whom we did not want to see die in prison. He expedited such cases through his office and followed them up until action was taken."

An unpublicized result of Lindsay's term in the Justice Department was a major reorganization of the method by which Presidential pardons were granted. Under a system that had been in effect since George Washington, the President had to sign each pardon twice. "It was one of those idiotic holdovers," says Lindsay, "that made the Presidency so burdensome. Huge backlogs gathered, and I remember being told that Franklin Roosevelt sometimes had to take a large batch of pardons to bed in order to cut down on at least some of the delay. The majority of the cases involved men who had proved themselves thoroughly rehabilitated and had been in civilian life for twenty years and more after having served time for the federal offense for which they had been convicted. And yet, without a pardon, they couldn't vote. Besides, they wanted to clear their records for their families' sake. I finally convinced the Attorney General and the White House to agree to a mass signing by which one signature would pardon several hundred people at a time, and that system has been in use ever since."

In another of his roles at the Justice Department, Lindsay from time to time had to appear before the Supreme

Court. I mention one such case because it reveals the man's capacity to brood even about victory and thereby remain the more open to change. In *Jay* v. *Boyd,* Lindsay presented the government's arguments for continuing to allow the Attorney General the use of confidential information in connection with his discretionary power to suspend or not suspend deportation—under certain circumstances—of aliens who were otherwise deportable. Such a suspension amounted to placing the alien in question on probation, and Lindsay had at first persuaded himself that these cases were similar to probation and parole problems in the regular courts where judges have traditionally been able to consider confidential information in reaching decisions on suspended sentences.

Lindsay won the case by a 5 to 4 margin, but by the time the arguments were concluded, he had become increasingly uneasy at continuing a system whereby aliens could not face their accusers. Accordingly, he soon arranged with the then Commissioner of Immigration, Joseph Swing, that the practice of using confidential data in suspension proceedings be dropped for all practical purposes; and the relevant regulations were rewritten.

"It's interesting," Lindsay told me as a footnote to the agreement with Swing, "how human relationships can affect the administration of justice. J. Edgar Hoover was all for utilizing confidential information because he was convinced that otherwise many of his agents might be exposed. But Swing and Hoover disliked each other so much that it was all the easier to get Swing to support the right of aliens to know who was fingering them. I'm not saying that Swing— for all the controversies about his own insensitivity to civil liberties in which he used to get involved in the administration of his office—didn't honestly see our point, but the fact that Hoover was against the idea helped our cause considerably."

In his last months in the Justice Department, Lindsay was deeply immersed in the drafting of what later became the 1957 Civil Rights Act which he considered a "significant breakthrough—the first important civil-rights legislation since Reconstruction days." The bill was weak in many respects, but it did establish a Civil Rights Commission and it gave the Attorney General power to institute action for an injunction to prevent interference with the right to vote.

From the time he entered Congress in 1959, Lindsay kept trying—with gradual success—to have much stronger civil-rights measures enacted. The details are in Daniel Button's book on Lindsay, including a full account of the climax of those efforts, Lindsay's essential work as a principal architect of and floor manager for the 1964 Civil Rights Act. That legislation too had deficiencies, but as Button notes, "it was the most sweeping law of its kind since Reconstruction."

VII   That Lindsay was able to enter Congress in 1959 was due in part to the torpor of the Republican organization in the City of New York, and particularly in the Seventeenth Congressional District, where he took residence again in 1957 after having left the Justice Department. Although the Seventeenth had elected Democratic congressmen on only three occasions since the First World War, there were clear signs that the Republicans would be in trouble in 1958. Frederic Coudert, the incumbent—colorless, mechanically conservative, with a high absentee record in Congress—had been steadily losing the confidence of the electorate. In 1954, he had been able to defeat his Democratic opponent, Anthony Akers, by only 314 votes. Akers ran against him again two years later, and although Dwight Eisenhower carried the District by 24,000, Coudert had been just

2,478 votes ahead of Akers. It was evident that Akers would try a third time.

Lindsay was rather ambivalent about the idea of a political career when, toward the end of 1957, he began to think seriously about entering the Republican primary the next year. He was happily married and had three daughters, Katharine, Margaret, and Anne, whom he missed greatly whenever he was separated from them. Furthermore, he was moving rapidly ahead in his law firm, and his partners were distinctly unenthusiastic at the prospect of his going into politics. His father also tried to convince Lindsay that he could make a greater contribution to the community as an independent professional man. It turned out that George Lindsay wanted warriors other than members of his family to do battle with Tammany. "Politics," George Lindsay counseled his son, "is unsound. If a person wants to go into public life, he should first become established and financially successful. Then, if he still feels the urge, he can try to become Secretary of State—if he can afford it."

On the other hand, John Lindsay's two years in Washington had reawakened his own postwar conviction that he had to justify his education and other advantages by becoming engaged in public service. "Some people's community," he later observed in an interview with a New York *Herald-Tribune* reporter, "is themselves; others, their family; others, General Electric; others, their law firm; others go beyond that into the state. That's for me." He had, moreover, much enjoyed being part of the Washington scene, and had become restive away from it. "You can't be part of what's really going on," he began telling his friends, "by going home to your wife and bitching over what you read in the *Times*."

Lindsay was also frustrated by what he considered to be the rapidly accelerating decline of the Republican Party in Manhattan. "We've all been talking about rebuilding the party," he grumbled, "but that's all we do—talk." It was true that since Fiorello La Guardia's years as mayor, there had been a dearth in the city of energetic young Republicans who were willing to make the financial sacrifice to try for public office.

Lindsay and his wife discussed his decision for many evenings. Some nights he decided he would not run, but a few evenings later, he had changed his mind again. Gradually, Lindsay knew he was definitely going to make the race. Beginning in January 1958, five of his close friends, one of them a seasoned Republican politician who is now a federal judge, constituted themselves, with Lindsay, an informal "executive committee" to plan his campaign. They met weekly, and soon more often, in Lindsay's apartment. Mary Lindsay became expert at determining the consensus of each meeting by the angle at which the strategists were sitting when she came into the room. "I knew they had temporarily lost all hope," she recalls, "when I'd see all six of them with the backs of their necks on their chairs, their feet sticking straight out, their hands in their pockets, sitting in utter silence."

The experienced politician in the group continually emphasized that a primary was a "one plus one" operation. Primary voting is usually small, and therefore, an intense effort had to be made to get at every voter. The tactician estimated that 8,000 out of the 39,000 registered Republicans would cast a ballot in the primary. "If you win the election, John," he said, "you'll be representing close to a half million people, but your immediate goal in the primary is to get four thousand votes—plus one." As part of the preliminary strategy, the politician instructed Mary Lindsay and the wives of the other committee members in how to map out the entire Seventeenth District, house by house, street by street. They were proceeding according to the venerable battle plan of an earlier Republican, Abraham Lincoln, who had said before the party was formed: "Divide the county into small districts and appoint in each a committee. Make a perfect list of the voters and ascertain with certainty for whom they will vote. Keep a constant watch on the doubtful voters and have them talked to by those in whom they have the most confidence. . . . On Election Days see that every Whig is brought to the polls."

As word spread of Lindsay's candidacy, it was clear that even if Coudert, the incumbent, chose not to run again, Lindsay would not have the backing of the official Republican organization headed by County Chairman Curran, who had been trained under Thomas Dewey's harsh code of party regularity. Lindsay had announced as an insurgent. Many potential recruits to Lindsay's campaign were reluctant to be placed by Curran in the same catagory of exiles. "Besides," one of them urged Lindsay in front of his "executive committee," "primaries are divisive and you'll rock the boat in a district that is already dangerously marginal." The old pro on Lindsay's "committee" snorted. "How can you rock a boat when it's already sunk?"

Further complicating Lindsay's ambitions was the New York State Legislature's decision to hold the primary on August 12. "A fine time," Lindsay mourned. "New York's heat and humidity, a half-empty city because of vacations, and absentee voting not permitted by law." The advantage, it seemed, would decidedly be with the regular Republican organization, which had the hard-core strength, while Lindsay would have to educate the voters with what volunteers he could muster.

Lindsay formally announced his candidacy on April 15, before Coudert himself had declared whether he would run for re-election. Most of the party's professionals and veteran political reporters gave Lindsay little chance. "You won't win," an elderly newspaperman told Lindsay flatly. "Your fingernails aren't long enough." Paper ballots were still being used in the primaries and, the reporter explained, under state law, a ballot marked other than in the proper box would be automatically voided. A broken-off pencil point under the fingernail could invalidate a lot of insurgent ballots. "As it turned out," Lindsay remembers, "very little of that sort of thing happened. There were a few attempts to get legitimate votes disqualified, and not just by old guard guys, but by young men in old guard suits."

Lindsay opened his headquarters at the Roosevelt Hotel ("named for Theodore," he carefully told the press). Former Attorney General Herbert Brownell strained a thirty-year personal and political friendship with Curran to come out openly for Lindsay, and a few other prominent Republicans —Mrs. Wendell Willkie, John Roosevelt, and former Congressman Bruce Barton among them—also declared themselves for him.

On May 15, Coudert announced that he would not stand for re-election. The Republican organization met, and a majority, representing over eighty per cent of the district, selected Elliot "Pete" Goodwin, a young, personable, "regular" Republican as the official party choice in the primaries. Only three Assembly District leaders—representing forty-four election districts—were for Lindsay; the other six, with one hundred and seventy-five election districts, supported Goodwin.

Externally, Lindsay and Goodwin seemed quite similar. Both were rising lawyers. Both came from Ivy League schools (Goodwin was a graduate of Harvard), both had been Navy lieutenants, and both were communicants at St. James Episcopal Church on Madison Avenue. Both, moreover, were former presidents of the Young Republican Club. (The board of governors and the officers of the Young Woman's Republican Club endorsed Goodwin, while Lindsay just barely won the endorsement of the all-male New York Young Republican Club.) The two candidates were divided primarily on how best to strengthen the Republican Party. Goodwin's campaign literature frequently emphasized Lindsay's insurgency, and Lindsay happily countered with charges of "bossism."

On June 30, Lindsay read a poem he had written to three hundred members of the Young Republican Club at a party in the Belmont Plaza Hotel. It was called "The Regular," and ended with the refrain:

> *Be regular, be regular*
> *O hear our loud refrain.*
> *Arm in arm, all in step,*
> *Together once again.*
> *O put my tombstone at the place*
> *Where the roadway took its bend,*
> *And on it carve this mournful trace,*
> *"He was regular to the end."*

Lindsay's campaign swiftly gathered momentum. He soon had attracted more than five hundred volunteers, primarily young Republicans who also felt that the party's leadership in the district had become sluggish. Most were participating in active politics for the first time. "Nobody," said one of them, "had ever invited us before." Directing the volunteers was a twenty-five-year-old law student, Bob Price. (He had become a captain in a Republican district at seventeen. Two years later, he applied for membership in the New York Young Republican Club and was rejected as too young. Price appealed to the then president of the club, John Lindsay, and the decision was rescinded. From a follower of Lindsay, Price became his principal political adviser and his campaign manager up to and including Lindsay's run for mayor in 1965.)

Price worked out an elaborate table of organization and assignments so that there was no wasted effort. All the formidable energy on hand was focused with maximum efficiency on the one-plus-one goal. Until Primary Day, August 12, Lindsay was constantly on the streets, in the stores, and in the apartment houses of the Seventeenth. He was often accompanied by lissome young ladies with an apparently unlimited supply of shopping bags, and balloons for children. On both items, Lindsay's name was prominently printed, and if the shopping bags didn't work, the balloons occasionally served as an introduction to the moppets' mothers. The district had been so stirred by the Lindsay whirlwind that of the almost 14,000 new voters who had registered for the primary in the city as a whole, nearly 10,000 were added to the rolls in the Seventeenth. Most of the latter were Republicans.

On the day of the election, the old political pro on Lindsay's executive committee was proved wrong. Not 8,000 but over 10,000, or more than twenty per cent of the registered Republicans in the district voted, some of them interrupting vacations to travel into the city for Lindsay. He defeated Elliot Goodwin by 6,129 to 4,052, and went on to win over Anthony Akers on November fourth by 53,674 to 45,956. One of Lindsay's more telling arguments in the campaign against Akers was his repeated reminder that although he and his opponent were running for a federal post, a congressman also has a responsibility to the electorate on local matters. "In this city," Lindsay declared, "if a Republican does not supply the challenge, who will?"

The day after Lindsay's victory, *The New York Times* noted that "John V. Lindsay emerges as one of the bright hopes of the Republican party." A similar estimate had prodded a Greenwich Village Democrat to abandon Akers for the first time. "I heard them both at a meeting of the Greenwich Village Association," the man said, "and I figured that if Akers won, we'd have a very good Representative. But if Lindsay won, we had a potential future Presidential candidate."

VIII By 1964, whatever his potential for the presidency, Lindsay had certainly won the respect of a larger and larger majority of the voters in his district, as was evidenced by his having taken seventy-one per cent of the vote in the election that year which won him his fourth term. The Seventeenth C.D. takes in the core of Manhattan—north as far as 110th Street and south to Stuyvesant Town. The wealth of some of the Upper East Side constituents has given the district its "silk stocking" sobriquet, but also included in the Seventeenth are most of Greenwich Village and even some poor areas—on the north in East Harlem and on the western margins down Columbus, Ninth, Eighth, and Seventh Avenues to Bleecker Street. As one index of the district's heterogeneity, during Lindsay's tenure, nearly ten per cent of the electorate were blacks or Puerto Rican, and there were high concentrations of Jews, Czechs, Poles, and Italians. In addition, its boundaries encompass the garment district, Times Square, the greater number of the city's theaters and art museums, and such non-voting tenants as the United Nations and nearly all the foreign consulates.

Essentially, for most of those in the Seventeenth who cared about politics—and there are proportionately more such than in probably any other district in the country, given the presence within it of Greenwich Village and the Upper East Side—Lindsay was exactly the kind of congressman they wanted. Bright, hard-working, articulate, independent—and accessible. If a constituent came to Washington, there was no problem seeing the Congressman, and Lindsay spent nearly all of Saturday every week back home listening to

complaints, problems, and demands. On those Saturdays, he
was always behind schedule. "If I didn't keep reminding him
there are people waiting," one exasperated secretary told
me, "he's quite capable of spending the whole morning with
just one voter." Lindsay had overheard. "I know, I know I
get behind, but I get so goddam interested."

Along with his interest, there was usually considerable
candor. A friend of mine, a pacifist from the Village, felt
Lindsay didn't go far enough in his opposition to the nuclear arms race and visited him on occasion to press him to
support unilateral American moves toward disarmament.
She always failed. "Still," she said to me, "at least you always
know exactly what his stand is, and why. I get angry as hell
at him sometimes, but there's nothing of the con man about
Lindsay."

In addition to his accessibility in the Washington and
New York offices, Lindsay also kept in contact with his constituents by regularly mailing out, at his own expense, carefully prepared newsletters in which he discussed the major
issues before Congress, explained his own positions, and
tried to indicate the failures as well as the accomplishments
of the House as each term went along. And there were also
frequent questionnaires to the electorate. In discussing these
questionnaires with constituents, he made it clear that final
responsibility for voting on issues was his alone, but that he
did consider the opinions of the voters in his district as
guidelines. As a congressman, Lindsay strongly agreed with
the doctrine of "virtual representation" which developed in
England during the eighteenth century and which maintained that a member of Parliament was free to exercise his
independent judgment. He was not simply a mechanical
agent of the majority of his constituency. Some congressmen,
Lindsay used to point out, still consider themselves delegates
who must carry out the mandates of the voters back home.
Others act as free agents, but regard their responsibility as
being primarily to their own districts. A third category, in

which Lindsay included himself, concurs with Edmund Burke, who told the electors of Bristol in 1774, "You choose a member indeed, but when you have chosen him, he is not a member for Bristol; he is a member of Parliament."

It was this lack of parochialism, along with his independence, which particularly impressed many voters in the Seventeenth C.D. because, by continuing to elect him, they were able to give themselves credit for recognizing the worth of so singular a congressman.

In 1960, for example, Lindsay's Democratic opponent was William vanden Heuvel, a thirty-year-old lawyer, a Kennedy-style liberal, and a skillful debater. Vanden Heuvel was photographed receiving Presidential candidate John Kennedy's endorsement, and speaking for him in the district were Adlai Stevenson, Harry Truman, Chester Bowles, and a considerable number of show-business personages. Lindsay meanwhile was running on the same line with Richard Nixon. (The latter's name, however, was conspicuously absent from Lindsay's campaign literature.) Largely because of the growing thrust of the Reform Democrats, Democratic registration in the Seventeenth had risen—there were 70,759 self-acknowledged Democrats and 2,695 members of the Liberal Party as contrasted with 61,355 enrolled Republicans. But Lindsay, again depending primarily on volunteers—more than a thousand in comparison with the five hundred of 1958—made sure all 225 election districts were carefully canvassed and he himself marched through the streets and supermarkets in addition to accepting all challenges for debate from Vanden Heuvel.

Lindsay won handily with nearly sixty per cent of the votes. One fairly characteristic response to Lindsay was that of an earnest young lady in her twenties attending a debate late in the campaign at a junior high school on the East Side where, as *The New York Times* noted, "women in minks and diamonds vied with working girls in trenchcoats and men in Brooks Brothers suits jostled men in bargain-basement outfits for standing room." The young woman whispered to her male companion as the debate neared its close, "I *know* I've never voted Republican before, but I just *trust* Lindsay more."

Another less instinctual indication of the trust in Lindsay in the Seventeenth was an article in the *Village Voice* by David McReynolds, a member of the National Committee of the Socialist Party and one of the national leaders of the peace movement. In the piece, McReynolds spoke for many of the district's political dissenters, and in the process, he also indicated why Lindsay was able to draw support from so many diverse sources in a district that especially prided itself on its own singularity:

> In my mind Congressman Lindsay reminds me of no one quite so much as the late Robert Taft. Who else but Taft himself would have had the good sense to suggest that when a severe housing shortage exists, housing be treated as a public utility? Official liberalism would not dare suggest anything so sensible for fear of being called Socialists. Lindsay's lone vote in Congress against the "obscene mail" bill can only be compared to Taft's historic stand in the Senate when, arch-conservative that he was, he stood up to Harry Truman and said this was a free country and that not even the President of the United States had the right to draft the striking railway workers. Lindsay's strong and consistent stand for civil liberties recalls Taft's lonely voice when he said, in the midst of hysteria, that he saw no reason why Communists should not be free to teach in public schools so long as they did not misuse their posts. And Lindsay shares one other characteristic with Taft: he is that rare man in politics, a man with a real sense of civic duty, a man who has served his district and served it well, whatever his stands on foreign and domestic policy. . . . I hope that, however liberals vote for President, hundreds and thousands of liberals and independents will join in backing Lindsay in November, and do it not under any illusion that Lindsay is a "liberal," but because they are tired of the kind of verbal games the Democratic Party has been playing.

Winning in 1962 was easier for Lindsay than the 1960 contest had been, and 1964 was a runaway. Clearly Lindsay could have continued to be the Seventeenth's congressman for many years to come. But he was becoming restless. As an irregular Republican, he could only go so far in the House—and, in fact, he had probably gone about as far as he could.

In the summer of 1964, I asked Lindsay's response to a comment by Washington reporter Robert Donovan: "If Lindsay is ever to become a national leader, his immediate problem is how to break out of the obscurity of the House."

Lindsay shrugged. "Oh, I don't know how to answer that. Whatever I say now about the future may be wrong, because this is one field in which chance is so large a factor. I'll tell you though, if I don't run for Congress next time, the main reason will be my family. This kind of life begins to bind the kids especially after a while." I remembered Mary Lindsay telling me about the children wondering why their father seemed to have so much time for everybody but them. And at a Sunday dinner at the Lindsays a few months before, one of his daughters, snapping a wishbone in two, announced her wish. "I wish Daddy would get out of Congress." Mary Lindsay had her own way of coping with the Congressman's lack of extra-congressional time. At one point, after having failed on a number of occasions to get him to allot her enough time for a discussion of family finances, she had called his secretary and had been given an appointment at the office.

"And there'd be another reason," Lindsay said, "in addition to getting to know my children again. I might stop just to get recharged. That was Henry Stimson's approach to public life. He kept going in and withdrawing all the time so that he could come back to earth and get sharpened up. He always felt, and I agree, that you can render your best service to government by keeping an independent base. The most effective public servant is a guy who is free to put on his hat at any minute and walk out. It's sad to watch a man come to the point where he needs the job. Then it's awfully difficult for him to follow through on what his conscience dictates. In my case, I can always go back to practicing law."

A close associate of Lindsay to whom I spoke at the time hoped that the Congressman *would* decide to withdraw for a while from public life. "The great danger John faces at present," he said, "is that maybe he's come too far too fast. On the surface, he has all the credentials for the big time, and with the Republicans so painfully short of appealing national figures, he may get thrust into the ring before he's ready. John, though not a profound thinker, is a thoughtful man. He needs time to reflect on his political philosophy. He could well profit from a year of reading which would give greater shape and substance to his beliefs and ideas. If you stay in Washington too long without a break, you may become like most politicians—creatures rather than shapers of events. But I doubt if he'll retire from public life voluntarily. He likes politics too much."

A Democratic congressman from the Northeast, who had great respect for Lindsay, also told me in mid-1964 of his conviction that Lindsay should not stay in the House much longer, but his reasons were different. "John might well get ground up in time," the Congressman said, "because as an irregular in a party controlled by conservatives, he cannot avoid being put into all kinds of awkward positions on votes. So far, John has been able to remain relatively independent without unduly antagonizing the party leadership, but he's been under considerable strain, and the strain will increase. With this kind of continuous pressure on him, even John could eventually become a political juggler. I worry about John because he's such a classy guy. From my point of view, Jack Javits has a more impressive record, but he gives me the impression of being a political I.B.M. machine. When you talk to John, however, you feel the very marrow of the man.

He's intensely human and open, but if he stays in the House, how long can he keep that quality alive? And the longer he stays here, the more he'll lose of that youthful flair of his. Other bright men will come along, and he'll have lost his chance. Timing means so much in this game. My own hope is that he'll be able to go on to the Senate where pressures of party discipline are less and the traditions allow more room for a freewheeler. Historically, in fact, men such as John usually make the most effective Senators."

But there was no likelihood of Lindsay being nominated for the Senate for some time to come. With Jacob Javits of New York City already in the Senate, the state Republican Party would not nominate another man from the city for whatever opening occurred. Traditionally, so long as Javits served—and he gave no signs of tiring of his job, short of a chance at the vice-presidency—the party would give its nomination for the other Senate seat to a man outside the city. The only other possibility for Lindsay was the governorship, but Nelson Rockefeller intended to hold on to that post as his base for another try at the presidency in 1968.

"What about running for mayor of New York?" I asked Lindsay in that summer of 1964. "Murray Kempton tried to start a movement for you as Fusion candidate for mayor four years ago. Do you think next year might be the time?"

There was a long pause. "Okay," he said, "the big cities are becoming more important in national politics, particularly after the redistricting that has been setting in after the 1962 Supreme Court decision on reapportionment of state legislatures. So being a mayor can have national impact. And God knows the cities have problems, especially this town.

"What bothers me," he went on, "is that New York isn't just Manhattan. There are four other boroughs, and while I think I could win in Manhattan, I have strong doubts about the others. The Seventeenth C.D. is one thing. Queens is quite another. I don't know. The odds are so high. Well, even if I don't win, I think I'd do well, and that might be worth it."

That fall I spoke to a constituent of Lindsay, a leader of the city's Reform Democrats. "I hope John runs," he said. "I might even vote for him—in the privacy of the booth. He'd make an excellent mayor." The Reformer grinned. "And as a good Democrat, that's exactly where I'd like to see him. Hopefully, for life."

A few weeks later, I was in Lindsay's Washington office. The Congressman was on the floor of the House, and an assistant was talking to me about Lindsay as politician. "I don't know if he's going to go for mayor," he said, "but he's ready for that kind of battle now. The guy has learned a lot about practical politics. He hasn't lost his sincerity, but I don't think you'll find him going out of his way to cut his throat. What I mean is John still doesn't shirk a touchy issue if he feels it's an important one, but on lesser matters that may stir up a fuss in the party, he'll keep his opinions to himself. And he has learned something else he'll need in order to move on up. You remember that one of the lovely qualities about Stanley Isaacs was that he didn't assume anyone was bad. He never thought about what people might use against him. But as a result, he was disarmed all the time. Okay, it didn't hurt Stanley. There weren't that many people aching to be Republican minority leader of the City Council in New York City. But when the stakes are higher, that kind of open faith in all men can be a big, big problem. I used to worry about John in that regard. But he's come to recognize what human beings are, not what he'd like them to be. Sure, he's outgoing, but he's learned to protect himself quite well. He's going to have to do just that if he ever does become mayor."

The Congressman strode in, waved to me to follow him into his office, and took a call. It was about a behind-the-scenes battle in the New York Republican organization and Lindsay was being asked to come into the fight. As the conversation proceeded, Lindsay's voice hardened. "No," he said sharply, "I'm not going to come out against him. He was with me in 1958. Where were you in 1958 when I was going against the organization? No, I'm not holding it against you. I just want to remind you of facts you may have forgotten."

After he had hung up, Lindsay was silent for a while. "The techniques of politics," he said as if to himself. "That guy," he gestured toward the phone, "is making a mistake. He's going to lose, and it's not as if it were a matter of principle. It's just a power play. You sure have to keep learning an awful lot about politics. About timing. And how to maximize your effectiveness. The danger is that you may get so involved in the learning that you become more expert in the means for staying in office than you remain concerned with why you're really supposed to be here. I'm always worrying whether I'm letting various pressures and political considerations work on me so that I'll wind up functioning like an I.B.M. machine and my positions will come out like fudge. I don't think I've let it happen, but rationalization is one of the great perils in political life. In all life. In this business especially, if you lose the capacity to think and act clearly, you'll be discovered in the end.

"There are some techniques though which you've just got to remember," Lindsay went on. "One of the main ones is that when you're campaigning, you have to ask and thank, ask and thank, again and again. For money. For support of all kinds. No matter how sophisticated they are, people like to be asked, and they like to be thanked. Some politicians have no compunctions about continually asking. It still kills me to do it, but that's a rule you have to learn.

"Anyway"—he leaned back in his chair—"aside from that part of it, I like campaigning more now than I did at first. I don't have to spend so much time justifying myself. After all, I've been elected to office four times, and there's reason for me to shake hands and introduce myself. At the beginning, I used to feel somewhat presumptuous. I figured that when I put out my hand, people were thinking, 'Who the hell are *you*? Haven't you something better to do with your time?' "

"If you do campaign for mayor," I asked, "how important is the Republican organization going to be to you?"

"I can't depend on it for any kind of basic support. I speak at their clubs and show up at their affairs but the core of my political strength has to remain with the volunteers. I have to continue to rely on the new generation. Nobody can argue with young people. Even an old guard election district captain can't argue with boys and girls pushing doorbells. My own test of how well I'm doing in politics is the enthusiasm I can maintain among youth. They're so damn important, the young. I don't mean only to me, but in terms of the direction the country is going to go. Hell, the Seventeenth is supposed to be exceptionally sensitive to political issues, but despite the newsletters I send out and the speeches I make, I doubt if the majority of my constituents—the adults, I mean—know what my positions are on most issues. The thing to do is to get at the young people while they're still in school. If you once put the flea in their ears that politics is exciting and important, it'll never really leave them. Anyway, in answer to your question, if I run for mayor, you're going to see a lot of young people around the streets."

Lindsay declared for mayor of New York on May 13, 1965, as a Fusion candidate on a ticket that would eventually have one Democrat (Milton Mollen for Controller) and one member of the Liberal Party (Timothy Costello for president of the City Council). The city had 2,400,000 registered Democrats and only 700,000 registered Republicans. Registered in the Liberal Party, which was to support Lindsay, were 60,000 voters.

Oliver Pilat, who left the New York *Post* to be Number 2 man—under Harry O'Donnell—on Lindsay's press staff during the joust for the mayoralty, began his political diary, *Lindsay's Campaign,* with this entry: *"Thursday, May 13,*

1965: John Lindsay began running today for president by way of New York's City Hall. Naturally he did not disclose his ultimate goal. His immediate prospects are dim enough without an unnecessary handicap. In this Democratic town, no Republican, even one as young (forty-three) and as lucent as Lindsay, is given any chance of being elected mayor. He has no machine, no troops."

It is not within this book's intent to summarize that campaign. It would be superfluous, in any case, in view of the existence of Pilat's remarkably complete and candid book. I would only mention that under campaign manager Bob Price, 120 Lindsay storefronts functioned throughout the city, and there were more than ten thousand active volunteers, most of them young. (In addition, there were another 20,000 tangentially involved.) By October 26, the volunteers had canvassed seventy per cent of the voters. "I do not believe," Pilat wrote in his diary, "that any party or combination of parties ever canvassed that high a proportion of the voters in any previous corresponding election."

Lindsay defeated the Democratic candidate, Abraham Beame, by 102,000 votes. His running mates, Costello and Mollen, lost. The last entry in Pilat's diary, dated Wednesday, November 3, ends: "For Lindsay an impossible campaign was already merging into an impossible administration which would break him or make him a national leader. John Lindsay would rule an almost bankrupt metropolis facing almost incurable problems, yet New York was still full of money and of people with great vitality and creative talent. I remembered Harry O'Donnell approaching the winner several hours ago to say: 'Congratulations, John. You have only yourself to blame.' "

The Mayor:
1966-7

I I paid my first call on the one hundred and third mayor of the City of New York early on a Monday morning toward the end of February at the start of his term. During his seven years as a congressman I had seen him under considerable stress at times and had been impressed by his resiliency. But never in his political life had he experienced such persistent turmoil as during his first seven weeks as mayor—a transit strike, many-pronged opposition to his plans to reorganize city agencies, sharp criticism of some of his appointees, and the accelerating pressure of financial problems so severe that new taxes, with attendant controversy, were inevitable.

There had also been difficulties with the press. The dry humor and spontaneity that had characterized his relationships with most reporters in the past were absent in the interviews with the taut John Lindsay I saw on evening television news programs. And newspaper friends had told me of the names City Hall reporters had given him—Mr. Clean, Captain Marvel, Sir Galahad, Prince Valiant.

At a quarter to nine I walked into the Mayor's office in City Hall, a high-ceilinged room with white walls, red carpets, and red drapes on tall, arched windows. The day was gray and damp outside, but the room was warm and cheerful. A crystal chandelier with six globes was lighted, and so were the two brass lamps on the Mayor's federal desk. The Mayor, sitting behind the desk, also looked bright, and not nearly so tense as I'd expected.

"All I need is a good night's sleep once a week or so." He smiled. "And on weekends especially, I try to get some exercise. Mary and I played tennis last night at the Heights

Casino in Brooklyn. It's canvas stretched on wood. *Very* fast courts."

Several small lights on his telephone were flashing on and off while he spoke. As fast as his secretary in the outer office deflected a call, another took its place. He glanced at the phone, ran his right hand through his dark-blond hair, and stretched out his legs. "Two things I've found the hardest to get used to. One is the goldfish bowl life here. You can't go to the bathroom without being observed. There's no such thing as a private conversation or a private visit. You're being watched all the time. But even more surprising, if that's the word, is the massive collection of relatively small things that zero in on the mayor. And that's because of the absence of coordination and planning that had become chronic here. It's all Scotch-taped together," he said in exasperation. "I find decisions have been made in the past by various personalities and often the rest of the municipal structure hasn't known anything about them. So when I look to find out who agreed to what, there's no record. In a sense, I suppose, that was the only way to do business here the way things have been. The bureaucracy has become so big and insensitive. The way these ninety-nine or so agencies are set up, they're often dealing with fractions of problems, fractions that sometimes transcend what the agencies' jurisdictions should be. The system is so damn divisive that city departments have to deal with each other almost by treaty. Imagine three different departments have jurisdiction over paving streets, depending on whether they're in parks or on bridge approaches or in midtown Manhattan. And does it make any sense to you that sick-baby clinics are under the Department of Hospitals while well-baby clinics are the responsibility of the Department of Health? That's why it's so important to reorganize all this into maybe ten super-administrations to cut out all this ridiculous overlapping. With each of those administrations taking charge of a definite and integrated field, and with clear lines of control and communication, I could know

what's going on all the time. And we can save a lot of money
that way too.

"Maybe then I'll get a little more time to think. We're
always battling time. But"—the Mayor leaned back in his
black leather chair—"I *am* avoiding as many luncheons and
dinners as I can. A lot of people have been annoyed because
they'd never been turned down before, but I'd rather be working as mayor than sitting on a dais in a midtown hotel. For
me those daises are like a plague. Toward the end, Bob
Wagner was making three or four luncheons a day and two
or three dinners at night. I don't want to criticize him, but
the trouble with Bob was he couldn't say no. And I've cut
out a great many of the ceremonial appearances. I send out
deputies—and Mary too has been handling a lot of that."

The Mayor paused, shook his head affirmatively, and
said, "Mary's wonderful. I don't know how she does it—taking care of the children, overseeing the redecoration of Gracie
Mansion, and making all these appearances. And at night it's
marvelous to have someone with her humor and toughness to
share your problems with."

A young assistant to the Mayor came in, consulted with
him briefly, and was almost immediately followed by another
assistant.

"For all I've been saying about time," the Mayor said
when the second assistant had left, "it's equally important to
have enough people who have complete access to me so that
I can get honest advice and information as things happen.
This job is like picking your way through a minefield. But
building a staff is so damn frustrating. It takes endless telephoning and a lot of interviewing. I've looked all across the
country; and when I do find people I want, some will consider
the offer for two or three weeks and then decide they can't
come. Their family doesn't want to move or they'll lose their
pension rights. So the telephoning starts again."

Increasingly, as we talked, there were telephone calls
that could not be held by the Mayor's secretary. As the Mayor

alternated between the phone and talking to me, the buoy-
ancy with which he had begun our conversation gradually
gave way somewhat and there were signs of strain on his
face. But there was occasional laughter in response to something a commissioner or another aide said to him over the
phone, and Lindsay himself often spoke with gusto. "All you
have to do," he said to one caller, "is tell me what you want
and I'll bash heads together until it's done. We've got to get
moving! What's happening with Operation Head Start? I
think we ought to act like De Gaulle—go in and *do* it and
answer questions afterward."

The call over, he turned back to me. "We have to have
doers. Sure, you need thoughtful people who understand the
depth and complexity of the city's problems, but if they allow
themselves to be picked to death by all the competing
interests, we'll get no place. There'll be no movement. You
need doers because there's always such resistance to change.
Like my plan for Little City Halls. I'd like thirty-five or thirty-
eight of them around the city, places that could be bridges
to the city government. Instead of having to go to a variety
of departments down here, anybody could go into one place
in his neighborhood and get any questions answered or complaints acted on. It would be like a one-stop seat of municipal services. I *know* people want it. I plug the little city halls
every time I go to a poverty hearing, and the whole place
breaks into applause. And sooner or later we're going to get
them. There has to be direct communication between the
people and the Mayor. The Mayor is always being blamed
for not being in touch with the people's needs and wants, but
now that I want to open a direct line, the Borough Presidents
and the City Council are against it."

"They're afraid the Little City Halls will supercede
them," I said.

"Well," the Mayor answered, "I think the City Council
will eventually go along with us if it finally understands that
in the long run, *it* will survive and the Borough Presidents

will not. Those Borough Presidencies are anachronistic and too costly. Meanwhile"—the Mayor looked at the flashing telephones—"I'm trying to make the various departments more accessible. Like you can call City Hall at night now and make a complaint that will be followed through. Before, you couldn't get any answer here that meant anything after 4:30 or 5. There are a lot of lonely people in this city and this way, they feel someone is watching over them at night. And I keep checking to find out how people are received on the telephone in all the departments—so we can just get some politeness in the way people are answered. Of course, it's taking some of them a while to get accustomed to my calling."

He laughed. "Two nights ago, around eleven o'clock, I called the Police Department to find out if anyone had been killed or raped or if there had been a major fire. It took quite some time before anyone answered, and then a girl came on.

" 'This is the Mayor. May I speak to whoever is in charge?'

" 'All right, honey, everything's going to be okay.'

" '*Who is in charge?*'

" 'The sergeant is around somewhere.'

" 'Where?'

" 'I don't know, I can't find him.'

" 'You *find* the sergeant. This is the Mayor on the phone.'

" 'Well, he's busy. He's playing checkers.'

" 'You tell him John Vliet Lindsay, the Mayor, is on the phone and wants to talk to him.'

"Maybe it was the Vliet that shook her up. Anyway, the sergeant finally came. He wasn't sure that I might *not* be the Mayor, so I got the information I wanted. The next day they gave me a special number to call when I wanted to reach the police, but I told them, 'That doesn't mean that from time to time I'm not going to call the number the public uses to see how long it takes to answer.' And I do. It still takes too long, but it's better."

On a table behind the Mayor's chair I noticed a compact battery of communications devices, including another telephone with rows of buttons. He looked at it too, and grinned. "Direct lines to all the commissioners. I had the phone company do it. The previous administration had the most cluttered, the slowest system you ever saw of routining calls through switchboards. But now these calls are picked up by the commissioners themselves. Let's see whether Henry Barnes is in his office." With obvious delight, the Mayor pushed a button. The Traffic Commissioner was at his desk. They talked for several minutes, and at one point, the Mayor exclaimed, "Oh hell, don't worry about that! Just stay in touch with me, and there'll be no trouble."

The Mayor was enthusiastic about all his communication devices. "Look at this gadget," he said, pointing to what resembled a very small television set, even smaller than a Sony portable that stood on his desk. "I'm putting all the phone numbers in my personal book into an index attached to that. When I want someone, I get his name on the screen, I push a button, pick up the phone, and he'll be on. Your number will be on it too." I didn't know whether to feel honored or computerized. "And I've got a mobile phone in the car, a two-way radio so that I can talk directly to the office here, another Sony television set, and I can even dictate directly to here from the car. I call a certain number, and as I do, the light goes on in the outer office, and they know I'm recording. That way I can answer at least some of the mail while I'm traveling. Including some of the mail that comes in here from the citizenry. I'll often pull out fifteen or twenty of those letters and answer them. Here's one from this morning." He reached into a folder, found the letter, and read sternly: " 'Sir, the tax rebellion is drawing near. It probably won't lead to shooting but it will lead to a quiet movement of people and businesses out of the city. I am unalterably opposed to new taxes.' "

"Aside from that kind of criticism," I asked, "how does

it feel to open the paper every day with the prospect of reading one or more critical stories and editorials?"

"It's certainly different from my experience as a congressman. Here the press is commenting on you all the time. I've
gotten cold-blooded about it. Well, not entirely. Once in a
while my blood begins to boil a bit. But listen, I figure I'll
do my best, and that's it. There's no sense getting coronaries
about criticism. There's no point lying awake nights about
a newspaper story or a mistake that's been made."

Another commissioner called. "Isn't there *anything* we
can legally do?" the Mayor asked in irritation. "You mean
we might be battling windmills? . . . Well, keep on it."

"That was something the previous administration agreed
to that I'd like to undo," the Mayor said to me. "We find
layers and layers of deals. Tom Hoving says he feels like a
new cook coming into a kitchen where there's a huge stove
on which the old cook left a lot of pots simmering. Every
time he picks up a cover, he feels like dropping it down again
immediately—the stench is so bad. Some of the contracts
that were let out—and not only in the Parks Department—
are appalling!"

I asked how strong a sense he had of the power of his
office. How much could a mayor actually change the way the
city is governed? The Mayor laughed. "As Napoleon said,
it's easier to conquer a territory than to hold it. One thing
we have to deal with is the colossal depth of the bureaucracy
and the way it has of digging in even deeper into old
habits—its tendency to say, 'You can't do that, it's never
been done this way before.' And many of the people in the
middle echelons of the government are so afraid of taking
the responsibility of making decisions, even decisions that
just require a little common sense. So the red tape goes on
and so do the delays. That's hard to change because these
people are locked in. The civil-service system needs looking
at. You're so limited in the degree to which you can hire and
transfer people. Furthermore, so few jobs are exempt from

civil-service requirements. In my own office, out of some ninety to a hundred jobs, only about twenty were exempt. Hoving didn't have *one* he could fill without having to go by the civil-service regulations. And so we had to go to foundations to get the money to hire people we felt we needed but for whom there was no provision under civil service. Eventually civil service will have to be restructured, and that's a legislative job.

"But meanwhile, by the kinds of appointments I make, by reorganizing the agencies so that things can happen faster, and by trying to make all city employees *want* to work harder and more efficiently because they feel part of a real attempt at change, I think we can hold the territory and improve it. And one thing I'm sure of. The office of mayor needs a lot more dignity than it's had in the past. I think the mayor of New York has usually tended to be kicked around, and he'd accommodate himself to being treated that way by saying yes to everything without delivering. As a result, the mayors didn't move around with any style. You have to lift the joint up. How? By the way you handle press conferences, for one thing. By the way you use television. By refusing to say yes even if it's going to make people angry. The Mayor has to walk a little taller than he ever has before. Look at the Board of Estimate hearings—the way people come in and are literally rude to the Mayor. It's unbelievable. That kind of behavior wouldn't be tolerated anywhere else in the legislative or the executive branches of government. But you can't hammer those people down and tell them to learn some manners. You have to control yourself, be dignified, and be very disciplined about not allowing them too much time. My heavens, if you're arguing before the Supreme Court, you're limited to half an hour in presenting a case that could change the nation. You certainly ought to be able to limit speakers before the Board of Estimate. Little by little we'll bring dignity back to those hearings, but you can't do it all at once."

   The Mayor paused, brushed his hand through his hair again, and said, "Being mayor, I'm beginning to realize, involves your having to do three things simultaneously. One, I'm aware of the fact that I'm a public symbol and therefore must do enough symbolic things that will produce a feeling of leadership. That means being seen around the city. At poverty hearings. Walking in the neighborhoods. At schools. At least once a week I want to visit a different school or college. Two, I have to resolve the clashes and collisions between people that are constantly going on while I'm also deciding on appointments, budgetary matters, and all sorts of daily problems. Like I had to get rid of a fireboat the other day. I never had to do anything like that before. Third, there's the matter of developing long-range plans for New York. Where do we go in five years? In ten years? Those three areas of concern are in my mind all the time. They're in my mind early in the morning, as I'm trying to get myself out of bed. Sometimes it's hard to face the day, but once I start—and so long as I keep going—it's all right. There are times when the problems do seem overwhelming, but when I get into them, they work themselves out."

   The Mayor stood up. "Since we've been sitting here I've been feeling today's pressures building. The door opening every once in a while and then closing. The phones flashing like crazy. As soon as you leave, they'll complain I've fallen too far behind. Thank God I've got some wonderful people working for me who are really moving in their areas."

   The Mayor asked about my family, and I asked about his. He frowned. "Time. Time is the problem. Last night, Annie, my third child, was trying to communicate with me. I just wasn't focusing. She turned to me and said, "Mr. Mayor, do you hear me?' I felt a little badly. I must have more communication with them. Little snatches of time are all you can do. That, and what can be saved on weekends. And we'll have to get away every once in a while."

The Mayor's secretary came in and told him that Robert Price, who was then a deputy mayor, wanted to see him in his office next door. And, she added, there were a number of visitors and a list of calls to return. The Mayor and I shook hands. He looked past me into the outer office, not focusing, and the signs of strain on his face were now quite evident.

As I started along the corridor leading back to the entrance, I passed two of the Mayor's young aides. "Moving into this government," one was saying, "is like trying to sort out a waterfall. It's just pouring down and you have to catch it as you can."

The Mayor's office is in the West Wing of City Hall, which is separated by a gate from a large rotunda in the center of the building. Out in the rotunda, a dozen men and women, volubly angry, were gesticulating at a city detective who stood impassively inside the gate. Heading toward them was Woody Klein, the Mayor's press secretary at the time. "Everything that has been wrong with the city," he said to me, "they want us to straighten out *now*. Don't they realize this is a new administration?"

II For the rest of the year and into the next, I followed the Mayor's attempts to hold the territory he had conquered and, more importantly, to convince the populace that his was indeed a new administration. I watched the news reports, talked with many of his associates, and had more conversations with the Mayor himself.

At first there was considerable confusion. One day early in the Lindsay administration, when a holdover from Robert Wagner's staff was trying to explain the intricacies of the payroll for certain departments—admitting in the proc-

ess that some of the names on the list and their functions
were unknown to him—Harvey Rothenberg, a mild-man-
nered man in his forties who had been a full-time shirt
manufacturer until he volunteered his services, at a dollar
a year, as the Mayor's administrative assistant for appointments, sighed and said, "If I owned this business, I'd sell it
immediately."

"I know what you mean," said Barry Gottehrer, a former newspaperman who had become an assistant to the
Mayor and whose responsibilities included setting up sports
programs for young people. "Eight departments have youth
programs, and not one of them knows what the others are
doing."

Late in that first winter I asked Gottehrer his initial
assessment of the Mayor and of his chances of bringing some
order out of the administrative confusion. Gottehrer, an
alert, energetic man in his early thirties, looked at the mass
of papers on his desk, and answered, "Well, one thing I can
tell you is that he has the temperament to get things straightened out. I always knew he wanted to do the right thing
and that he was good under pressure, but it wasn't until I
began working closely with him that I realized how strong
he is. Like the other day, he met with a delegation of
Puerto Ricans. They wanted assurances of more policy-
making jobs for the Spanish-speaking community. Five were
supposed to come but seventy-five showed up—some of
those running the show obviously figured he wouldn't be
able to resist that kind of pressure from a minority group
so early in his term. But the Mayor made it clear that he
was not going to play the game under the old rules. He
told them no city job belonged to a particular nationality.
If a position could best be filled by a Spanish-speaking appointee, fine, but he wasn't going to be pressured into doing
anything he didn't want to do. If he can stand up under that
kind of pressure, I think he can deal with the other obstacles
to change in this city. Anyway, he's convinced me he has

the capacity to get things done. That's the only reason
I'm here."

Behind City Hall in the dingy old courthouse that
stands there on Chambers Street—it is usually called the
Tweed Building, because its construction, begun in 1862
by William Marcy Tweed, entailed considerable profit for
him and his colleagues—I was talking to a man with long
experience as a political reporter in New York. Now on the
Lindsay staff, he took delight in telling me, as so many
officials had once told him, that anything he said was for
nonattribution.

"He's going to have trouble at first," my anonymous
friend said, "getting used to the hazards of being so damned
exposed. You know, it's not like it is with a governor or
senator. Anybody feels he has a right to grab the Mayor.
And you can't just flick them off, because then you get the
reputation of being arrogant. But the biggest hazard is the
press. Here's a group of highly critical reporters who know
every angle and they're trying to force a guy stewing over
a hundred problems in his head to shoot from the hip. If
he does talk off the top of his head on any issue, he can get
into a lot of trouble. The other day, we were at the airport
and a pushy TV guy wouldn't let up on him. Lindsay didn't
shoot from the hip, but he didn't do himself any good by
getting angry and stalking away. Later he asked me how
he did. I told him there was another way of handling that
kind of situation. You look at the guy, you smile, and then
you say, 'That's all the comment I have to make.' I'll tell
you where else he's going to have trouble. He's had no
experience in Albany, in dealing with the way that legislative scene works. Albany is a rattrap of the worst kind.
Its processes are devious, and many of the practitioners of
those processes are, to say the best of them, callous. Things
operate indirectly there; even if you know the score, you
can hardly see what's happening.

"But I think this guy has a good chance to do more

than survive. For one thing, he has an enormously effective constitution. I mean he can take a lot physically. And he's well-organized mentally. Just as important, for all that so-called Boy Scout image, he's a pretty tough guy. Once he gets into a fight, he's without fear and his mind keeps functioning clearly and well. Of course, there *is* a certain boyish quality about him, when he's free of pressure. During the campaign, for instance, we were walking in the Bushwick section of Brooklyn, past a line of three-story buildings with stores on the bottom. At one corner, leaning out of a third-floor window were two of the most beautiful girls you ever saw—one with a man and one alone. They weren't too well dressed, but man, they were delightful. One was tousled, flimsily dressed, and looked as if she'd just awakened. John looked up, grinned, kept on grinning, and then, looking at his wrist watch, he said in a loud voice, 'I'll be right up.' That made me feel I was working for the right guy. I've also seen him in a reverse kind of mood. One night we'd gone through a very exhausting session. He'd been finding out where the bodies are, the layers and layers of arrangements that had accumulated over twenty years. One group accustomed to naming a staff member at a certain institution; another having the inside route somewhere else; the tie-in between one department and the union most directly involved in it, so that the union had taken the right to shift people around. John suddenly turned to me and said in a tone of complete discouragement, 'How can you make a city like this honest?' But he snaps back and uses what he finds out. He's already shaken up a lot of areas, and he'll cause more consternation as he goes along.

"Sometimes I think John is the last surviving example in town of a good man. He really wants to do good. You know, all my life, I've distrusted people I call Christers. Most lack subtlety or *something*. They're not quite human. And because I'm not sure myself anything will ever do any good in the long run, I've figured the wise man is the one who's objective and doesn't go over too far. And that kind of man is also the more comfortable man to work for. But this guy, I don't know. He's not prissy; he can be very funny in private; and he's a hell of a good boss. He has extraordinary tact. God knows, there've been some awful blunders around here these first few months; but he binds up these kids' wounds from day to day so they can go out and do battle again. People around him have enormous affection for him. He has a capacity for pleasing people. And if you can get close to him, he has more personal impact than you'd think because there's so little in him that's phony. I tell you, even if he were the most vacuous guy in the world —which he isn't—you'd still have a decent administration because people really *work* for him."

The former newspaperman stopped, suddenly embarrassed at his outburst of enthusiasm for his employer. "But remember," he added, "I'm not saying he's going to work miracles. He's only one man, and this city is on the verge of so many sad and tragic things. It's in very vulnerable shape. If he can keep it on an even keel for a year and then go on to improve it—and I don't know whether he can or not—he'll legitimately be a national hero. But do you know what he needs to make any real improvement? He has to get at least a billion bucks in new money for starters. Try that on your harmonica some day. Where is it going to come from? *That's* his basic problem."

Also in the Tweed Building was the office of Constantine Sidamon-Eristoff, a compact, round-faced, pipe-smoking man in his middle thirties, who was then the Mayor's assistant on personnel—a post involving patronage to some extent. "It's taking a while to sort things out," he told me after my talk with the former newspaperman. "I found a man's title, for example, didn't necessarily relate to what he was doing. And then there was the matter of finding out who the no-shows were—people who draw a salary but are hardly ever seen where they're supposed to be working."

I had noticed that a number of campaign workers for Lindsay were being added to the administration and I asked Sidamon-Eristoff, who had been the most important figure after Robert Price in managing the mayoralty campaign, to what extent party affiliation was a factor in deciding whom to hire. "Well," he said, "we have roughly four political groupings. Democrats, mostly Reform Democrats. Republicans from the organization. Liberal Party men. And, primarily—this is my own bias—people who worked within our structure in the campaign no matter what party affiliation they have. I try to do this as idealistically as I can, but I would say that if there are two equally qualified people, I'll try to get a commissioner to pick the devoted campaign worker."

I asked about the impact of the Mayor on the staff, both on the hold-overs and the new appointees. "He's in command," Sidamon-Eristoff said with a smile. "I think that was a shock to many people. Some expected Bob Price to be the real decision-maker and others just didn't know whether this young ex-congressman could be an administrator. But now we know. He can really chew you out. And he's quick to tell you what he wants. 'No, not that way, *this* way!' But he'll always end with some touch to show you haven't been cast into outer darkness. And he's got a knack of sensing whenever you're very tired or low. 'By the way,' he'll say, 'let's have dinner.' We get there and chat about nothing in particular, but you finish buoyed up. Basically, however, the guy is tough. He's very considerate, but he's not patient with failure. He'll give you a fair chance, but after that, if you keep making mistakes, he'll find someone else to do it. What makes him particularly impatient is wordiness. You're better off with him if you can think and talk concisely."

Sidamon-Eristoff's secretary came in with a message and he asked her to stay. "This is Leslie Booth—Betsy Booth—she worked for John in Washington."

Miss Booth, a soft-voiced, attractive woman in her early thirties, took a chair and looked tentative until Sidamon-Eristoff waved her on to reminisce. "I'd been a teacher," she said, "and that was my first office job. What first impressed me was how quick and direct he was. When I took dictation, he never paused. He shot it right off the cuff. But then, every little thing had to be checked afterwards."

"The lawyer's eye," said Sidamon-Eristoff, puffing on his pipe.

"Another thing was that he wanted what he wanted *when* he wanted it. And that was that!"

"And you get quick reactions from him too," said Sidamon-Eristoff. A memo comes back with 'No!' or 'Hell, yes!' scrawled on it."

"He didn't worry about how the office was run," Miss Booth continued. "He knew he had devoted girls who wouldn't get things fouled up, even under the terrific pressure there."

I remembered that staff. In Washington, his secretaries often put in a ten- to twelve-hour day without overtime, and would take turns working Saturdays, when at least half the staff was usually on hand. Occasionally they'd take work home. And despite those wearying hours, the morale in Lindsay's office had been extremely high, with very little turnover in personnel.

"What made the pressure bearable," Miss Booth said, "was that feeling that revolves around him—the feeling that whatever had to be done could be done, no matter how difficult it was. What he himself loved most was getting on the floor of the House and into a fight. That he ate up with a spoon. Then, there was also his sensitivity to people. Oh, he's toughened up, it seems to me, in recent months, but he's still very sensitive. He doesn't want *you* to know he's sensitive. He'll go to all ends sometimes to pretend he's not. And when things get rough, he sometimes has a shrug-of-the-shoulder façade he doesn't always mean. But he does want you to know what's happening and what he thinks. He'd sometimes get us all together—the secretaries, everybody. Like after the Republican Convention that nominated Goldwater, he tried to explain what had happened and how dismayed and baffled he was."

Miss Booth looked at Sidamon-Eristoff and then at me. "The pity of big-time politics," she said, "is what will happen to a nice guy like this?"

"I still think it's possible," Sidamon-Eristoff said judiciously, "for a man to make it and still be a nice guy."

"Well," Miss Booth was doubtful. "Perhaps I'm too new at this, but it seems to me the nice guys get so hurt they have to toughen up to survive.

"But he does have to be tough enough to command," Sidamon-Eristoff persisted.

"A lot of people who surrounded him in Washington," Miss Booth said, "looked at him with a Kennedy type of worship. But I never felt like that. I don't think he's a perfect man or a perfect answer to the problems of New York or the nation. I do think he's energetic and sincere, and he seems to be honest. What bothers me a little is that to this point, he's been a little too sheltered. That wonderful staff in Washington may have served him too well. They shielded him too much. Now he's going to have to judge people for himself."

"Yes," said Sidamon-Eristoff, "I sometimes worry that he's not harsh enough in judging people. He tends to have a good impression of people the first time. Eventually he comes up with the correct impression, but now he has to make so many judgments so quickly, maybe he has to get more cynical. On the other hand, I don't want him to get too hard, to lose his sensitivity. I hope too he can get enough good people around him here so that some of us can also take some of the lumps. But I don't believe he has to cut off the human part of himself to do a good job. The city is cold enough as it is, without a cold personality on top."

Miss Booth had become noticeably gloomy. "Another thing that bothers me," she said, "is that a young man like Lindsay really needs to bump into a big storm. So far he's always been rolling along, the fair-haired boy who could do no wrong."

"He ran into quite a storm on that transit strike," Sidamon-Eristoff said emphatically.

"Yes, but he got out of that okay. I feel somebody like him in public life has to stub his toe sometime, and maybe it's better if it happens early in a career. I'd hate to have it happen at the brink—just before he might get into the White House, for example. That is, if he wants to get there. God, I wonder why he would want to. And quite apart from all this, I wonder about his family. He really enjoys his children, but with the hours he has, how can they remain a family?"

Miss Booth rose, but stayed to hear me tell Sidamon-Eristoff about Elliott Shapiro, the principal of an elementary school which Lindsay had recently visited, who had observed what he called a "glazed look" in Lindsay's eyes through most of the speech making and while touring the classrooms. "But," Shapiro had added, "in our private conversation later, he was quite different—very lively, curious, informed, irreverent about the school system's hierarchy."

Sidamon-Eristoff laughed. "When he focuses on you, he focuses hard. But he doesn't always focus."

"He has a marvelous ability to shut his mind off," Miss Booth agreed. "He can be looking *right at you* and be somewhere else. In Washington, I'd come in with phone messages, hold them in front of his eyes and get no response. Finally I'd have to put them in his hand."

In a conversation shortly after my afternoon with

Sidamon-Eristoff and Miss Booth, I asked Theodore Kupferman, who had succeeded Lindsay as congressman from
the Seventeenth Congressional District, whether he thought
the Mayor had yet learned to be sufficiently tough.

"Oh," said Kupferman with good-humored briskness,
"I wouldn't use that word. I'd say he's become more practical. When he began, he had interesting ideas of how things
ought to be, but he's found out it's very difficult to attain
a lot of those goals. I think that through the years he's come
around to John Kennedy's concept of trying to do what's
possible, what's practical. He's come around more to the
idea of compromise."

I remembered an afternoon in Lindsay's Washington
office four years before. I had been asking him speculative
questions about his political future and wondered aloud
whether he'd ever go after the support of the Liberal Party.
"No," he had said quickly, "they operate by trading, by
making deals. And that isn't my style."

"But," Kupferman brought me back into the present,
"he's still very much in the Stanley Isaacs tradition. You do
what's best for the greatest number of people, and that
means you don't do everything the party says you ought to
do. After all, the worst thing that can happen is you'll lose
an election. On the other hand, you do accommodate yourself to the needs of the party where you can, providing those
needs are not significantly different from what you believe
to be right."

I asked Kupferman his reaction to the concern expressed
by several friends of Lindsay that the Mayor's good looks
and breezy manner might actually be a hindrance to him in
that they connoted to some of the electorate a lightness of
intellect and an insufficiently complex personality. One
writer had asserted, for instance, that Lindsay lacked the
depth of perception and the tragic sense of life he ascribed
to Robert Kennedy. Kupferman did not agree. "Actually,"
Kupferman said, "he's been able to get away with a lot

of things among some conservatives because they just like him as a good-looking figure, the epitome of the Wasp. Don't forget that in this country you can make up for a lot of provocative ideas you may have if you also look good and can express yourself well. If John had been short and fat, I don't think he would have been able to take some of the positions he has and still gotten some of the Republican support he needed. Nobody gives *that* kind of political science course—how genetic accidents affect politics."

III   In the spring of 1966, I paid a call at City Hall on Robert Price, who was then one of the two deputy mayors. Price, intense, his egg-shaped face dominated by horn-rimmed glasses, shifted his attention between me, his two telephones, and stacks of papers on which he kept making notes. "It seems to me," I said, "that the Mayor came into office as a unique political phenomenon in that he's not tied to any of the established power groups, such as the labor unions or a strong party organization. Even the banks and the rest of the business community are opposed, in various degrees, to his tax plans."

"That's true," said Price, "and it makes it easier in that you can move more freely. But, not being plugged in anywhere also makes it easier for you to get shot at as you do move more freely. You're speaking to an expert on that. It especially happens in New York because this is a show town. People here like to eat up politicians. And there's a very persistent press which doesn't entirely realize that you can't make real changes to accommodate a.m. and p.m. deadlines."

"What about the Lindsay image?" I asked. "The names

the reporters have for him all come under the Boy Scout heading."

"He's had that problem before, running for Congress. But people came to realize he had solid achievements in civil rights, civil liberties, housing, foreign affairs. They'll find out about his substance as mayor within the next two to four years. This business about his being an intellectual lightweight is absurd. I probably know him as well as anybody. Do you think I would have invested as much time in him as I have if he weren't able to handle complex problems quickly and flexibly?

"But the problem here involves more than what one man can do. I'm trying to explain that problem in a speech I'm writing. I'm calling it 'The Urban Frontier.' But what do you think of 'Riding with John Lindsay on the Urban Frontier'? Or maybe better yet, 'Riding Shotgun with John Lindsay on the Urban Frontier'? Anyway, there are basic changes that have to come in the relationships between the cities and the states and the federal government. The cities now are stepchildren of both the states and the federal government and the country as a whole has not yet fully grasped the fact that this is an urban society. But it's going to be forced to during the next ten years. And what happens here in the next four years can have a great effect in terms of showing what *can* be done to save cities. Cities all over the country are watching us because John is now identifiable. He's known throughout the country."

Price took off his glasses, stared at me, and continued. "Everything's happening wrong here. Our streets and subways are dirtier, people and businesses are moving away, the streets are less and less safe. In four years John has to turn this around and move forward. Now how is he going to do that? First he has to eliminate the inertia that is so rooted in many of the three hundred thousand city employees. That and their fear of making decisions. Second, he has to eliminate the inertia among the citizens at large

—the feeling that all politicians are the same, that nothing is going to change anyway. He's already shown at least some movement to the people on the side streets. There's action. They're not sure if it's good or bad, but *something's* happening. Third, there have to be some sizable physical signs of change—like a passenger center for ships on the West Side or more new schools, vest-pocket parks, rehabilitated housing, industrial parks. At the end of these four years, people are going to have to be able to *see* changes."

Price turned to the phones, assuring his children on one that he would really be home for dinner and saying simply, "No!," to another caller.

"Okay"—he turned to me again—"what are the chief obstacles? The special interest groups, to begin with. They want change, but for other people, not for themselves. It's fantastic how many of them there are. Labor leaders, even good government groups, who are accustomed to getting more than their share. Firms that are accustomed to getting business from the city without bids. Or they're accustomed to setting up special requirements for a bid with a city department—requirements only one company can fill. "We're constantly finding this kind of thing under the woodwork. Or let me give you another example. Political leaders and civic groups who are not accustomed to having *their* neighborhoods thought of for public housing.

"You mentioned John not being plugged into any of the established power groups. That's what these people are finding out. He can't operate any other way. Lindsay is Lindsay. When he was a congressman, he'd consult his constituents and he'd consult experts but not political organizations or other vested interest groups. Okay, that independence has been useful so far politically, but I wonder about now and in the years ahead. I think he's come to the point where he needs a structure of support behind him—either that of a political party or a structure built for him personally. His always acting alone doesn't always get him the support he might need to get something important done. We *are* a political government and a political leader *has* to trade and bargain. Look, suppose you badly need a legislator's support for something his constituency isn't so hot on. If you're going to get his support, you're going to have to give him something in return so that he can then say to his constituency, 'See, we got this for that.' But without a structure, a party, or something behind you, what *can* you give him?

"So, if John does continue as a total independent, he may wind up having headed the best four-year administration in New York City history—an administration which would then not be re-elected. Because this is still a Democratic town. Or, within those four years, if he stays totally independent, he may propose many very good programs which the City Council or the state legislature will then destroy because he doesn't have a structure of support. Now *he* can't build that structure because he's too busy working on substantative problems. And *I'm* not going to do it. What he has to do is find people who can work on forming a structure. Maybe he thinks that's part of my job. But if he does, he came to that conclusion without consulting me."

Leaving Price's office, I saw the former newspaperman who these days speaks only anonymously. "Have you seen Mary Lindsay yet?" he asked. I hadn't since before the election. "You ought to. In some ways, Mary is the best thing in the administration. He talks practically everything over with her. She has considerable influence, and that's a good thing because she's a remarkably decent woman. Of course, her main concern is keeping him alive."

On a sunny, cool spring morning, I went to see Mary Lindsay at Gracie Mansion. The family had moved in only a few weeks before, having stayed previously at the Roosevelt Hotel while the Mayor's official residence was being repainted and redecorated. The refurbishing was still not completed but the upstairs quarters had been in good enough shape to make the move possible. The spacious rooms downstairs were bare, without furniture or rugs. In the front hallway I saw a pedal-operated fire truck and a fire chief's hat, the property of five-year-old John Lindsay, Jr.

Mrs. Lindsay, hugging herself against the chill, literal and figurative, of the emptiness downstairs, greeted me at the door. I told her my five-year-old had exactly the same fire truck and hat. "But it can't stay," she said rather sadly. "I told Johnny that when the red carpet comes, the fire truck will have to go. Come along, there's some heat upstairs." She led the way to a sitting room on the second floor. Her new role, I noticed, had caused no discernible changes in her appearance or temperament. Lithe, quick, with brown hair and an unusually mobile face, Mrs. Lindsay is much more attractive than photographs indicate. And although she is usually as politic in public as her new role requires her to be, a natural candor still asserts itself from time to time on ceremonial occasions, as when, cutting a red ribbon to open a Greenwich Village art show a few weeks before, she had burst out, "Isn't this silly?" Another time, when asked by a reporter how she felt about being recognized on the street, her instant reply was that while it was pleasant in one sense, the fact that strangers called her and her husband by their first names was something that she rather resented.

In the sitting room, there was a spaniel sleeping on a brown couch, snoring lightly. Mrs. Lindsay sat down a few feet away on a chaise longue, and I took a chair across from her. "It's impossible to realize the demands of being mayor until you live it," she said. "John could work twenty-four hours a day, seven days a week, and he'd never be finished. So the most important thing is to set your priorities. He's been very tough in limiting his schedule of appearances, but he still gets home late nearly every night—usually around midnight—and he brings along a folder four inches thick with just the most essential stuff he has to work on. Some of that he may do in the car riding back and forth, some he roars through with his secretary at the office, but some he

has to do here. We try to work it out so he can have dinner
with the children *one* night a week. That's my highest sight
at the moment in that respect. Even when we got away for
a few days skiing in Stowe this winter, he spent a large part
of that weekend on the phone. I try to keep Sunday free, but
take last Sunday. At four in the afternoon, there were still
three men waiting to see him. Sure the children miss him,
but they're resigned to it."

I asked her when the Mayor's day begins.

"He's usually off by seven thirty or eight. If he hasn't
left by eight, he says he's late. I tell him he never looks very
happy in the morning. He never goes bouncing out, looking
forward to the day ahead. You can see in his face the innu-
merable things facing him. It's especially bad now, at the
beginning, because he has to make most of the decisions
himself. I'm hoping that eventually the administration can
be structured so that more of the people around him can take
on more responsibilities on their own. Yes, he often does
talk about problems with me, but I try hard not to ask him
about anything to do with the city unless *he* starts it. I figure
there are some nights when it would be a relief for him *not*
to talk about what's gone on during the day."

The phone rang and Mrs. Lindsay made arrangements
for her son to have lunch at a schoolmate's home the next
day and then go to the park with him and his mother. "If
you see a big, tall, nice-looking man following you," she told
the mother, "don't get nervous. He's a detective."

As she hung up, Mrs. Lindsay said to me, "I don't mean
to sound as if it's all crisis or pressure. A week or so after the
transit strike was settled, John and I took a Saturday afternoon walk from Fourteenth Street down Broadway to City
Hall. People stopped him, of course, but everyone—people
looking out of coffee shops, kids looking out of windows—
had a smile for him. That felt good. And do you know that
during the transit strike with which his administration began,
when he'd be walking downtown to the office, there'd be

people at the doors of restaurants, holding out a cup of coffee for him. So when he gets discouraged at a particularly bad morning's mail, I tell him the people who write are usually only the angry ones. I like to see the mail, to see what people are saying. I get twenty-five to thirty letters a day here, and I read them all. And others are addressed to me at City Hall. If someone doesn't like something, and if the complaint is something I can answer and *if* there's a return address, I answer.

"I said he sometimes gets discouraged, but actually he gets more worried and concerned than discouraged. I'm sure, though, that little by little things will become more workable. Being mayor may never be *fun,* but it'll be something he'll be able to cope with. It will take time. Even in a little way, I can see how hard it is to *move* people out of rigid patterns of thinking and behavior. During the decorating, for instance, we heaped together a pile of terrible lampshades that were no longer going to be used. And the pile stayed there. I asked the Parks Department man why he didn't get rid of them. 'I can't,' he said, 'I have to go through channels.' Well, after a while, I just threw them out the door and said, 'Let channels come and get them!' Goodness, they're like pack rats. They save *everything.*"

After another telephone call had been taken care of, I asked Mrs. Lindsay how she felt about the occasional criticism of the fact that her children weren't in the city's public schools. "I said at the very beginning—and I even said it on the Today Show—that our children have always been in private schools, and when we came back to New York, there was never any question that they'd stop going to private schools. One of the girls did spend a year in a public school in Washington. It was a happy time for her, but they didn't put enough pressure on her academically. I also feel—and this has been the experience of many people in public life who have children—that the children have to be kept out of the limelight as much as possible. It's not good for them to be made much of, and that would certainly happen in our case if they went to public school. The private schools, however, bend over backwards in this respect. They pay *no* attention to whose son or daughter it is. They're all there to get an education and that's all there is to it."

But, I said, the children couldn't escape the limelight entirely. She smiled somewhat ruefully. "Oh, I don't think our lives will ever be what you could call normal or peaceful. But when people say, 'How do you *do* it?,' I tell them it's not a question of that. Long ago I made up my mind this was the way life is going to be and I'd better enjoy it. Otherwise we'd all really be miserable. That is, I enjoy it as much as I can. I don't know any woman in public life who *really* enjoys it."

Mrs. Lindsay had to prepare to attend a luncheon, and she led the way down the stairs. It was even colder than before on the first floor. "There's only one thermostat for this whole, huge house," she said, grimacing. "But we did get some storm windows put in. Well, I have to think of what to say at this meeting. It's one of those occasions when I stand in for John. I try to limit them to the daytime because I like to be here when the children come home. I feel they need at least one of us around. And tonight," she said cheerfully, "John and I are going to the theater. It's not only a pleasant respite for us, but everytime he goes, it shows people in the theater how interested he is. It gives them a little boost. But do you know that we get letters criticizing John because he does go to the theater once in a while? Why, the theater industry is one of the largest contributors to the city's economy—and there are also the taxis and restaurants. I think it's important that the Mayor is interested in the theater."

We said good-bye, and walking down the path to the sidewalk, I thought it was rather sad to feel it necessary to justify an evening at the theater.

After talking with Mrs. Lindsay, I decided to get an appraisal of the early stages of Lindsay administration from the Democratic wing of City Hall. I called on a Reform Democrat who had had a high post in the Wagner administration and now held a staff job with the City Council, which has offices in the east wing of City Hall. By contrast with the bustle in and out of the gate leading to the west wing, it was quiet at the entrance to the east wing. I was shown to a comfortable office, and soon, the official, a graying and urbane man in his forties, came in. "Wagner," he said as I sat down on a couch opposite his desk, "was not fully understood by the public, but in retrospect, his skills seem to me to have been all the more valuable. He was highly intelligent, extremely knowledgeable, and his mind worked almost like an I.B.M. machine. A proposal would be made to him, and thirty seconds later, he'd tell you who'd be for it, who'd be against it, and how the opposition could be neutralized, if that were possible. But Lindsay . . ." He lowered his voice. "I voted for him, and so did my wife, but I have a lot of regrets now. For one thing, he doesn't figure out carefully enough in front who his allies and his opposition may be to specific proposals. Thereby he doesn't do enough planning with allies or potential allies, nor does he attempt to chip off the opposition. That's why he's run into so many frustrations. Look at the way he handled his attempt to reorganize the transportation system. There are people in this wing and in the legislature who would have worked with him on that if he'd called them in early enough and consulted with them. And look at the unnecessary hassles he created for himself in pushing for his tax bills by trying to bull them through. Sure, Wagner procrastinated, but sometimes there was method in those maddening delays. He was waiting for the particular time when he could get a particular plan through.

"I've also been disappointed—amazed, really—at the attitude of Lindsay and some of those immediately around him. I mean self-righteousness, arrogance, claims to omniscience. He comes on as if he's bearing the white man's burden. With him, it's a matter of noblesse oblige rather than facing people as people. I'm not talking about the mistakes they've made. Those are inevitable. In some ways, the government of New York City is as complex as the federal government, and you know it takes any President two years to master the mechanics of that government. The same is true here. This municipal government is a monster. Working for it are three hundred thousand people, addressing themselves to a myriad problems one step a time, but not in any orderly sequence. What bothers me about Lindsay is his lack of humility in trying to conquer that monster. He doesn't seem to know what he doesn't know. There were other ways of trying to get the Little City Halls through. Again he didn't consult early enough or fully enough with some of the people over here. So he exacerbated relations with the City Council. That could have been avoided. That's a deadly combination—ignorance linked with an assumption of knowledge. Maybe it's his insecurity at suddenly being placed in charge of this administrative maze without having had experience in that line. But if that's the explanation, he would have been wiser to have kept quiet until he'd learned something."

The critical Democrat stopped, lit a cigarette, leaned back, and said, "On the other hand, let me be as fair as I can. No mayor of this city can fully deliver so long as the resources of our society are allocated as they are now. One plain fact is that whereas the mayor of New York City has tremendous powers governmentally, he has practically no power to solve the ultimate problems of the city because he doesn't have the money nor the means to raise enough of the money. Certainly the answer, or a large part of it, is much more federal funds. But I don't see any sign that we're going to get enough of those funds fast enough. Yet, unless this society solves the problems of the cities, we won't have to worry about the dangers of war from abroad. We'll explode because of the tensions in our cities. And even if there were enough money, you need time. You cannot wipe out in four or eight or twelve years the effects of decades of poverty and poor planning and no planning.

"This man is in trouble, in great trouble. Even if Lindsay had been all I'd expected, much of what he could do—with resources allocated as they are now—would be limited to dramatizing the problems of New York, to calling attention to them in the hope there would be enough of a cumulative impact on the society to get the help that's needed before the tinderbox explodes. But with his own disadvantages, and with the current priorities in Washington, consider what the Lindsay administration is going to have to face in its last two years. Inevitably there'll be some attrition in the top levels of his administration by then, particularly if not enough money is coming in to enable them to get things done. So how many first-rate people—not that he's gotten so many up to now—will he be able to recruit then? In two years, this won't be nearly so glamorous, so attractive, so trail-blazing an adventure. Yes, sir, I do not envy Mr. Lindsay."

IV There were days when I didn't envy the Mayor either, particularly those days when City Hall seemed to be under siege from cadres of homeowners, sanitation men, or various vanguards of the poor claiming the war on poverty was being directed at them. And the assault troops were usually accompanied by television cameras. As on a morning in May of Lindsay's first year in office when a joint hearing of the Board of Estimate and the City Council's Finance Committee was to start considering the Mayor's proposed expense budget.

As I walked up the stairs of City Hall, about a hundred

sanitation men, most without ties and all looking aggrieved
and bellicose, were massed to the left. At the top of the stairs,
several television cameramen were setting up their equipment. Inside, in the rotunda near the entrance to the Mayor's
wing, I saw William Booth, the wiry, energetic chairman of
the city's Commission on Human Rights. The former New
York State chairman of the National Association for the
Advancement of Colored People, Booth had been arrested
for picketing craft unions in the course of demonstrations
at Rochdale Village, in Queens, during the previous administration. This morning, he was getting his shoes shined. I told
him I was impressed that Gilberto Garena Valentin, an especially militant Puerto Rican leader, had just been appointed director of the business and employment division
of the Commission on Human Rights' staff.

"Yeah," said Booth, "but I'm getting some flak. He's a
controversial guy."

"You mean flak from inside the Puerto Rican community?"

"No, no. From some of those so-called liberals. He's too
strong for them. However, we're moving along. There's a
real change of attitude in the Police Department, I'll tell
you. I got a call from Leary, the commissioner, and he wanted
to come to *my* office to talk to me. That's unprecedented. In
the old days we couldn't even get through to high police officials. This man Leary seems to *want* to have better relations
between the police and minority groups."

Just inside the gate to the Mayor's wing, in the office of
the Mayor's press staff, I met Alfonso Troche, a new assistant
press secretary. Not yet thirty, Troche, born in Puerto Rico,
had been graduated from high school and college in New
York and had gone on to become an Army officer and a newspaperman. On the wall over his desk, he had Scotch-taped a
quotation: "I do the very best I know how—the very best I
can. And I mean to keep on doing so until the end."

"Abraham Lincoln," Troche told me. "He kept me going through the Army."

Troche's shoes were being shined by a Negro in his late forties. A slim, brown-haired secretary came by and Troche said to her, "I bet you don't know I used to have the shoe-shine beat on 145th Street. I used to average thirteen dollars a day."

"How old were you?" the girl asked.

"Thirteen, fourteen. Then I got promoted to an exclusive franchise in a barbershop and then I graduated to shining shoes in a shoe-repair shop. *There* I was really making money." The shoeshine man stood up, finished. "Hey," said Troche, "can I use my American Express card?" The Negro grinned. "I still have my shoeshine box," said Troche as he paid the man. "I save it as a relic."

I asked Bob Laird, another young assistant press secretary, what the Mayor's schedule was like. "All full, as usual. We tried to hold out a chunk of time in the afternoon, but it got filled."

"When does he have time to think?"

"That's a good question," said Laird. He looked at his watch. "He's already behind schedule. Every one of his aides has something that will take just two minutes. That's one of the reasons."

A private meeting had been scheduled for ten o'clock in the Blue Room, just outside the Mayor's office, between Lindsay and a delegation of Negro ministers and other civic leaders who were preparing the agenda for a White House conference on civil rights. A TV cameraman, with his equipment all set up, was waiting in the Blue Room, but a press aide told him there was to be no TV coverage. "That's all right," said the cameraman, dismantling the camera, "I'm used to it. You used to be able to set up anywhere around here, but not now."

The delegation was already seated at a long table. At twenty past ten, they were joined by William Booth. At ten thirty the Mayor strode in, looking fresh and ready for business in a dark gray suit, a white shirt, and a maroon-and-silver-striped tie. After introductions and handshakes, he asked for specific information about what the White House conference was to cover. Arms folded, eyes roaming the table, he listened as the visitors spoke of urgent problems in housing, welfare, transportation, job training. Then he was asked what else he thought should be on the agenda.

Somber, Lindsay looked around the table again, and said, "The best contribution New York can make is to make it clear to the White House and to Congress that if the Demonstration Cities program, as small as it is, doesn't go through *intact,* you might as well forget about this conference. We don't have enough money for established programs, let alone new ones. Mitch Ginsberg alone can lay out twenty-five different areas in his Welfare Department in which the federal government can be of specific help in race relations, in making real changes in the way people live. The same is true of housing and jobs. I wish you'd tell the White House that my conviction is this is an economic problem more than anything else. There's so much that has to be done here and that *can* be done if we had the money."

At quarter of eleven the Mayor was on his way upstairs to the quarters of the Board of Estimate. He moved so quickly that two accompanying staff members and I almost had to trot to keep up. "You're getting soft," the Mayor said to me. "I bet you slept till nine. Start off with me at seven some morning."

In the spacious chamber where the Board of Estimate meets, the Mayor took his seat at the center of a long semicircular table. In the audience in front of him I saw about forty of the sanitation men. They looked, if anything, more aggrieved and more bellicose. Also around the table were the President of the City Council, the Controller, the five Borough Presidents—these officials, plus the Mayor, make up the Board of Estimate—and the members of the City

Council's Committee on Finance. Hovering behind each
official was at least one staff member. As the hearing got underway, a succession of middle-aged men, representing civil-
service unions and other groups, rose to make statements.
Nearly all were insisting on higher pay. The Mayor, with
a slight, somewhat grim smile, listened without comment
until a spokesman for Local 300 of the Building Service Employees International Union, pointing vigorously at him,
finished loudly, "We must then, Mr. Mayor, assume that if
the sum you have allocated, sixty million dollars, for salary
adjustments, is not sufficient, that additional funds will be
made available to provide a just and living wage for the
competent, dedicated employees you stated are needed to
translate well-meaning intentions into workable programs."

The Mayor had put on his glasses and, leaning forward,
he said, "Let me ask you, as a leader of this fine organization,
have you taken a position on the Mayor's tax program?"

The spokesman was somewhat flustered but quickly recovered. "We have not taken a stand on *how* you raise taxes.
We are *for* taxes if the money received is used wisely, but we
don't want to get into a controversy as to how they're going
to be raised."

The Mayor laughed. Although the lights in the chamber were on, it was sunny outside, and my attention wan-
dered during the next witness's statement as I looked at the
first leaves of spring on the birch trees in City Hall Park.
The Mayor suddenly stood up and rushed out. Downstairs,
he strode to the Blue Room to preside at a ceremony for
schoolchildren who had won awards in an art contest sponsored by the Department of Parks and the school system. As
he handed out the savings bonds in front of the television
cameras, Alfonso Troche, leaning against a wall, shook his
head. "If I was Mayor," he said, "I'd cut *all* this stuff out
and just do business."

After looking carefully at each winning painting and
congratulating the children, the Mayor sprinted up the stairs

again. "When do you get time to read?" I asked him. "Oh, I get it in," he turned around without breaking step. "Like I read the early edition of the *Times* at midnight and then, in the morning, I look at the late edition to see if there have been any changes."

Some turbulence had been created upstairs by a proposed appropriation of forty thousand dollars for green uniforms for building inspectors, who had previously worn civilian clothes. The reason, I was told by an aide to the Mayor, was that a considerable amount of bribe-taking had been detected in the department and the theory was that in uniform the inspectors would feel themselves more visible and therefore be less likely to risk breaking the law. I thought it a rather ingenuous theory. A heavy-set man, a patch of gray stubble on his chin, his round face flushed and sweating under the television lights, stood before the table of city officialdom. "I was ordered by my doctor to stay home for a month and rest," he said hoarsely, "but this is a *burning issue.* I've been an inspector for eleven years, and I've seen commissioners come and go. Each one thinks *he* will be the one to do the proper job for the Buildings Department. But they're all the same. However," he forced his voice to a strangled shout, "I want to commend this mayor because he is the first mayor to back up *any* idea of his Buildings Commissioner, no matter how asinine it may be."

The Mayor pressed a pencil to his lips to control a smile. He leaned over to listen to an aide. Frank O'Connor, the then President of the City Council, was also being whispered to. "Gentlemen," cried the protesting building inspector, "pay attention to this! Don't talk among yourselves. These uniforms are going to take MONEY! It's forty thousand dollars now. In future budgets it will mushroom to over a million dollars! Do you think we're going to stink away in one uniform, one tie, one shirt, one pair of shoes? You're going for broke! And look," he took a handful of change out of his pocket, "where is the money coming from? The money for the uniforms and the money for the generals and assistant generals and aides and aides to aides that our commissioner has appointed? From me, that's where! It's *my* money! It's *my* taxes!"

Out of breath, he paused. Stepping close to the table, he went on. "Almost everyone who worked in your campaign is being rewarded," he looked directly at Lindsay. The Mayor's smile was now tight. "I ran a grocery store. My mother did. My father did. *They* never got a reward for running a grocery store. And I, after eleven years, I'm making the same salary as men who are just coming into the department. Where is my reward, Mr. Mayor?"

"I hope," the Mayor broke in, "you notice that for the first time in many, many years, people in the ghetto neighborhoods are beginning to feel that the Buildings Department works for them and—"

"From what money, Mr. Mayor? From what money? From what *money*?"

"—to the extent you people are cooperating in that effort to make the people in the ghettos feel there is movement, the city is deeply grateful."

"Mr. Mayor." The inspector threw his shoulders back and smiled in a manner he presumably thought was ingratiating, "You don't expect us to shirk our jobs?" He put a hand on his heart. "If this be my last act on earth, I will be happy knowing I have served the City of New York. But do not put uniforms on us. We are not dirty. We should not be demeaned, disgraced, dishonored. We should be handled as human beings, not as dirt and filth the way the newspapers and some commissioners handle us. Many of our sons are doctors, priests, nurses, lawyers. And now are we to be demeaned? Gentlemen, if I were younger, I wouldn't mind dying in a green beret!"

Controller Mario Procaccino, who had appeared more interested in his cigar than in the proceedings, sat up. "Atta-boy!" he shouted.

"If God grants you life," the building inspector was now so hoarse he had to whisper as he pointed a finger at the Mayor, "remember re-election."

The Mayor looked at him without expression. "Thank you," he said, "for your well-reasoned and constructive statement."

As the next speaker rose, the Mayor asked him if he could be brief. He was. Handing the Mayor a piece of paper, he said, "I am the attorney for six taxpayers in an action in Supreme Court, Queens County. This is an order restraining the issuance of uniforms to building inspectors on the grounds that the Buildings Commissioner ordered men into uniforms in February without appropriations for those uniforms having been voted." Flash bulbs popped as the Mayor looked at the restraining order with distaste.

Another speaker came forward, and I went outside to talk to one of Lindsay's press staff. When I returned five minutes later, the Mayor was gone, and Robert Sweet, then the Mayor's executive assistant (and now a deputy mayor) was in his place. "He's got a luncheon," said the press aide. I imagined that for once, the Mayor welcomed a dais, so long as it wasn't in City Hall. Downstairs, at the gate leading out of the Mayor's wing to the rotunda, Woody Klein had just finished a heated colloquy with a group of Negroes from Bedford-Stuyvesant who were bitter at the red tape they claimed was delaying the start of several anti-poverty projects. Workers hadn't been paid for weeks, and some had already taken other jobs. Klein had finally arranged an appointment for them later in the day with one of the Mayor's assistants. Klein looked tired. "Everybody comes to that gate," he said. "I tell them they're right. I know how they feel. Okay, we've got Sviridoff coming in to integrate all the anti-poverty programs into a Human Resources Administration. He's supposed to be a great guy. And we've got studies, reports, analyses. But these people still go home from that gate to some crummy apartment. And so many people in this city still don't have jobs. I tell them, 'Give us time to get started.' And they say, 'We've heard that before.' And they have. And then they insist on seeing the Mayor. Everybody wants to talk to the Mayor. And that's the way it should be. But he can only see so many people in a day."

Late that afternoon a budget problem—though somewhat less than the forty thousand dollars for building inspectors' uniforms—was concerning Dr. Donald Shaughnessy, at the time an assistant to the Mayor for economic development. I was in Shaughnessy's office in the Tweed Building, becoming depressed by the institutional dun color of the walls as Shaughnessy spoke on the phone. "I have to get a budget line for this man," he was saying, "I need this guy. It's absolutely essential."

Shaughnessy, who had been director of the Foreign Scholar Program at Columbia University before he joined the Lindsay administration, had prepared Lindsay's position paper on the city's economy and had written speeches for the candidate during the mayoralty campaign. A vigorous man with a beaked nose and bushy hair, Shaughnessy gave the impression of being in control of a great deal of information which, unlike some city officials, he was eager to discuss. His eyes are piercing but his manner is relaxed even when, as on this occasion, he had to cope with a stream of phone calls as he talked.

"I don't think," he said, "anyone—least of all the Mayor and the people around him—was aware of how bad a fiscal mess this administration inherited. Nor were we aware of how much rigidity was built into the budget—how great a lack of flexibility because of the civil-service rules. You can't move bodies from A to B without stepping on twelve toes, even if what you want to do is for the best of reasons and for the best interests of the city. It may take four years to do it but we're going to get this government reorganized into a sensible system. Meanwhile we *are* breaking down some of these little feudal hierarchies that have been built

up over twenty years and more. And we're doing such unprecedented things as calling interdepartmental meetings
between agencies with similar interests. I've created, for instance, an interdepartmental committee on industrial development, bringing together agencies—Housing and Rede-
velopment, the City Planning Commission, the Department
of Marine and Aviation, the Department of Real Estate, the
Mayor's Office—whose responsibilities include the city's economic growth. That had never happened before. It was a
revolutionary concept."

Shaughnessy shook his head. "It's a nutty situation. People have been talking about the number of manufacturing
jobs New York is losing, but we've been *driving* them out
by not doing a goddam thing to keep these industries. Look,
let me give you an example. You'd think that someplace
the city would be able to find out how much of the land it
owns is zoned for industrial purposes. I need the information
because I want to set up, among other things, vest-pocket
industrial parks. About fifteen acres. That's a nice piece of
land. So I went to the City Planning Commission for a breakdown of what we had available. They didn't have it. It's the
City Planning Commission! Why don't they have it? Because
it's never been requested. Now we're assembling the information ourselves, but it's an arduous job. Meanwhile, corporations have been calling the Department of Commerce
every day wanting to know where they can get more space.
If they get an answer they can use, it's only by accident.

"Another thing. When I started, I wanted to find out
how bad things really were with regard to jobs. But try to
get reliable figures on the civilian labor force. Try to get
reliable figures not only on the number of people in New
York who are unemployed but also on the number who have
been unemployed for twenty-five weeks or more. Try to get
precise figures on unemployment among Negroes or teen-
agers by contrast with the overall unemployment rate. You
can get data on the national level from the Bureau of Labor

Statistics, but we did not have reliable data for the city. Why? I guess because nobody really gave a damn. And that's because, I would guess, there was a built-in assumption all these years that New York is and always will be a major center of economic activity, which would never have problems of job development and economic growth. You know the theory—in a city like New York, there will always be jobs for people who *really* want to work. So what happened? Since 1960 the whole country has enjoyed a period of prosperity, but as of the time Lindsay took office, New York City had not shared in that growth. Not so far as jobs were concerned.

"We can change that, but it's going to take a lot of work and new perspectives. I'm sorry, for example, that City Hall is in Manhattan. It should be in Brooklyn or Queens. Maybe there ought to be a portable City Hall that would stay six months in each borough. It's one thing to see New York as the fancy shops and nice buildings on Fifth and Park Avenues. But there's quite another perspective when you get out to East New York, the South Bronx, or South Jamaica."

I asked Shaughnessy why he, a Reform Democrat, had had sufficient confidence in Lindsay to leave Columbia to take such a difficult assignment.

"I admit," he said, "that when I first became aware of Lindsay in the late 1950's, I had to conquer my first impressions of him. When I saw him, I saw Cary Grant, and I thought nobody has the right to be that good-looking, charming, and affable. But I gradually got to know more about him. In 1963, I did some work for the United States Commission on Human Rights and I found out that Lindsay had played the most active civil-rights role in the minority party in Congress. Then I looked into his record on housing, civil liberties, and foreign policy and I saw that a lot of things he was doing required guts. So I worked in his 1964 campaign

as co-chairman of Democrats for Lindsay. After that, John
and I corresponded about different bills and I did a few
research chores for him. In April 1965, he asked a number
of us whether he ought to run for mayor. I was pretty much
opposed. I thought he'd get clobbered, and even if he got
in, he'd have a Democratic Board of Estimate and a Democratic City Council. I told him to go teach somewhere. Become chairman of a department of political science, write,
enjoy yourself. But he foolishly declined my advice, got me
involved in the campaign, and then asked me to stay on.

"An interesting thing about working with Lindsay"—
Shaughnessy reached for a pipe on his desk—"is the way his
mind works. Whenever I begin to explain some concept that
is rather imprecisely formed in my head, he invariably comes
up with a disturbing question that penetrates to the heart
of the problem. He not only grasps concepts quickly, but he
also grasps the way they interrelate. He'd make an excellent
teacher. And he learns all the time. He's a perpetual student.

"And he keeps surprising me with some of the things
he's found out," Shaughnessy continued. "Every month, for
example, there's a meeting of the City's Science and Technology Advisory Council—a high-powered group of engineers,
technologists, scientists, headed up by John Dunning who
is in charge of the School of Engineering at Columbia. Recently Lindsay was sitting in at one of their meetings. They
were talking about econometrics, which is to economics what
linguistics is to English literature these days. It's a way of
using computers to study economic measurements in order
to develop and test economic theories. Well, during the
meeting Lindsay referred to some work being done in that
field at the University of California. I don't know where
the hell he found out about it. And then he linked what
was being done out there to whether the city should continue to support the Health Research Council's studies to

the degree it has in the past. 'Why don't we try *their* way to find out?' he said. Nobody else there had seen that relationship.

"Okay, that part of him I can understand. He has a good, quick mind. But he has another quality that impresses but puzzles me—the fact that he cares very deeply about things you wouldn't have expected him to care about. Like civil rights, and what it's like to be poor. He didn't grow up in East New York or Bedford-Stuyvesant. I wouldn't describe his boyhood as having been deprived although there was no inherited wealth. His father was a self-made man. Anyway, I've watched him with people, and that concern of his is real. That's why he can communicate with Negroes and Puerto Ricans on a nonverbal level. And that concern of his is not like the kind Franklin Roosevelt, let's say, had. Roosevelt's was the Hudson River–patrician approach that delivered baskets of fruit to families down the road every Christmas. John has empathy, and a very strong belief that everyone has a *right* to be able to develop himself to his fullest potential."

"What about Lindsay's own political potential?" I asked, telling Shaughnessy about Robert Price's fear that if Lindsay did not develop a political structure of support he might not last beyond his first four years.

"I don't believe that's so," said Shaughnessy. "I'm beginning to think that voters in urban areas are becoming more sophisticated than they were in the past. Their level of education is rising all the time, and therefore, a lot of those people in New York who have been claiming for so long that they can deliver blocs of votes may turn out to be wearing the emperor's clothes. Take the labor leaders. I'm not impressed by Mr. Harry Van Arsdale and the voting power he supposedly controls. Oh, sure, he can get two hundred people to walk around City Hall, but you've got to remember that union members are many other things besides cardholders—they're tenants or homeowners and members

of social and religious organizations. They can't be manipu-
·lated as if they were one homogeneous mass.

"I don't think it's necessarily going to be fatal to John
that he's not plugged into any of these so-called power blocs.
It seems to me, as a matter of fact, that what you have to be
especially careful about in politics is choosing your enemies.
It's important to have good enemies. I'd like John to keep
some of the enemies he has—Van Arsdale, the craft union
leaders, the president of the Stock Exchange—because we now
have a stock-transfer tax. That kind of enemy. Also Lindsay
is plugged into something else. He has, as I said, empathy
into the way more and more people in this city feel about
certain things. The demographic shifts that are taking place
in New York—the growing numbers of Negroes and Puerto
Ricans—make it all the more important for him to maintain
certain enemies. That's why his shake-up of the Police Department—bringing in Howard Leary from Philadelphia,
promoting Sanford Garelik to be chief inspector, and going
for the civilian review board, even though it lost—was of
great political worth to him. The breaking up of the Irish
Mafia that's been in control of that department for so long
was a special delight for me. My father was a cop, and I have
firsthand information on the kind of name you had to have
to move up in the department. I'm not that worried about
John and the power blocs. Don't discount the possibility that
John may make it by just being a very good mayor."

V   Downstairs at City Hall was the office of another Reform Democrat in the Lindsay administration, thirty-
three-year-old Donald Elliott. At the end of the year he became chairman of the City Planning Commission, a logical

development since when I saw him several weeks after my talk with Shaughnessy, he was involved, as counsel to the Mayor, in developing the capital budget, in governmental reorganization, in housing and urban renewal, and in anti-poverty operations. Tall, lean, confident, Elliott appears incapable of being ruffled or visibly angered. By contrast with some of the restless young men around the Mayor, he is uncommonly calm and even cheerful.

I told Elliott about Dr. Shaughnessy's conviction that the Mayor's empathy with the poor and with minority groups was more genuine than many people realized.

"You should have been at a meeting we had the other day." Elliott smiled. "We've been having a difficult time getting a program of legal services for the poor going. Some high-class lawyers have been involved but they've been resisting giving some of the control of the program to poor people in the community-action groups. These lawyers come from the kinds of firms John was in and I was in. They have enormous affection for John, but they don't understand anything about poverty or poverty programs. So the meeting began with their lecturing John for half an hour on the necessity that the law be left to lawyers. He listened, but then he got tough and for fifteen minutes he lectured *them* about the way the world is going in the twentieth century and about *their* need to stop being paternalistic in their approach to the poor. 'This program is not,' he told them, 'a dispensation from on high of good things for poor people. You have to look at the law as more than a tool by which to continue the status quo. Otherwise you'll be in trouble, because if you lawyers don't go into this program, it will be done without you and you won't have a say in it at all.' It was quite a performance. They were stunned."

I asked Elliott how sanguine he was that the Mayor would be able to bring basic changes to the city, changes more pervasive than providing legal services for the poor. "He made a lot of mistakes at first out of not knowing enough," Elliott said. "In Congress, he had learned a great deal about civil liberties, foreign affairs and matters of national policy, but he knew much less about the specific problems of New York City. To be sure, the Seventeenth Congressional District is heterogeneous, but it doesn't really have as many difficult problems as the poorer districts in the city. John had not been subjected to all the nitty-gritty fights you have to go through to change patterns in housing and jobs and education in a city like this. But he keeps learning. As of now, however, he often looks for sharply increased productivity without a sufficient basis of reality for his expectations. But that's certainly preferable to what the city's been used to. Yet we also need more than activity. All of the government has to be made more responsible to the Mayor. Operations like urban renewal and the poverty program have to be coordinated so that they reinforce each other rather than compete as they do now. Most importantly, we have to do the kind of long-range planning that has never been done before. One example is: how many housing inspectors should we have and where should we put them? We don't have nearly enough now, but even if we were to get the money for more, how can we use them most efficiently? Does it make sense to use them to inspect buildings which can't be brought up to code standards by the present owners? Or instead should we develop a detailed program to take those buildings away from the present owners? But then, what do we do about those buildings into which the city can put seventy-five thousand dollars and they'll still be slum buildings?

"Or take garbage removal. In some neighborhoods a lot of garbage piles up in backyards and hallways. But the Sanitation Department doesn't have the manpower now to take care of those areas. At present, the sanitation trucks go down the streets, sweeping, collecting, six times a week. Maybe it would be better for them to go down some of those streets three times a week and use the other time to take care of the hallways and backyards. Should the criterion of their effectiveness be the number of miles of streets that are cleaned or the number of pounds of refuse carried away? We have to rethink every one of those areas. And that means program planning, including program evaluation and review, and it means cost-benefit analysis so that we're able to compare the cost and benefit of alternative programs. We need to find out, in short, how to get maximum payoff for the money we spend. Program planning has never been done in this city before.

"At the same time," Elliott continued, "you have to balance what you're doing so that there are also short-term results. That's why there are occasional crash programs— like cleaning up East New York. But there are very real limitations on what crash programs can accomplish. I know that the test in June 1969, if John decides to run again, will be what basic changes have been made through long-range planning.

"Look at the schools. In 1963 the Board of Education made an agreement—and I'm for it—by which they have control of their own budget. It's still made up of specific lines, but they can change the lines. The Board's budget, however, is over a billion dollars a year—a fifth of the whole budget—and since the Mayor has to produce the money, the city has the right to find out what kind of results the use of that money has produced. We have a right to find out what happened to the new money that was put in last year—especially that proportion of the new money which was supposed to have improved the system. Why have we been unable to solve the problem of educating the children of low-income families, the Negroes and Puerto Ricans? What use has been made of the money allotted for *that* purpose? If, for example, the More Effective Schools Program—under which class sizes are cut and considerable special services are given to specific slum schools—if that works, why isn't it spread to include all slum schools? We have the right to ask questions like this and we have the responsibility to set up ways to get answers, to get the kinds of data which will allow us to determine whether real improvement has taken place. Then if one program isn't working, we have the right to say that more money ought not to be allocated next time for that. And if we can get those kinds of answers, we'll be able to demonstrate to the national legislature that even New York, with all its enormously difficult problems, knows how to begin solving them if it can get enough money. And that way we'll also be helping other cities."

Elliott was late for an appointment. "One other thing will have to be accomplished," he said as we were going out the door. "Most of these programs will have to be decentralized. It's possible, for instance, to create a program which will decide which roads ought to be paved, but then people in the various communities have to be given a voice in determining paving priorities. If the people in the neighborhoods don't have a say in what's going on, we'll have failed."

In the summer, I decided to get a somewhat different perspective on the administration than could be obtained from inside City Hall. I visited the Mayor's twin brother, David. (The Mayor has two other brothers. George, two years older than John, and also a lawyer, is a past chairman of the Planned Parenthood Federation of America; Robert, the youngest, is a senior vice-president of the Morgan Guaranty Trust. Their parents and a sister are dead.) Though affable, David Lindsay is more reserved than the Mayor and is less given to expressions of enthusiasm. His hair is somewhat darker than that of his twin, but there is a clear resemblance. The East River was serene as seen from his office in a large law firm on an upper floor of Chase Manhattan Plaza near the tip of Manhattan, and for a moment, the city itself seemed less turbulent from that height.

As a matter of fact, the city's affairs were somewhat less disordered at that moment than they had been before the

Mayor succeeded in getting his tax program through the legislature in Albany. The program was based on the first city income tax—also including commuters, at a lesser rate —and a stock-transfer tax. That morning's *New York Times,* however, had chided the Mayor for having "neglected to some extent the enlistment of support, understanding and good counsel from the business, financial and industrial community" during his tax battles. I asked David Lindsay's reaction to the criticism. He shrugged. "There could have been more meetings and breakfast conferences if John had nothing else to do. But he did do a great deal of it. There was one fellow, though, whom John didn't have time to get to, and he gave out with a blast considerably sharper than the one in the *Times.* And that fellow got a phone call from John: 'What's the matter—don't you have my telephone number? Have you ever asked to see me?' That toned him down—toned him right down.

"The tax problem is revealing, however, because it's one of many, many examples of the fact that when you're running a city, there are so many issues that touch people in ways they can immediately see and feel. On the other hand, what their congressman does seems much more remote to his constituency, and besides, you often get a long lag between the enactment of legislation in Washington and its impact on people in a particular district. There's still another factor that makes being a mayor so much more difficult. While your actions do have much more immediate personal impact, many people in the city seem able to focus on only one issue at a time. So you may solve the financial crisis; but if the next big issue is the Police Civilian Review Board, the people who don't like that say you're no good, regardless of what you've done in terms of finances."

I asked David Lindsay if he felt the Mayor had been forced to compromise too much on his tax proposals.

"What he got through is about half of what's needed," David Lindsay answered, "but it's fantastic he got that much.

It's always abrasive, getting taxes through. A national program usually takes two years—one for the House and one
for the Senate. This was done in a matter of months and
during a year in which everyone was running for office. Nor
do most people realize how small a staff John had to work
on the tax program in all the phases it went through. We
hardly have a Treasury Department in this city. It was rough
in Albany this June. During those last days and nights in the
Governor's Mansion while the tax agreement was finally
being hammered out, there were times when, if you'd struck
a match, the whole place would have blown up. Not that
there weren't some moments of relief. Frank O'Connor was
being given a tour of the paintings by one of the Governor's
aides as John happened by. 'Frank,' John said, knowing
O'Connor was surely going to run for governor, 'the paintings don't go with the house.'

"John's humor hasn't been affected by all these pressures. During the transit strike, I got a call from him one
morning. City Hall was being picketed. 'Hey, Dave,' he said,
'they just hung a guy in effigy. He looks like you. How are
you feeling?' And he hung up. The biggest difference I've
seen in him is his acute consciousness of time now. He's
always budgeting time, even to seeing how few words he
can use to get a point across to me. And that, of course, leads
me to do the same unless there's a joke I can tell him. But I
don't think John's tremendous concern with time now is
linked to any fear of failure. I mean the political implica-
tions of failure. He wants to do the best he can, but he's not
in trembling fear every day of losing the next election. Besides, losing has its own kind of victories. There are a lot of
satisfactions to be had that have nothing to do with public
life—like enjoying privacy and your children. John loves to
read, he loves other people's company. I don't think he'd
consider the end of his political career a tragedy."

I wondered if this sudden turn in the conversation
implied that David Lindsay felt the city couldn't be basi-

cally changed, even by as much application of energy and enthusiasm as his brother was applying. "I was talking last night," he said, "to a man who had been in the Wagner administration for a long time. When he started, he brought some people in with him who shared his own crusading spirit. They came in early and stayed late but eventually they got to the point where they didn't expect to accomplish too much. It was just too hard getting real work out of all those people locked into all those jobs in the lower echelons. I think though a lot can be done, but in answer to your question, I shall quote Lincoln: 'With high hopes for the future, no predictions will be ventured.' "

Some weeks later, in search of auguries, I looked in on the headquarters of the Department of Buildings on the tenth floor of the Municipal Building. It was toward the end of summer. As I entered a large outer office crowded with desks, I saw Charles Moerdler, the young, intense Commissioner of Buildings at the time, in conversation with the even younger Sidney Davidoff, an assistant commissioner. There were only about half a dozen other people in the room. It was quarter past nine in the morning, but Moerdler already looked as if it were five thirty in the afternoon. "This doesn't make sense," he was waving a piece of paper at Davidoff. "But it happens every day. *Every* day."

Tacked to the door of Moerdler's office was a sign in big red letters: "STOP THE WORLD I WANT TO GET OFF!" Seeing me, Moerdler said wearily, "Welcome to Fun City. If you're looking for anyone in my department today, they're on a boat ride. It's an annual event of the employees' welfare organization. To be more precise, most people in the department have a day off. Whether they take a boat ride or not, I don't know."

Moerdler went into his office, and Davidoff led me to his desk in the outer office. A Lindsay enthusiast, Davidoff has been working for the Mayor on and off since the latter's first campaign in 1958, and often accompanies the Mayor during his breaks for physical exercise in the gym at the Downtown Athletic Club. At the moment Davidoff was exasperated by what he called "the civil-service attitude." Two weeks before, he had organized a voluntary expedition, headed by Mary Lindsay, to Welfare Island to pick up paper and rubbish as the start of a citywide clean-up program. "I wrote to each of the commissioners," said Davidoff, "and asked them to post a notice of the expedition in their offices for anyone who wanted to come. All day I was getting calls. 'Do we get lunch money?' 'Do we get traveling expenses?' 'Do we get credit for the time?' 'Will we be covered by Workmen's Compensation?' That's some difference from that small, dedicated staff he had in Washington. I'm not saying they're all just time-servers here. We have some who are great, but by and large, if they've been in the system for any length of time, their spirits get defeated by the system. Somehow we've got to find a better method of providing incentives. We do have a program of merit increases now, but some time ago I put in an increase for a stockroom clerk who's been here more than thirty years. It still hasn't been processed, and it may sit on somebody's desk for a year.

"The system is really something. The time clock in our office upstairs has been out of order for more than two weeks. To get it fixed you have to go through channels. Both the people who are the channels in this case are on vacation, and nobody else will take the responsibility."

A young man in his early twenties who had just sat down at an adjoining desk broke in to say, "That clock was fixed," he told Davidoff. "But it's still not being used."

"Why?" Davidoff asked.

"Because the sign saying it was broken stayed on."

"Why?" Davidoff bellowed.

"I *told* them it was fixed but they said, 'The sign says that it's broken, and nobody has been authorized to remove the sign.' *I've* been using the clock, checking in, but they're all angry at me for doing it."

Davidoff rolled his eyes toward the ceiling. Then his phone rang, and while he was talking, Moerdler came out of his office and began discussing with the young man at the adjoining desk the results of the local and state primary elections in June. He had been pleased by the victories of several Reform Democrats and disturbed that a number of other Reform Democrats had lost. I told him I was somewhat surprised that he, a Republican, was rooting for members of the opposition party. "Opposition party?" he said. "I'm a former president of the New York City Young Republican Club. I'm a city commissioner under a Republican Mayor although this is a Fusion administration. But in Bronx County I'm virtually shunned by the Republican organization. They're eighteenth-century conservatives out there. It's a strictly clubhouse organization that can't get people elected. They have no base in terms of public support. But they treat us liberal Republicans like lepers. I mean that literally. Yesterday I saw one of the Republican leaders in the Bronx walking down the street and he wouldn't even say hello to me."

"You should be in Queens if you want to know how a leper feels," said the young man he had been talking with.

"Do you realize," Moerdler turned to me, "that this is the first administration in New York City in many years that is totally without any political-party base outside of Manhattan? So when you find legislators in the Democratic Party whose goals are similar to yours, you support them. I'm still a Republican, mind you, but the New York City Young Republican Club has long supported Democrats when we felt they were right. These days I don't get involved personally in the campaigns; I don't have time. But many of the people who worked for John have been working for Reform Democrats in the Bronx and elsewhere. That's the way we can get a real Fusion political base. After all, that's how we got a Mayor. If the Lindsay administration and the Lindsay style are successful, we will either have made a basic change in the two-party system in New York by creating a Fusion base or we will have created a Republican Party that's responsive to the people."

"Yeah," said the young man from Queens, "but how are you going to do that second thing? Young people now are gravitating to the Reform Democratic clubs."

"That's what I mean," said Moerdler. "We do have the chance if we remake the Republican Party, to give them an alternative. Look, I'm a lawyer. Once I finish a few major things here"—he looked in the direction of his office—"I'm going back to the practice of law as fast as my feet can carry me. But I'm also going to keep working in an attempt to create a twentieth-century Republican Party—what we really need is a twenty-first-century party—that will be responsive to the needs of large numbers of people. I take very seriously that section of the charter of the Young Republican Club that says—wait a minute." He rushed into his office and came back with a small green book, from which he read: "We must correct in our own party that tendency of all parties to make organization an end rather than a means."

Someone across the room summoned Moerdler, and I returned to Davidoff. "The system," he was muttering. "A few weeks ago, John was out in front of City Hall for some ceremony and he looked at the flag. It had forty-eight stars, and was old and dirty besides. 'Hey,' he said to the custodian, 'there's only forty-eight stars.' 'I know it.' 'What do you mean, you know it? Why hasn't it been changed?' 'It's still a good flag and we have so many, I hated to waste it.' That's part of the system too—if you have it, use it. But if you don't have it, and if you can't get it through channels, nothing happens.

"I was out in the Bronx at Morrisania City Hospital the other night. They'd run out of diaper pins. Why? Because they were short a stock clerk. So they were using adhesive tape instead. Another night, I was there with Bob Price and they were down to their last tube of penicillin. He asked why. The week before, they told him, two of the men in the supply room had called in sick. Price got mad. 'Do you mean to tell me,' he said, 'that in a city of eight million people, if two men get sick, you can't get essential supplies?' 'Well,' said the hospital's administrator, 'one drove the truck and the other loaded it.' 'If you can't get another truck driver here,' Price told him, '*hire* one for twenty dollars a day. Even if you have to pay for it out of your pocket before it goes through channels.' 'But that's not correct procedure.' 'Correct procedure,' Price said, 'is making things *move!*'

Davidoff sighed. "Another problem is that a lot of the people in the system aren't clear as to what they're allowed to do and what they're not. Shortly after we came in here, Moerdler saw a school which had a number of obvious violations of the building code. He asked an old-timer in the department whose job it is to inspect the schools. 'It's ours,' he said. 'When was this one last inspected?' 'Oh, we don't inspect schools.' 'You just finished telling me we did.' 'But we made an agreement with the Board of Education's Division of Maintenance and Operation not to inspect schools.' That's all changed now. We go into the schools. And to make sure that everyone we hire knows what all our powers are, Moerdler has started a training school for building inspectors. It used to be that the old-timers would break them in. Now they learn in a classroom as well as in the field. They get lectures from the legal department on what they can do, and they get lectures from the administrators here as to what we're trying to accomplish in the overall sense. I hope that academies like this one will be instituted in the other departments too."

Davidoff was called away, and the young man from Queens, grinning, said to me, "The Board of Education was furious when Moerdler started going into the schools. One of the men at the top told Lindsay to get Moerdler the hell out of there. Moerdler heard about it, and he said, 'When

John tells me to get out, I will, and then he can get a new commissioner.' "

"We've got a lot of reorganizing to do," Davidoff said when he came back. "That's one of John's main themes at the weekly cabinet meetings. 'How can we cut red tape? How can we build a four- or five-story school in less than seven or eight years?' But we've made beginnings. Hospital administrators and the people who run municipal health centers are finally going to be given authority to hire people and buy equipment without first having to get approval —which sometimes took years—from the Hospitals or Health departments. This way you give a hospital administrator the powers he needs to administrate. *Then* you're able to tell if he's any good or not. And if he isn't, you get another one.

"But one of the hardest jobs we'll have is getting the people all the way along the system to move. It's one thing to change the procedures; it's another to get people to implement the procedures. Time and again, they look at me with blank stares. 'That can't be done,' one of them says. 'Why?' 'Because it's never been done.' 'Is there a rule or directive that *says* it can't be done?' 'No, it's just never been done.' You can waste a lot of time that way."

Davidoff looked out the window. "If John can get a sense of real movement going, maybe we can move these civil-service people too. I wish he'd get out of City Hall more—that's one way to get that sense of movement across. When a judge is sworn in, he ought to be sworn in in his own neighborhood. If John is going to commend someone in the Sanitation Department, he ought to do it in the area in which he works. And he ought to hold press conferences in the street in each of the boroughs. He does do a lot of walking through the city, and that's a big help. I've seen him walk into neighborhoods in East New York, in Harlem, with no advance publicity. He just starts talking to people about their problems, and the whole area seems to change. Everybody's smiling; there's a new feeling in the air."

"That's this year and maybe next," said the young man at an adjoining desk, "but if the neighborhoods don't really change, I doubt he'll be able to get away with strolling in Harlem two years from now. He'll get something instead of smiles then."

Downstairs I saw my anonymous friend, the former political reporter who had been on Lindsay's staff since the start of the administration. He seemed cheerful. "We have a long way to go," he told me, "but John's on top of things now. Those weekly cabinet meetings are a big help, both for him and for the commissioners. Everybody has a much better idea of what everybody else is doing than ever happened under Wagner. And then he's in touch with them during the week. Wagner almost never called a commissioner directly. There was one commissioner," he laughed, "who had not talked to Wagner once in five years. Well, at least we've got some communication going."

VI   Early in the fall of that first year I had another appointment with the Mayor. I arrived in his outer office at eight thirty. A few minutes later, he walked in rapidly, handed his secretary a list of things to do, and waved me into his office. "I was in the car in front," he said, "getting some paperwork done. That time in the car first thing in the morning—if there's no one with me—is very useful. Yes, the hours are still about as long. I've been averaging five hours of sleep a night, but on Saturday or Sunday, I try to get seven or eight. It's funny, the few times these past months when I could have gotten to bed earlier—like when I was away for a short time this summer—I wasn't able to. One thing always leads to another. I watch the late news, read the papers, get a beer, and before I know it, it's one thirty."

The Mayor seemed to me to have changed somewhat from when I had seen him in February and at various times in the spring and summer. It was, I decided, a difference in confidence. He now had a more noticeable air of command and of enjoying command. I told him so. "Yes," he said, leaning back in his chair, "I think I've got a grip on the monster now. At least I have a hold somewhere on most of the tentacles. They're still writhing, but they're not strangling me at the moment. I'm much more certain now about how the structure should be changed, and I think I'm staffing the government as best I can. That's terribly important. I still spend a lot of time on it. It won't make any difference how sound the structure gets to be, and even how much money we get, if there aren't pros to run it. There's a rare beast known as an urbanist, and because they're rare, there's intense competition for them among the cities.

"I've been getting most of the people I go after except for some from other areas in the country who are anchored. I mean a wife is anchored to a white picket fence and the man is anchored to a bloody pension system that's frozen. I still run into that a lot. I've been trying for three months to get a guy out of the federal government but so far he can't get unsnarled without a massive loss of pension. Senator Muskie, of Maine, has submitted a very good bill—I've testified for it—that would make it possible for a man to go from the federal to local government without this problem. Pension systems have to be made more mobile."

"Aside from problems of staffing," I asked him, "what about money for the city? When you testified in August during Senator Ribicoff's hearings on the problems of the cities, you said New York City alone would need fifty billion dollars more in federal aid during the next ten years. But Robert Kennedy, among others, said you were being totally unrealistic in expecting that kind of money."

Lindsay smiled. "I remember reading in Justice

Holmes's memoirs of his years on the bench a line that's stayed with me—'I do expect a rough equation between isness and oughtness.' In testifying before the committee, though I wasn't requested to do it that way, I was focusing on 'oughtness.' But I'd accept a rough equation. Nobody can put a thoroughly specific figure on what we need, but I do know that if I'd said ten billion for the next ten years, I'd have been in error. If I'd said twenty-five billion, I might have been in the area of the rough equation. What I was trying to do, however, was to lead Congress, which is just beginning to recognize what's happening in the cities; and therefore I had to give them shock treatment. They especially needed it in so far as New York is concerned. The only budget larger than New York City's in the whole country is the federal budget. Our population is larger than that of sixty-six of the hundred and eighteen members of the United Nations. And yet, with all of our problems—like a welfare budget of seven hundred million dollars, which Mitch Ginsberg, the Welfare Commissioner, says we have to increase to eight hundred and sixty-seven million for the next fiscal year—we contribute something like fifteen billion dollars a year to the federal government in personal and corporate income taxes. Do you realize that represents more than ten per cent of all federal income taxes even though it doesn't include revenues from Westchester and the Connecticut and New Jersey areas that are part of Greater New York? But in any one year New York City has never gotten back as much as a billion dollars in direct or indirect federal assistance. This year we'll get about eight hundred and twenty million, or less than six per cent of this area's contributions in income taxes alone. But New York is accused of asking for a disproportionate share of federal aid.

"We're in a fiscal crisis, and so are the other big cities. And without a vastly increased commitment of federal resources, it's going to get worse. We've got to wake up Congress. There are thirty-six standing congressional committees and not one—not one—represents the needs of the cities. That's why I keep speaking up for the creation of committees on urban affairs in both the Senate and the House. And that's why I keep saying the federal government has to reexamine its priorities. Instead of making cuts in appropriations for the cities, it ought to see what cuts can be made in all those funds pouring into Vietnam. What it comes down to is which is the more important in the long run— funds for Southeast Asia or for Brownsville? I'm for Brownsville."

The Mayor's secretary came in with some papers for him to sign. When she left, I asked him whether, with all his inescapable concentration of city affairs, he had any time left to pursue the strong interest in foreign affairs that he had developed during his years in the House of Representatives. "I try to," he said. "I seem to find out best what I want to know from the *Economist*. Even about America. Its American survey is frighteningly accurate. I also read the Paris *Tribune* every day to find out what's happening in Europe. And my friends send me articles. Some of them in the State Department with whom I've worked on Atlantic affairs, for instance, send me things they've been writing. My reading still covers a very wide area. I try not to miss the *Congressional Record*. In a way, it's like reading the Sears Roebuck catalogue, but it's so entertaining. God, it's wonderful! And about New York, Al Troche in the press office goes through all the city's foreign-language papers and weeklies and puts together a book of significant items every two or three days. I go through the whole of that damn thing. And other people compile articles about New York from papers across the country."

"When do you get time to do all this reading?"

"Mostly at night. There's a nice chaise longue in our bedroom where I sit and listen to the radio or TV and read. I've taught myself to read very fast. And, traveling around the city, if I'm not dictating or if there's not a conference going on in the car, all I do is read things. This moving around is important. I don't mean only the walks I take in the ghetto neighborhoods. I've been involved in an educational program in the business community. There have been meetings after meetings of groups of fifteen to twenty or thirty people. I must have talked to a couple of thousand businessmen by now, trying to convince them not only to keep but to expand their investment in the city. Some are afraid that New York is being strangled by the poor and their needs, but I explain to them that with the increasing industrialization of the South and of Puerto Rico, immigration has lessened considerably; and by contrast with other cities in the North, we've stabilized the problems we do have in that area. Chicago, for example, has never really coped with its welfare problems. It has a bad plan. In fact, other cities are now sending teams to our Department of Welfare to learn how it should be done. And I also tell these business people that we've lost sight of the fact that in some of the so-called ghetto neighborhoods, a solid middle class is developing. There's more black ownership on 125th Street, for instance, all the time. I tell them there's a whole world of exploration and development possible in those areas. And as for the city as a whole, I remind them of the immense labor pool we have. Blue collar, white collar, all kinds. I think these talks are making a dent, are making businessmen realize what the city's potential is.

"And for the first time, I think there's an awakening among some of the labor leaders to *their* responsibility to be more flexible. And that's a big step—a very big step. We've still got problems with the municipal unions though, particularly with regard to our right to move men around, and that's an essential right. Take the Fire Department. I was struck with luck in the appointment of Bob Lowery as Fire Commissioner. He turned out to be a brilliant administrator. Furthermore, he knows when to roll with a punch and when not to. And he's very sensitive to what the pros call the high-hazard areas. However, over the years fire companies have put down deep roots into certain neighborhoods. For a long time the men were given limited privileges to moonlight in neighborhoods where they were stationed and those part-time jobs made for even deeper roots. Until Bob, no Fire Commissioner has moved them, even when more men are needed in the high-hazard areas. Since he *is* doing that, he's anathema to the heads of their unions. When Bob took men who weren't needed after dark in Lower Manhattan and put them in Bedford-Stuyvesant, where there are twelve fires a night, Gerald Ryan, the president of the Uniformed Firemen's Association, was appalled. I told him, 'Gerry, isn't it logical we do this shifting around?' 'Well, no, not exactly,' he said, 'these people are part of that neighborhood. They have their cars there. They have to get those cars washed at a certain hour—that kind of thing.' It hasn't been easy and Lowery, while skillful, *is* a Negro dealing with a largely white organization. So sometimes he needs reassurance, and that's why I spend a good deal of time with him. I told him, 'If it gets to that point, crack Ryan over the head publicly, and I'll support you.'

"This business of trying to get the separate parts of the administration working at maximum efficiency leads to all kinds of resistance," the Mayor said with some relish as if at the prospect of more head-cracking to come. "For example, in the Human Resources Administration, under our reorganization plan, there'll be a major division advising me on public-education policy. The Board of Education resisted the idea, but we told them it wouldn't kill them. I've finally gotten the Police Department responsive to the Mayor, and now the Board of Education and its empire cannot continue to travel in *its* own orbit. Education has to be made an integral part of community development, and therefore it has to be subject to a good deal of guidance from City Hall. No matter how many asbestos walls are put between me and the Board of Education, at the end I get the blame, and so I bloody well ought to have something to say about what's going on.

"God, they're slow in that empire. You remember when Freeport, on Long Island, refused a federal program based on teaching machines? The government was going to supply not only the money but bodies to go with it. You couldn't get a better package. We read about it in the paper and I asked the Board for an immediate decision. No, they said, they needed a month to decide. Bernard Donovan, the Superintendent of Schools, was in Europe; someone else was away. I told them they had twelve hours. You never saw such a crisis and so many telephone calls. But they came to a decision within those twelve hours, and we got the program.

"Then, there was the time the people filming *Up the Down Staircase* wanted the use of a school building. The Board said it would take months to come to a decision, and that besides, the picture might present a poor image of our school system. The filming was to take place during the summer, mind you. The schools were empty. So what if they showed a brick going through a window? At least, that would indicate a little activity. Anyway, I called Moe Iushewitz, a labor official who's on the Board. 'Do you realize,' I told him, 'that you're losing a million dollars in jobs by taking this stuffy attitude? How would you like to see *that* in the paper, Moe?' I signed him up, and then delivered the rest of the Board." Lindsay broke into laughter. "Yup, I've got a new slogan. Wasp Power! Thought of it the other day. Someone was teasing me about the number of Jews in the administration but I said, 'We Wasps may have only eleven per cent of the vote in this city, but one day we're going to rise.'"

A phone call was put through. Lindsay, hitting his desk with a pencil, listened for a while and said, "Well, do what you have to do. I'll back you up." He turned back to me. "The things you have to deal with. We had a very interest-

ing one a few weeks ago. We got word that the Ku Klux
Klan in Baltimore planned to march through Harlem.
Howard Leary, the Police Commissioner, sent a couple of
smart guys to talk to them—to tell them they were damn
fools and they'd get their skulls split open. I thought they'd
been convinced, but two weeks later, Leary got a telegram
signed by the big Grand Wizard saying they were coming
by way of the George Washington Bridge in full regalia,
and since it was to be a peaceful march, they demanded
police protection. Leary called me. 'Well, chief, what do I
do now? What are the rights and liberties on this one?'
Rankin, the Corporation Counsel, was in transit somewhere
and couldn't be reached. But I happened to be talking to
Bruce Bromley. He's a former Court of Appeals judge who's
now a partner in Cravath, Swaine & Moore. He volunteered
to research this one himself. The next day, he called me up
in triumph. He'd found an old statute that goes back about
a thousand years. 'Does Rankin know,' he said, 'that it's
illegal to walk through New York City with something on
your head other than a hat?' Well, we didn't actually use
that statute. Leary sent the Wizard a telegram that said,
'You are coming to New York only to incite racial disturbance. Don't come. If you do, we'll lock you up.' That settled
it. And here I'd had visions of a great scene on the George
Washington Bridge. Before we were sure they wouldn't
come, by the way, Leary asked me what to do if they did
come. 'Surround them with Negro cops,' I told him, 'and
you and I will go up to the roof of a tenement and throw
bottles at them.' " Lindsay roared with laughter.

"What have been the really rough times so far?" I
asked him.

"Those last days and nights in Albany getting an agreement on the city-income-tax program. It was a brutal, bloody
show. It was like a Mack Sennett movie, little groups in different rooms caucusing and caucusing. That was a rough
three days."

"You've been criticized," I said, "for having been too aggressive when you first proposed your tax program and thereby unnecessarily exacerbating the legislature."

The Mayor looked skeptical. He thought a moment and said, "Some say I wasn't aggressive enough. It probably *was* a tactical error for me to say I'd go into the constituency of each guy who didn't go with us on taxes and campaign against him. It doesn't work to *say* that. It may be a good idea, under certain circumstances, to *do* it, but it's not effective to *announce* your intentions along that line. And I suppose my charge of legislative cowardice did inflame some of them. On the other hand, all that aggressiveness, if that's the word, may really have helped. It got a lot of people behind us. The non-white community especially supported us all the way. Joseph Zaretzki, the minority leader in the Senate, told me he'd never before seen a Mayor come up to Albany asking for more taxes with real backing from his people. That made it look as if Albany, if it didn't give us more taxes, would be *denying* the community. I'll tell you, the taxes we did get—and especially the fact that a graduated income tax was involved—were the subject of a lot of conversation at the conference of mayors I attended at Dallas not long ago. All the cities need new ways of taxing, and perhaps what we achieved encouraged some of the other mayors.

"But even so, this city still has very limited taxing powers. I'm pushing for a very high measure of home rule in the Constitutional Convention that starts in April. As much home rule as we can get. We may well need, for example, to adjust the taxes we have as we go along, and we ought to have the right to do that *here*. Also, there's no reason to have to wait for approval from two sessions of the legislature —plus a referendum—every time we want to propose any change in the real estate tax rate. And I'd like to put out bond issues on public housing without the need for public ratification all the time. Another thing I hope we get out of that Convention is a greater share of state revenues for education—higher and lower."

The Mayor ran his hand through his hair and frowned. "A very important thing to push for in the Convention is a way of getting judges out of the election business. The setup we have now leads to trading and dealing by party leaders so that if you do get an outstanding judge, he's not so much a product of the elective system as he is one of its survivors. There are various approaches which are better than what we have now. One might be an adaptation of the Missouri system under which judges are appointed by the governor or the mayor or both with some guidance from bar associations. The judge serves for a period of time and then, having made a record on the bench, he goes on the ballot without an opponent so that if he's proved himself incompetent, he can be voted out. But for the courts located in New York City specifically, I'm supporting a constitutional amendment mandating that all our judges be appointed under a merit selection system. You'd have a nonpartisan commission—representing the courts, the bar, the public, and the appointing authority—which would make recommendations. And no judge could be appointed who was not on that list.

"Actually, I've been following a procedure like that in anticipation that it will eventually become the law. I have a fifteen-member Mayor's Committee on the Judiciary, the majority of whose members were selected by Justices Botein and Beldock of the Appellate Division of the Supreme Court. The chairman is Louis Loeb, a former president of the New York City Bar Association. It's a voluntary system, it doesn't have legal status, but I give them the names and they decide. I haven't made a single judicial appointment that wasn't approved by that group. I do give my opinions when I feel I ought to. Like I've appointed about fifteen Negro judges, and in some cases, we've made certain allowances. This business of people's qualifications at the bar is all relative.

I had it out with the committee. 'Certainly standards have to be high,' I told them, 'but if I send you the name of a Negro lawyer in Bedford-Stuyvesant, I would hope you would not find him unqualified simply because a downtown lawyer, let's say, who's been to all the right schools and has worked with the most prestigious firms is also available.' The committee understood."

I had been in the Mayor's office for a little more than an hour and, as in February, I had been feeling the pressure rise—on him, and on me as an obstacle to the furthering of city affairs. The lights on the Mayor's phone had been flashing almost continuously, and frequently the door would open, a head would pop in, look at me—reprovingly, I thought—and pop out. But I did want to find out in the time I had left how much progress, if any, had been made in making certain that new policies, however venturesome, were actually being carried through on the lower levels of the administration.

The Mayor sighed. "Sometimes I feel I'm pushing my shoulder against a mountain. My feet are churning away and the mountain won't budge. But I'm determined to blast things through. Every Friday morning I tell the commissioners at the cabinet meeting to get out of their offices into the streets to find out what their departments are doing with *people*. And I'm always on them to *act* and follow through on the action. I'd rather they made three errors out of ten decisions so long as they make decisions, and get them into operation. I know it's tough, and sometimes the bottlenecks have nothing to do with the people in the lower echelons. I've walked by those rattrap buildings in East New York—the ones with rubble and beer cans inside, and at night, a few guys mainlining it. They've been abandoned by owners we can't find. All the city can do is board them up. Three days later, the boards are down. The logical thing to do would be to tear down those buildings, blacktop the area, and put a basketball or a handball court there. Or a place to get cars off the street. But by law you can't pull the mess down without going to court over the damn thing. And if you do finally get court permission, you have to have competitive bidding. But I did see one terrible block and I told the Public Works Commissioner to just pull down the buildings. I don't care about finding the owner or about competitive bidding. 'You'll back me?' he said. 'Who'll sue us?' I told him."

Lindsay laughed. "I wish we would get sued. Then we'd know who the owners are. Sometimes that's the way you have to operate. I learned that in the Navy. Before I became gunnery officer on my destroyer, I was in charge of damage control. I was the housekeeper. My job was to get the necessary repairs done, get the guns we needed, get the ship painted, and get out to sea. You stole from the next guy, you borrowed from somebody else, but you got it done. Cumshawing, we called it. If you'd waited for the paper-work to get to you from this agency and that agency in Washington, you would have never gotten out to sea again." Lindsay suddenly looked glum. "Of course, you had a great advantage in the Navy. You could shove off. Nobody could do anything to you once you were in the middle of the Pacific. But," his spirits were up again, "the thing is to keep moving and to keep others moving. We'll break through. And that's one of the reasons I go out into the streets as often as I can—to show movement, to show concern."

"What if you're just raising hopes in the ghettos when you're out in the streets," I asked, "hopes which will lead to even deeper frustration if movement doesn't lead to visible change?"

The Mayor frowned again. "I've done a lot of thinking about that, but I honestly believe people are reasonable. They don't expect miracles. They do expect some under-standing and knowledge of their troubles. And when I'm around, they do see some signs of visible change on some level. I was in a Bronx neighborhood where a kid got killed

because there was no traffic light. When I left there, I called
Henry Barnes, the Traffic Commissioner, and made sure it
wouldn't take the usual four months to get a light where
the people wanted it. I will *not* walk out of a situation like
that without being able to assure the people in the neighborhood there'll be immediate action." Lindsay grinned. "Sometimes there's even action before I get there. The Sanitation
Department, for instance, has a real information system. If
they find out I'm going to be in a certain neighborhood,
they'll clean it up before I come. That's what they've always
done with mayors. But I don't always tell them where I'll
be. Sometimes I don't tell *anyone* where I'm going. And
then, when I get there and see they haven't been moving
their butts, I yell and scream to get the trucks into that
neighborhood. And I go back, or I send someone back, to
see if they've followed through.

"Also, going out on those streets is of immense value to
me. It's the one way I can really find out what people are
sweating about, what they care about. I wouldn't have had
those houses in East New York torn down if seeing them
hadn't hit me in the guts. You see so much grief on those
streets."

Harvey Rothenberg, the Mayor's assistant for appointments, came in. "You're all backed up," he said to the Mayor.
I rose. "One more question," I said. "When you see all that
grief, and when you read and hear about what's happening
in the hospitals, for example, isn't it an enormous weight
to have the responsibility you have? I would think the pain
and frustration would be constant."

He looked at me, ran his hand through his hair, and
said, "Mary's good at handling that. She's tough. She reminds
me whenever I get very upset that I'm only here for a visit
and I can't change the world."

VII From the Mayor's office I walked down a narrow red carpet to the office of Robert Sweet, who at the time was the Mayor's executive assistant and was responsible for, among many other things, legislative liaison between the Mayor and the City Council. (He later became one of the two deputy mayors.) Sweet, who went to Yale College with Lindsay and was one of his roommates at the Yale Law School, is a tall, slim man with a fierce black-and-gray mustache, who is unfailingly composed and courteous. Even during the times of greatest friction between the Mayor's wing and the Democratic enclave on the other side of City Hall, Sweet's relations with the opposition have been cordial.

"The name of the game here," he told me as I settled into a chair opposite his desk, "is to find out what the hell the questions are. In the campaign we kept saying that New York *can* be governed and made a better place to live in, but once we got in here, we had to find the right questions to begin organizing around. At the start the key question was: 'How do you begin restoring confidence that the city can indeed be governed?' In trying to answer that one, we've gone some way toward putting the city on a sound fiscal basis. And we set up the concept of the Night Mayor to indicate that someone will always be available for complaints. It was also to answer that question that so much time was spent deciding on appointments. You certainly can't say John has loaded the city with political hacks. Another part of the answer is reorganizing the structure of the city government, and that's why it's so important that we get the City Council to pass our reorganization plan to combine dozens of miscellaneous city operations into ten super agencies.

"Of course, some questions come up you know are the right questions, but the answers aren't immediately apparent. How do you get movement below, where the tendency is to let things function as they always have? What's the answer to that question in the Sanitation Department, where only six positions out of fourteen thousand are exempt from civil service? The Mayor's personality is such that he wants things to happen *now*, but it will take time to get that kind of spirit down below. My own belief is that the one way you can really change established patterns of performance is by example. You can't do it very well by directives or with all the hortatory language in the world. If it's going to be done, it'll happen through real leadership on John's part. As I found out in college, he's a very determined man. And he has that very important element of leadership that has to do with the ability to make controversial decisions and not back down.

"I'll give you an example. There's a very thorny problem of where to put a public-housing project in the Bronx. If you put it in an area that's already disadvantaged, the people in the project won't be moving out of the ghetto. If you put it in a mixed area, you might tip the balance. If you put it in an all-white neighborhood, there's going to be a lot of furor. Now, this project had been on the Board of Estimate's calendar for approval for two years before we came into office. But it was so hot a question no one would touch it. The last time it came up under Wagner, it was put aside without date. Meanwhile, the federal government was pressing the city. If you're not going to do it, they said, give us back the money. So John simply went ahead. We proposed the project be built outside the ghetto in a white neighborhood, and the Board adopted the proposal. There's a lot of opposition, but that's his way of leading. Wagner's was quite different. He had superb political judgment; it

wasn't that he was indolent. His technique was to let conflicting pressures cancel each other out over a period of time
unless one pressure group was able to build up a big enough
head of steam to indicate to him that he wouldn't lose too
much politically if he moved. After all, he *was* elected three
times. His way may turn out to have been the better political technique.

"Another difference between Wagner and John, of
course, is that Wagner did have a political structure behind
him, and that made it much easier to be Mayor. When he
did decide to move, he could pick up the telephone and
tell the Democratic City Council and the Democratic Board
of Estimate, 'This is what I want done.' John is a loner.
Anything this administration has gotten so far has been by
main strength and awkwardness. But I'm quite confident
you'll know at the end of four years that we've been here.
I can't believe men of good will can't accomplish *something*."

"Do you think," I asked, "the Mayor could be more
effective a leader if he were more politic, less abrasive at
times?"

Sweet shook his head negatively, and smiled. "Oh that's
John's personality. It's part of his integrity, and this administration is going to stand or fall on whether enough people
believe in his integrity. Okay, so he made some of the legislators sore during the tax battle. Maybe that was bad politically, but at least it was refreshing to have a guy who says
what he thinks. In that particular case though, I don't think
it mattered how he came on. He could have sung 'The Star-
Spangled Banner' on top of City Hall for all the difference
his style would have made. It was an election year and the
decisions were made during those three days in Albany not
on the basis of temperament but on the basis of what was
possible under those conditions."

The Mayor's style and its contrast with his predecessor's
also figured in a talk I had later in the year with a man who

had been on Wagner's staff through two of his terms and
was now working for the state of New York. The former
Wagner aide prides himself on being a political technician
and as such, was not impressed with the first year of the
Lindsay administration. "Lindsay's attitude," he began, "and
that of the people he brought in with him is that if you're
intelligent and your heart is good, all you have to do is
take over and there'll be change. They're so naïve. And being both naïve and without experience, they didn't have the
sense to phase the old-timers out of the administration. Some
they got rid of instantly and others were told they were on
the way out. That's why there was so much unnecessary
confusion down there." He laughed. "When Lindsay and
those youngsters first came in, they didn't even know how
to turn on the lights. They literally didn't know how to
turn on the lights. No one from his team had contacted me
for transition advice during the period between election and
January, but I sure got a call the first day they were in office.
They wanted to know how the lights and the phones worked.

    "Okay, so they're in and the lights are on. Then they
start talking about the quality of their appointments as compared with ours. Do you remember the first new man
Wagner brought in, in 1954? Dr. Luther Gulick as City Administrator. A professor, a do-gooder without any political
connections. That was an unheard-of thing at the time—
bringing in a guy like Gulick. I'll admit there were a lot of
things wrong with the Wagner government, but don't forget
he turned the tide of municipal government in New York
after O'Dwyer and Impellitteri by bringing in do-gooders
and academicians. You're too young to remember, but when
Jimmy Walker was Mayor, if you went out to Belmont Park
on a weekday afternoon, there'd be a line of cars with city
seals on them—the cars of heads of departments. Wagner
put professional career men in the key agencies. But the impression the Lindsay people give is that Wagner's administration was entirely dominated by political interests. Good

Lord, the grip Alex Rose, the power in the Liberal Party, has on John Lindsay is a lot stronger than the influence any individual had on Wagner. I'm not saying Lindsay hasn't made good appointments. His top ones have been excellent. But look at many of the middle-echelon appointments. They're as political as ever, except this time more Liberal Party hacks have the jobs. And another thing they say is that they're the first administration to get involved in long-range planning. I can show you files of long-range planning programs in the Municipal Reference Library that go far back to the beginnings of the Wagner administration. But we never had the money to implement them."

The office we were in was comfortable, thickly carpeted, quiet. The political technician spoke without passion, even as he went on to say, "And Lindsay himself is a very grating, ungracious man. I attended a meeting he had with Negro leaders who had worked in his campaign. They wanted to find out whether his administration would have more than a token few black faces. Lindsay started off with a complete lack of finesse. He blasted them out of their chairs. 'How *dare* you guys do this to me—put pressure on *me!* I'm your friend. I'm suffering. The city is suffering.' It was embarrassing. For a man who's had experience, after all, as a legislator, he has so little understanding of how to get things done. It's a matter of give-and-take. But he feels that if you're not for him, you're automatically against him. Any sophisticated man in politics knows that isn't the case. Everybody has his own interests to take into account and if you want something from him, *you* have to take those interests into account too. I was in Albany during that last stage of the war about his tax program. I will grant that Lindsay fought very hard for the City of New York, as a mayor should, but he showed a lot of petulance, too. It was not his finest hour. You know, to me this is the tragedy of John Lindsay. He will go down the line for the city, but a mayor needs more than determination if he's to be effective. He must have finesse. I knew he didn't have it. That's why I didn't vote for anyone for mayor. I got to the booth and I walked away."

"Where do you think Lindsay will go after being mayor?"

"I don't see the Presidency for him, I'll tell you that. Charisma is fine when you're a candidate, but it's not enough once you're in office, especially the office of mayor. The cruelest thing about being mayor of New York is your extreme visibility. As the mayor, you cannot hide. Not ever. So performance as well as personality is essential. Now Wagner had hardly any charisma at all, but he could go into a room with a group of politicians and get something done. I have grave doubts Lindsay will get much done."

"The Mayor says," I interrupted, "that the way to accomplish change in the city is to make decisions quickly and forcefully, the implication being that Wagner was the Great Delayer."

"You can overdo that instant decision-making. Dilatory tactics are sometimes much wiser. Take the Lower Manhattan Expressway. When it was first proposed eight years ago by Bob Moses, it was generally agreed that an expressway was a necessary part of the city's arterial highway system in order to alleviate the tremendous traffic problems downtown. And Moses had the money—ninety per cent of the funds were to come from the federal government. It was a great bargain for the city. The federal planners had approved the idea, the State Department of Public Works had approved it; but then, as usually happens with physical planning, the local people involved suddenly emerged. About two thousand people and eight hundred businesses would have to be relocated, and no provision had been made for them.

"There was a lot of screaming at the first large-scale public hearing, so Wagner got his colleagues on the Board of Estimate to hold up the expressway. And Wagner told

Moses he had to take care of the people being displaced. Four or five months later Moses came back with a plan for low- and middle-income housing for those who'd be displaced. But meanwhile the Regional Planning Association, among others, had suggested that the expressway be depressed so that we wouldn't have a Chinese Wall down there. Moses said that would cost too much, and that if we waited any longer, we'd lose the federal money or he himself would take it and use if for some other project. Wagner cooled Moses down and arranged for another delay to find out whether the cost of depressing the route would be too prohibitive. Whichever way it finally goes, there's sure to be a lot less dislocation of people and a much better plan than if Wagner had been an instant decision-maker. So being a strong Mayor, if you don't also have finesse, isn't necessarily the way to make it.

"Okay, I'll grant Lindsay's done some good things. Like shaking up the police hierarchy. I never thought the cops should be above the Mayor's control. But much of what's been going on is *surface* performance—what he likes to call a sense of movement. That'll wear thin in a while. People will want results, not a show. Yes, he has held out a hand of hope to those in the ghettos, but that may turn out to have been a cruel hoax."

The political technician filled and lit a pipe. "Well, we'll know by 1969. I have one key index to go by: What will the condition of the non-whites in this city be by 1969? If Lindsay has failed there, he has failed the city. Public school enrollment—not only elementary school enrollment —will soon be more than fifty per cent non-white. That's a significant statistic. It could presage a largely black city, a city of the black poor. If he can change the employment picture so that non-whites can start moving up, and if he can change the school system and the environment as a whole so that middle-class whites will stay, he's made it. I hope he does, but I just don't think he's sensitive enough to the nuances of New York. There's no city in the world like this one in terms of the cruelty of its contrasts and the subtlety with which you have to play interests against each other to accomplish anything. And maybe—maybe what you most need as mayor of this city is an acute consciousness of your capacity to make mistakes. Wagner had that. Lindsay does not."

The political technician looked out the window. The only view was of another office building. "Of course, no matter what happens," he said, "the city will keep moving along. The babies will get born. All the grubby things that city workers do will keep getting done. The garbage will be collected. No matter who's on top, things do keep running. Good Lord, under Impellitteri, who was almost no mayor at all, the city ran. It'll be here after Lindsay's gone."

VIII I later mentioned the political technician's reservations about the Mayor and his administration to Jay Kriegel, a fairly recent graduate of the Harvard Law School, who, as an assistant to Lindsay, had acquired the reputation of being one of the brightest of the bright young men at City Hall. Kriegel, a slight, restless man of twenty-five, responded to my remark wryly. "It's amazing, the number of men on the inside of the Wagner administration who tell us they were grand fellows. Why didn't things move when they were here? As for John's personality, do you know where I first met this 'grating ungracious' man? I spent three weeks in Washington with some other law students, helping to draft sections of the 1965 Voting Rights Bill. Lindsay didn't know us from Adam, and he could have treated us summarily. We were mere law students. But very quickly we were on a first-name basis with him and were barging into his office whenever anything occurred to any of us. I was impressed by that, and also by his ability to listen. He picked things up very fast.

"And he's still amazingly open and accessible. A Javits or a Kennedy can travel around the world and pick out a crisis on which he expounds in the Senate. It's a lovely life. This poor bastard has a crisis every day. And the pressures! The other night he was a hundred phone calls behind, and he still had the usual phenomenal amount of paperwork to get through. That much he's learned—how to get used to full-time pressure. And I think he's also come a long way as an administrator since he started. By the middle of 1967 he'll really be on top of things."

"What do you think the likelihood is of going from a sense of movement to real change?"

Kriegel looked at me as if I were a freshman on the first day of the term. "If you break New York City's five boroughs into five cities, my friend, you have four of the eight largest cities in the country. And the Borough of Richmond, which we look on as a piddling country town, would be fifty-second in population among the cities—if it were a separate city. So it's a rough government to move. But John has the temperament to move it. There are people who think he's naïve. To me, that quality in him is the mark of an honest Puritan. I've been on some tours of dangerous neighborhoods with him during tense periods, and he's the kind of man who, if you tell him he can't walk down this street because it isn't safe, he goes ahead and does it. He figures he's the Mayor of the damn city and if the streets aren't safe for him, are they safe for anyone? And he wants action, all the time. If you're in the field and a decision ought to be made right there, he can get awfully mad if you take the time to check back with City Hall. I once said to him, 'Yeah, but if I make a mistake, the press will clobber *you*.' 'Hell, so what?' was his reaction. 'The main thing is to show the city government *can* act quickly.'

"And I agree with him about the importance of his being out in the field a lot. For one thing, it's an extension of his whole feeling about being mayor—that he ought to be into everything, not some magisterial being waiting to step in at the supreme moment. For another, until we do get the reorganization plan through and until program planning begins to show results, he has very little more he can give these people except himself. There have been twenty years of neglect to make up for. Sure, opening up a few more play streets and getting the Sanitation Department into a ghetto neighborhood is not in the same league as new housing and schools and jobs. He knows that. And he knows the people in the neighborhoods know that. But at least he's out there finding things out. And because of his lead, so are the commissioners. It's important for *them* to know what government can do, even now. They can change things, if they know what's out there that has to be changed. And another reason I like to see John on the streets is that getting away from City Hall is a great way for him to clear his head."

A light flashed on one of the phones on Kriegel's desk, and he took the call. "No," he said softly, "I don't appear on any radio or television programs. The Mayor speaks for me."

"How long," I asked him, "are you going to stay in the administration?"

"I don't know. I'm a Democrat. My first touch of politics was working for Bill Ryan in 1960. But I think I'll be around a while. I think we're on the way up. The first six to eight months were the lowest point that John is going to have. The press *had* to knock him down—the Ajax knight on a white horse. And, in a way, he and some of his aides deserved it. They did think they could change the world right away. But we came to learn the value of planning, and of time. You have to know what to wait for. You have to learn the need to set priorities. You don't try to change the whole city at once. You decide what you're going to change first. Just as, if I were to pay equal attention to everything that comes across my desk, and if I answered each letter as fully as I'd like to, that's all I'd be doing. *That's* the way to get movement—getting your priorities straight."

In December and January, I watched the Mayor on television and at several public meetings as he was being asked to assess his first year in office. In all these various year-end summations, he seemed, with some justification, to feel a sense of accomplishment. There had been reverses, he admitted, such as the defeat of the Police Civilian Review Board; but on balance, the first year had been a substantial beginning, "a time of tooling up so that we can start the production needed during the next three years." Part of that tooling up had involved putting the city on a markedly sounder fiscal basis which included the end of crisis borrowing and the achievement of an income tax he described as "the first really flexible one we've had since it rises as the economy grows. Equally important, it covers the entire region of people involved with New York City." Also basic to the "tooling up" process were the plans for reorganizing the city government. ("We've gone further than any city in the country to modernize our municipal structure.") He also claimed to have created a sense that New York was no longer in a state of decline. Of his associates in the administration, he said, "These are men who understand the most effective ways in which the federal government can be linked to the megalopolises of the country."

Watching him on these occasions, I felt again, as I had during most of his public appearances in previous months, that his personality underwent a kind of truncation under bright lights. In all the conversations I'd had with him, both when he was a congressman and after he became mayor, he had shown a perceptive irreverence along with a wry consciousness of his own vulnerabilities that seldom came through fully in his public appearances. And so, in order to conduct my own interim reassessment, I paid another call on him—this time at Gracie Mansion, late one Friday afternoon in early February of 1967. The day was cold and overcast; the streets and Carl Schurz Park adjoining the Mansion were nearly deserted. As a policeman stopped me at the small gatehouse on the way to the new reception wing, the Mayor stepped out of his black Lincoln in front of the entrance to the Mansion's new reception wing, which had been completed only a few months before. He was bare-headed, thinner than he had been the last time I'd seen him, somewhat harried-looking. He waved, signaled to the policeman to let me pass, and told me as I came up to him, "I'm running late. I have a meeting with the health people and then I have to get this make-up off. I've been on TV, taping a show for Sunday so I can go skating with the kids. Come in and relax."

I waited in a small room from which I could see, at the far end of the ballroom, a painting of Susan Wagner, after whom the ballroom is named. The wing, which the Mayor generally refers to as the Annex, had been appointed in eighteenth-century style, and while this resulted in an impressive atmosphere of subdued elegance, I felt as if I were in a museum after-hours. To bring myself back into this century, I read the *Times* by the dim light of the small chandelier. It was absolutely quiet. I wondered where the staff was. As it grew darker outside, an hour went by. Suddenly the Mayor loped in and motioned me to follow him downstairs to the office he uses in the new wing.

"Staff?" he said, laughing. "It doesn't exist. The staff consists of Mary and three people in the main house. Two of them are on the city payroll, and one is on ours. And this is a lot of house to keep, so they kind of run back and forth between here and the living quarters." The office downstairs, a small one, was brightly lit by a brass chandelier. In a corner was a compact telephone console with direct lines to City Hall and the Police and Fire departments. I took a seat in front of a large mahogany desk with ornamental brass handles at its sides. On the wall to the right of the desk was a cut-out picture of a turkey that had been vigorously colored in and signed by John Lindsay, Jr. Behind me on the back wall were shelves partially filled with lawbooks. The Mayor called the living quarters to ask for two Scotch-and-waters, and then took a seat next to mine. (The drinks were delivered a few minutes later by the Mayor's daughter Margaret.)

"A year ago," I said, "you laid considerable stress on the importance of getting the Little City Halls into operation. But the City Council insists they're dead."

"They're not," said Lindsay. "It'll take time, but I still think we'll get them. I've told the leadership of the Council that either we'll get the idea approved by the Council, or little by little, we'll get them opened one at a time. I've got four now, one of them officially in a Health Center in Brownsville and the others set up with foundation help and with volunteer staffs. One way or another, we'll cumshaw them through."

"And the reorganization of the city government—the ten superagencies—do you think you'll get that through?"

"Well, I've been able to do some of it by executive order. We couldn't have coped with Medicaid if I hadn't been able to cut through all the constituent agencies which would otherwise have been involved with that. But I do need legislation to do final budgeting for the ten new administrations we've planned. If we don't get it, we won't have as good a government as we could have."

Lindsay was drumming his fingers against the arm of his chair. "Of course," he went on, "I can't be certain I'll get all of the reorganization plan through. The City Council has emancipated itself. It's becoming an honest-to-God legislative body that feels it can be independent."

"Is that partly because you're a Republican?"

He laughed. "It's wholly because I'm a Republican. But although their emancipation brings about some problems, it's not such a bad development for the future." He glanced at his watch. "Look, I have to take a few minutes to execute a will with Mary. I'd been letting it slide until I finally realized it had to be done."

A few minutes later the Mayor returned. His wife came in to say hello. I asked her what had happened to John Jr.'s fire truck. "The new carpet did come," she said, "but now he rides the truck in circles out back. That's one problem we solved."

She left and Lindsay returned to his chair. "Now I can die in peace. I've got my brothers all lined up to take care of the kids. Everything's in order. The only thing is I've probably done it wrong."

He mentioned a speech he had to go over later that night and I told the Mayor of my feeling that the public Lindsay was rather stiff compared to Lindsay in private. I asked if he was conscious of the difference.

He looked at me quizzically. "It's hard for the subject to comment on something like that, but I expect there's a lot of truth to what you say."

"Why does it happen?" I asked.

"If I knew why, I'd be a wiser man."

Changing the subject, I asked, "What about the contention of some newsmen and some of the people in the Democratic wing of City Hall that you take the position if someone doesn't fully support a program of yours, he's automatically against you?"

Lindsay thought for a moment or two and he looked a little troubled as he answered. "I'm prepared to compromise more than people think. Within limits, of course. I wouldn't have been able to survive in the House for seven years if I hadn't learned how to compromise. But, remember, I came into a situation in which a lot of people had been used to getting their way for a long time. And I proposed a lot of things that were quite different from what had been going on, so I had to state my positions with some strength. Also, I don't know that people who say that really believe I'm all that inflexible. I know from my experience in the House that when a legislator doesn't want to do something, one way to cop out is to say that the executive doesn't know how to compromise, that he won't consult with you sufficiently. But I suppose I have left the impression with some people here and there that I won't meet them halfway. I hope there aren't too many who think that."

Lindsay got up and began to pace the floor. "There are some times, however, when that charge is a lot of nonsense. Like, I saw in the press that the President of the City Council and the Controller were complaining I hadn't consulted with them on a capital budget. I called each one in, independently of each other, and I asked them, 'What is this nonsense? You know how elaborate a process is involved in setting up the capital budget before it's time to consult.' Each one of them blamed the press, and said he'd been misquoted. One of them even said that, of course, a congressman wouldn't expect to go over to the Bureau of the Budget to see what's going on while the President is preparing his annual budget message. So I told them, 'Anytime you think you haven't been consulted, let me know. Don't complain to the press.'"

"Why didn't they hold a press conference to say they'd been misquoted?"

Lindsay smiled wryly. "They didn't choose to."

I mentioned Robert Price's concern that Lindsay needed a political structure behind him if he were to accomplish all he wanted in the years ahead, especially since he was dealing with an organized Democratic opposition.

"Sure he's right," said Lindsay. "I'm conscious of that all the time. But I went into the campaign without even a substructure, and we created one. Many of the people who were involved in the storefront organizations during the campaign have set up local organizations—in all the boroughs. We call them CIA's—isn't that a hell of a name—for Civic Improvement Associations. There are about fifty of them now in the five boroughs. The people in them come from all parties, they meet regularly in tiny headquarters, and they really are civic-improvement associations. When I needed help, for instance, during the fight to keep the Civilian Review Board, they came out to help organize support. And when we put public housing into Queens or the Bronx, they show up at Board of Estimate hearings on the other side of the yelling and screaming. Obviously, they don't have as much muscle as a strong political organization with a network of legislators in office would have. What it comes down to, as of now, is that my only real strength is what I have going with the people. And that goes up and down all the time."

The phone rang. It was the Mayor's secretary at City Hall. His schedule for the next day, already tight, would somehow have to be expanded enough to include a half hour with a commissioner who had pressing budget problems. When the call was through, I asked the Mayor about a statement he had made a few weeks before that the city's expense budget had increased more than one hundred and fifty per cent in the past ten years. (The expense budget, financed mainly by taxation, provides for the city's operating expenses. The capital budget, financed principally by borrowing, encompasses the cost of constructing public schools, libraries, and other buildings.) "At that rate of increase," I wondered, "how high will it be at the end of the next three years?"

He slumped in his chair, looking at his hands. "I don't know. I just don't know. I'm still guessing what the next budget will be, the one that theoretically has to be adopted by April 15. I know it'll be over five billion."

"How are you going to be able to keep raising revenues to meet that large an expense budget when the city's own taxing potential is so limited?"

The Mayor looked at the ceiling. "Oh it is indeed limited. I am constantly being reminded of that by the leaders of the City Council and by other people in the government. Well, the answer has to come from federal revenues. This terrible pressure on the expense budgets of cities is like a specter at these mayors' conferences I go to. We start to talk about long-range plans for urban development and invariably the discussion quickly distills itself into the No. 1 problem every mayor has—the expense budget. Take Theodore Mc-Keldin, the mayor of Baltimore. He's lost his whole middle class from the core city, and the state legislature not only won't give him any upward adjustment in real estate taxes but it's also seriously threatening to repeal his payroll tax. We asked him, 'What are you going to do if that happens?' He threw up his hands and said, 'I don't *know* what I'll do.' It's comforting to go to these mayors' conferences because the problems you think are unique to you turn out to be modest by comparison with what's going on in other cities.

"I do think, though, that mayors can work as a force to put pressure on Congress. It'll always be a fight to get the real money, but there are things you can do. You noticed, I expect, that I put twenty-five million dollars into our 1967–8 capital budget for the Model Cities program. The Congress passed that program, such as it is, but so far hasn't funded it. So my hope is that by doing this— and we're the first city to try this approach—we can embarrass the Congress to appropriate the federal money that's been promised. If they do, we'll qualify for a hundred million dollars more than that twenty-five million of our own money.

"We had another reason for doing it. Most of our twenty-five million is for the three areas that need the most attention—Harlem, the South Bronx and Central Brooklyn. But Robert Weaver and his team at Housing and Urban Development have been resisting our idea of focusing on three sections of the city. They told us that because Congress would probably appropriate very little money, we had to put all the funds we get into just one hard-core area. We had a meeting with them, and when we told them we were prepared to put up our own Model Cities money as a starter for three neighborhoods, that stopped them short. So if Congress does come through, we won't be limited to one area."

Mary Lindsay phoned from the living quarters. I was keeping the Mayor from dinner. He promised to be right over, but sat down again. "Relax," he said. "There's time."

I asked what he thought of a statement by Edward Costikyan, who had been the New York County Democratic leader for three years of the Wagner administration. Costikyan had said that although the Lindsay team had shown the "usual initial flurry" of energy, 99.8 per cent of government is unchanged by any administration, and the Lindsay administration would inevitably "go out tired," just as its predecessors had.

The Mayor shrugged. "I haven't been here long enough to testify as to the truth of that. But I do think the urban situation is changing. Here and in other cities. We are getting urbanists who are real professionals and only need the money to do the job. And I detect a change in those of the young who are interested in public service. Many of them are no longer rushing into federal service. They want to be in the front lines of the action, in the cities. I'm not saying there's a radical change of mood in the country insofar as the cities and their problems are concerned, but there *is* some difference in attitude. My deepest satisfaction in this job so far is that I think we've helped to strengthen that change of attitude. We've shown, I think, that there is the possibility of a first-class government in this city by the way we propose to restructure it. After all, consider the quality of the people who have been willing to come aboard. They wouldn't have come if they hadn't believed in the possibility.

"It is true, though, that the machinery is still so slow. That's a constant struggle. The goddan bureaucracy can drive you crazy. Hell, even among the people close to me, some don't always move their butts as fast as they ought to. Six months ago I gave instructions for a particular piece of legislation to be drawn up. It still hasn't been done."

"Why?"

The Mayor banged his hand on the arm of his chair. "Aagh! Legal problems, communication problems, they say. What it comes to is that it got stuck on a back burner and hasn't moved. You know that story about Eisenhower's first day in the White House after he'd been elected? He came into the Presidential office, and Harry Truman said, 'Well, there's the desk and there's the chair. You sit in it all day long and give orders and then you try to find out what's happened to them. Good-bye. I wish you luck." Lindsay laughed. "That's why I found out I had to be tougher than I thought I'd have to be. But there are times I worry I'm being too tough. There's the danger of being arbitrary and the danger of being wrong. There are times when you can't be sure you're going on the correct information. As in Congress, there's too much to know, so you're always skimming the surface more than you'd like to. It's particularly frustrating for a lawyer to have to do that. Lawyers like to get to the bedrock of things.

"Nevertheless you do have to set firm guidelines. I believe people would rather have someone say, 'This is the way you do it and if you don't like it you can leave,' than have someone equivocate because he's not sure. You've got to be tough because you keep getting collisions between people in government and being firm is the way to handle them. I've often had to say, 'If you don't have confidence in my decision, you can resign.' "

He was drumming his fingers on the chair arm again. "This need to be firm when you may not have all the information is the reason I like to have real professionals around me. And it's also the reason I've come to appreciate good staff work. But then, sometimes you can overstaff a problem. Take the towaway program—clearing the streets of illegally parked cars. That could have been talked to death. In a situation like that, you go ahead and *do* it and deal with the problems as they come."

"After a year," I asked, "are your hours any shorter?"

"It's not so bad now," the Mayor said. "I start at seven and usually wind up about midnight."

I remembered that was the same span of working time he had described the year before.

"And time with the children?"

"We're still fighting for dinner together one night a week but we're not too successful. We started dinner the night before last. Afterwards I was going to show the kids some home movies we'd taken when we went skiing in Colorado. They love to see themselves in home movies. But just before the ice cream, two fires blew. A warehouse went up in the Village and then there was one in Harlem. That ended that evening."

"Do you have to go to those fires?"

The Mayor frowned. "Oh God, a three- or a four-alarm fire? I ought to go. I really should go. Fires are fearful things."

"Are the children any more resigned to your being Mayor?"

"Johnny's too young. The others are not resigned. Margie, our thirteen-year-old, hates public life. If I have to do anything official when I'm with the kids and I go in the limousine, she screams about it. And when she sees the cameras, she runs away. Annie's somewhat the same way, even though she's only eleven. Kathy, who's sixteen, is away at school, and because of that, she's probably the most relaxed of the three. But when she's home she gets out of here fast and spends her time with a friend in the Bronx. Madame Gandhi, when she was here, told me that she sent her kids out of the country. 'They either made or lost friends because of me,' she said.

"How about the strain on you? Has that lessened?"

"Yes, chiefly because I've got the government shaped

up a little bit better and I've gotten confidence in the team so that I don't have to do every bloody thing myself as much as before. One problem that doesn't get any better is keeping myself accessible to everybody. They're all griping at me that I don't spend enough time with each one, but it seems to me that's what I'm doing all the time. Like in ten days I'm going to spend a whole week with Leary. I'll be involved in nothing but police problems—equipment, budget, communications plans, programs. I'll spend time in each precinct. And then I'll do a week of nothing but health and hospitals. And when it gets warmer, I've got to start getting out on the streets again."

"Speaking of that, did you see Saul Alinsky's charge that 'the average citizen in New York City has much less to say about things than in any other American city I have seen?' "

I half expected the Mayor to start talking about various community action programs and other forms of citizen participation by way of an answer. Instead, he smiled thinly and nodded in agreement with Alinsky. "That's because of the size of the city. Actually they'd have more to say if they really wanted to. I wish more people *would* start yelling and telling us what's bothering them. That's a real problem—how to excite them so that they'll insist on having a say on how the city is run. But that *can* happen if they get to believe you mean it when you say you're concerned. I've got something going now with Sid Davidoff, Barry Gottehrer, Jay Kriegel, and Jim Smith, he's the man who directs the Mayor's Information Center and Mobile Unit. They're my troubleshooters. They go out in response to complaints we get through the mail or from petitions or by calls from various people, and they try to straighten out what's wrong. They move out as fast as what looks like a legitimate complaint comes in."

It was nearly eight. Mary Lindsay called again. As we were leaving the office, I said, "At a meeting of the Newspaper Reporters Association, I heard you say, 'My present political ambition is to end my political days in this office.' "

The Mayor stood still and nodded. "That's about right. I can't imagine any other office as interesting as this one. I'm sure the Presidency is worse in terms of loneliness, exasperation, being misunderstood. But it has no greater problems. Except one. The President has the button, and that's a colossal difference. But after being here, the interest in any other office just isn't there. Not even the Presidency. Also I really think you ought to exhaust yourself in this job. Furthermore, if you try to do the kind of job you want to as mayor of New York, you have to forget about any other office anyway. Because, to do it right, you have to throw away all your credit cards."

IX   During the next few months, it wasn't always clear how many credit cards the Mayor was using up and how many new ones he was collecting. I did discover one new source of credit about which I intended to tell him. In Washington Square Park on a Sunday in May, two women were discussing the Mayor as their three-year-olds established rights to a corner of the sandbox.

"Well, really," said one mother, "what *has* changed?"

"I don't know what I could point to," her friend moved her hands aimlessly, "but he's brought the feeling—to me, anyway—that change *is* possible in this city. Well, look," she pointed, "we have sand now in that sandbox instead of dirt. Oh, what I'm trying to say is you never quite know what's going to pop up next these days. Before, you knew *nothing* could pop up—ever."

What popped up, however, was not always at the instigation of the Mayor. A strike of building service workers in late May and early June of his second year of office, for example, brought pressure on him both from tenants, who

were demanding that something be done about the absence
of elevator service and the accumulation of garbage outside
their doors, and from the owners of rent-controlled buildings, who were demanding financial relief if there was to be
a wage increase for the workers. Before the strike was settled,
more than six hundred owners of small rent-controlled prop-
erties stormed City Hall in an attempt to reach the Mayor's
office. They didn't succeed, but nine panes of glass in windows
and doors were broken during the attack, and the Mayor's
assistant appointments secretary, an attractive young woman
in her twenties, was slightly wounded on the ankle by a rock
that came hurtling through the double doors at the front of
the Hall.

The siege repulsed, the Mayor went on to further skir-
mishes, including several with the City Council over his reorganization plan and his executive budget. When the Council and the Board of Estimate removed from that budget
twenty-three million dollars intended to meet pay increases
for schoolteachers, police, and firemen, the Mayor characterized their action as "one of the most coldly calculated political maneuvers I have ever seen." In arctic answer, Frank
O'Connor, then president of the City Council, said the
Mayor's original budget had been "dishonest on its face."
This kind of exchange took place often during the Mayor's
first term, rhetoric being the only free commodity to which
both sides could have instant access.

In the middle of June, I received a telephone call from
the political technician I had talked to the previous fall. "I've
had some second thoughts about the Mayor since I saw you
last," he said. "Why don't you come see me?"

We met the next morning in his office in midtown. "I
was pretty harsh on the Mayor nine months ago," he began,
"because my reactions to him were based primarily on the
horrendous way in which he'd handled the transit strike just
as he took office and the way he threw his first tax package at
the legislature in Albany. I must say there's been a different

Lindsay in certain respects since the first of the year. When he went up to Albany on taxes during *this* session of the legislature, he was calm and reasonable, and showed much greater understanding of how things get done there. Why, at a dinner at the Executive Mansion, with leaders of both parties present, Lindsay praised the Governor, paid tribute to the sagacity of the leaders on both sides of the aisle, and made a big point of making clear how well aware he was of *their* problems. As we were leaving, a Democrat said to me in some astonishment, 'He's practically a new man.'

"However," the political technician looked at me severely, "there are still negative elements in this administration. I'm appalled by what seems to me a very serious, imminent breakdown in several key areas. Morale in the Health Department, for one thing, is at the lowest point in twenty years because of his bureaucratic thrust to create those umbrella-like superagencies. The people in the Health Department don't know *what* their functions are going to be. And from what I hear, there are similar morale problems in other departments with all this reorganization that's in the wind. Furthermore, I have my own worries about it. Superagencies are going to mean super-bureaucracies. Bureaucracies feed on themselves anyway, and this could become monstrous.

"On the other hand," the political technician now looked benign, "I will say that Lindsay himself has become more relaxed. That grating suspiciousness has largely gone. I think Lindsay now realizes that everybody *is* out to get the mayor, any mayor, and that everybody *does* have his own angle, and you might as well learn to live with it."

"But wouldn't realizing that make him more suspicious rather than less?"

"What I mean is that now his suspicions are more empirically grounded. It's always easier to cope with things you *know* are real. You see, he wasn't ready at first for the trauma of being mayor. Now he's gotten used to it, and gradually he's also acquired more confidence in his own judgment, especially, I think, since the end of last year, when Bob Price, on whom he used to depend quite heavily, resigned as deputy mayor."

"Nine months ago," I said, "you felt there was little chance of Lindsay going on to higher office, particularly the Presidency, after finishing here as mayor. He seems to agree with you. He talks about exhausting himself in this job and then going back to private life."

The political technician smiled. "No matter what he says, I don't think he intends to leave public life after having been mayor. And unlike the way I felt nine months ago, I'm beginning to believe he might move up in his party, especially if he has some moderate success as Mayor. The Republican Party has been changing since the 1964 convention when Rockefeller failed to liberalize it, to say the least. More and more of the new Republican governors and senators are young moderates, and they're altering the nature of the party. Sure, there's a lot of hard-core conservatism that still has to be dealt with, but it was Rockefeller who took *them* on directly in 1964, not Lindsay. Lindsay doesn't have that albatross around his neck, and it's conceivable that at some point— who can predict?—the party, including some of the conservatives, will be looking for an appealing moderate candidate for high office and will turn to John V. Lindsay."

"You say," I interrupted, "that he'll have to show some moderate success as Mayor. The last time we talked you didn't think he'd even accomplish that much."

"I've changed my mind about that. Now I'd say he has a good chance to get something done. Or rather, to leave the impression that there's been change. Basically he's a very attractive man. He does make his presence felt in the city. Sure, it's style more than substance so far, but so what? Very few voters go beneath the style and worry about things like all the bureaucratic problems that will come with his reorganization plan. Okay, so he'll have a success of style. That's at least some kind of success, isn't it?"

"You still think, then, that basic changes are unlikely?"

"With what you have to deal with in this city, it's going to be very, very hard for him to make any kind of dent in the real problems. As soon as you put a finger in the dike in one place, another part of it starts breaking down."

"What if he had more money to work with?"

"He's not going to get the money he needs from the federal government. In Washington, lip service is being paid to urban problems, and little more. That's why, under the present set of arrangements, no mayor can really make a dent. Look at congestion in the city—at how difficult it is to move around and do business. More than three million people enter the central business district of Manhattan every day, between Sixtieth Street and Wall Street. It's one of the largest daily movements of people in and out of one place in the history of the world. So three years ago, after ten years of debate, Congress enacted a federal transportation program that was designed to help cities with their mass transit problems. Do you know what the entire mass transit appropriation is for the entire nation for the next four years? Less than four hundred million dollars. What can you do with that? Or, take water pollution. The federal anti-water-pollution appropriation for the entire country for one year is only going to be about three hundred million dollars. And where's the federal money for fighting air pollution? Try to find it. It's practically nonexistent."

The political technician was silent for a while, contemplating an increasingly congested and polluted future. Then, with more enthusiasm than he had shown at any previous point in our conversation about the Mayor, he said, "In one respect, there *has* been substantial accomplishment in this city—the parks. Lindsay and his people have reversed Robert Moses's conception of the function of parks. They've made parks for people rather than automobiles. That really is an accomplishment. God, those iron bars around the sandboxes in the playgrounds Lindsay inherited! *There* was the symbol of Moses.

"And I'll give Lindsay credit for another accomplishment. The flush of enthusiasm created by him, by his style, has helped involve more young people in local government than I've ever seen in this city before. It used to be that young people would go into campaigns for somebody like Stevenson or would devote their energies to world federalism or something high-minded like that. When I was young, at parties someone would say, 'What do you do?' I'd tell them I worked in city government and they'd walk away as if I were some sort of hack. But now that's where the glamour is—municipal government. And there's still another thing he's done. I don't know how much political sex appeal there is in it, but he *has* devised a fairly rational tax and financial structure for the city to operate on. That's a very important precedent he set—bringing commuters into the city income-tax system."

The political technician paused. He seemed surprised at having arrived at a balance in favor of the Mayor after assessing the first eighteen months of the administration. "Yes," he said, "all in all, he's done more than I thought he'd be able to do. However," he was stern again, "I'm still disappointed, very disappointed in many of his appointments. He's not attracted the people of stature throughout the administration that had been hoped for. His single greatest appointment was Hoving, and now Hoving has left."

X   Toward the end of June, I went to see the Mayor once more. City Hall had been under siege again—by welfare workers, welfare clients, and by more than five thousand members of the United Federation of Teachers, who were serving notice that they and many of their colleagues would

resign in September unless the UFT won substantial gains
in its contract negotiations with the Board of Education.
Meanwhile, the Transport Workers Union had announced
that *its* new contract demands might cost the city more than
six hundred million dollars in the next two years. I made a
mental note not to plan to use the subways after midnight
New Year's Eve.

On the way to Gracie Mansion, I had been reading a
New York *Post* report on the annual convention of the
United States Conference of Mayors in Hawaii, where the
Mayor had unmistakably emerged, according to the *Post,* as
"one of the strong men of municipal government. . . . His
was the most influential viewpoint in the deliberations of the
conference platform committee." Moreover, the reporter
added, "he stops traffic among the tourists and is probably the
one mayor in the country who is recognized by residents of
a city other than his own."

I wondered how the Mayor had felt, coming back after
ten days as "one of the strong men of municipal government"
to the ceaseless crises which would keep testing that strength
for the next two and a half years. "The change in climate
wasn't that great," he said, smiling. "In Hawaii, I was on
the phone for at least an hour or an hour and a half every
single morning, being briefed on everything, every bloody
detail. You can't get away from pressure these days—not with
the telephone. But I did get a good rest out there, a lot of
sleep and swimming, and a long run on the beach every
morning."

Tanned, he looked rested, and thoroughly relaxed. We
were sitting on the long back porch of Gracie Mansion. It
was like being in the kind of old, comfortable, well-kept
country house that has usually been in the same family for
generations. There was green summer furniture on the porch,
some of it with bright-colored cushions, and from my chair,
I looked out into a small grassy playground with a slide and
swings. "That's not only for John Jr.," the Mayor said, fol-

lowing my glance. "In the summer, I sometimes hold the weekly cabinet meetings out there on the grass. It's much more pleasant than the conference room downstairs."

I remembered his recurrent concern during his first year as Mayor at not having enough time to think, and I asked him if that situation had improved. He took off his jacket, sprawled on a couch, and said, "Oh yes, I can delegate a lot of things now with confidence in areas I couldn't before. I still have a few amateurs here and there, but there are some good professionals. Staffing and administration is like marrying a woman—you don't really know what you've got yourself in for until you live with her for a while. There's a great element of risk and testing in many appointments. Some of the amateurs I started with developed into pros. Some didn't. And once in a while, a man who looked very professional from a distance turned out to be an amateur. But that's rare. On balance, I think the appointments have been on the plus side. There'll be some changes and a few additions, but the basic team is now pretty well set. And since I'm able to delegate matters to that team, I do have time to think, and to read. A good deal of the reading is on technical city stuff, but not all of it. I found a collection of Bernard Shaw's plays around here, and I've been zooming through that. And I've been rediscovering O. Henry. I grabbed it out of the library at the annex and I read a story or two before I got to bed. That and the *Times*. They send me a first edition now around eleven o'clock. The only thing is," he shook his head, "I still don't have any time to write. I'm a month late on a book review for *Life* on a study of wiretapping."

I told the Mayor of the thesis I'd heard that his ability to be relaxed these days resulted in part from finally recognizing that his suspicions about everybody's being out to get the Mayor were quite realistic. He roared with laughter. "You tell the man who said that he's not too far off base. That's the way it is, and you might as well relax and get used to it. No, I don't have much of a problem keeping calm now. But once in a while I still have my bad moments. Occasionally I'll wake up at three in the morning and fret and fume and toss around until six."

"What usually causes those bad moments?"

"Irritation. At the system—how hard it is to get the bureaucracy to move. At petty politics. At press-hungry commissioners."

The Mayor was called away to the telephone, and I watched the slow serene movement of ships on the East River until he came back. "You only have two and a half years of the first term left," I said, "and yet your reorganization plan, which you've insisted is central to bringing change in the city, hasn't moved out of the City Council. Don't you get irritated at that?"

He ran a hand through his hair. "Sure, but I think we'll get it through. I no longer get any negative talk about it from the City Council leadership, as I did for a long time. Now they say, 'Just give us some more time.' And they're about to give their approval for the first of the ten super-agencies—the Housing and Development Administration, which I've already set up by executive order. We'll get the whole package. There'll be some compromises, but they'll be compromises we can live with."

"But meanwhile," I said, "isn't there a morale problem among the staff in the various departments as they wait to see what will happen—in the Health Department, for example?"

"What you have," he said, frowning, "are certain members of the Establishment in all those departments who don't want any change at all. And there is, of course, some degree of uncertainty in the middle echelons. But that's inevitable when you do any kind of reorganizing. It happened in Washington when the Department of Health, Education, and Welfare was put together, and it happened when the Defense Department was changed over. But I'm more convinced than ever that we've *got* to have this reorganization in the city. I had doubts myself for a long time, for instance, over whether the Sanitation Department should be included in the administration that will be concerned with environmental control. The department is big, critical, and a uniformed force that has been on its own for a long time. But the more I went into the problems of environmental control, the clearer it became that you have to talk about air, water, earth, and streets all together. And you have to budget them all together. If you burn what the Sanitation Department collects, you corrupt the air. If you don't burn it, you corrupt the earth. And whatever you do, you need more equipment and more manpower in an integrated system that will deal with every element of the problem—in the air, in the water, and underground.

"Or take Health Services. That's one of the four administrations I've set up by executive order, along with Human Resources, Transportation, and Housing and Development. But I need changes in the City Charter before they can be fully functional administrations and before I can go ahead and create the other six. Even under an executive order, I'm limited in what I can do. The Hospitals Department, for example, *still* administers the sick-baby clinics while the well-baby clinics continue to be under the Department of Health.

"But during this transitional period, I've been conducting a series of meetings—six two-hour sessions—about health. Just as I did earlier about all aspects of police work. At the meetings I've had Harold Brown, the Health Services Administrator; Edward O'Rourke, Commissioner of Health; Joseph Terenzio, Commissioner of Hospitals; Marvin Perkins, Commissioner of Mental Health Services; and Milton Helpern, the Chief Medical Examiner. I also have the staff aide from my office who is the liaison between me and the Health Services Administration. When the whole plan goes through, there'll be nine other people on my staff connecting the Mayor's office with each administration.

"Anyway, we've had these meetings, and as they go on,

you cannot avoid seeing how all these departments inter-mesh. Once you start talking about your strategies and goals for health services, you have to consider the relationships between hospitals and clinics, between medical schools and the voluntary hospitals they're affiliated with, between well-baby and sick-baby clinics, and so on down the line. In addition, the whole area of preventive medicine is related to all these other functions. I swear to God, it's been idiotic to have lived so long with things the way they used to be—all the separate sections, with separate budgets, with over-lapping functions, with nobody in charge of the whole picture. The sections never met with each other, and in fact, they were all in jealous competition with each other. You simply cannot do any real, substantive planning—budgetary, physical, sociological—under that kind of setup.

"A fundamental goal of health care in cities now, for example, is delivering that care to poor families who don't have family physicians. That means bringing small, im-mediately accessible health-service centers into the neighbor-hoods, thereby relieving the burden on the out-patient clinics in the big hospitals, where the jamups take place now. The large hospital complexes, with full laboratory facilities and beds for people who need extended hospitalization, will be the hub of the health-service wheel, and the neighborhood centers all over the city will be the spokes. But you cannot get this done, you cannot get budget flexibility, you cannot plan in terms of priorities, you cannot assess the efficiency of each program in terms of the money spent on it, unless you have the kind of total reorganization we've planned."

The mayor had been leaning forward, making his points vehemently. Now he sank back on the couch, and I turned to the role he had played at the United States Con-ference of Mayors in Hawaii. According to the New York *Post,* Lindsay had been one of the leaders there in creating what he had described on his return as "an atmosphere of urban alliance to insist that the federal government put the problems of the cities in a position of No. 1 priority."

"Do you have any realistic expectations," I asked, "that the pressure from such an alliance will actually get the cities the amounts of federal money they need?"

The Mayor smiled rather wanly. "The most we can do is keep the pressure on and thereby get the little bit extra that comes from continued pressure. But realistically, so long as so big a part of the federal budget is gobbled up by the Defense Department, not much is going to change. The cities won't get what they need until there is first a change in what we do outside this country."

A press aide materialized on the porch. Five members of the Israeli parliament, in New York as advisers to Israel's delegation to the United Nations during the debate on the aftermath of the Six Day War, were waiting for the Mayor. "Is this a ceremonial or a substantive occasion?" I asked. The Mayor grinned. "Oh, there'll be a little substance to it. We'll talk about how nice it is to be alive and win wars. I did have a ceremonial occasion a couple of hours ago at City Hall. Some members of the Greek community gave me the Commander's Cross of the Greek Order of Saint Denis. They even did the bit with the sword. One of them kept whispering to me to kneel while that was going on, but I wouldn't do it. They tapped me on the shoulders anyway, so now I'm a knight. I'm Sir John, and don't you forget it. But," he sighed, "they didn't give me a white horse."

I had one more question. Despite the Mayor's disclaimers that he had any political ambitions beyond being Mayor, *The New York Times,* in an editorial at the end of May, had observed:

> Mayor Lindsay clearly has a future in national politics. The Republican party is not so richly endowed with intelligent, personable, effective candidates who run well in the big cities that it can afford to ignore him. His own interest

in foreign affairs will impel him sooner or later to return to Washington. In short, unless Mr. Lindsay decides that he would find greater personal satisfaction outside of public life, he has to be regarded as a potential candidate for the Senate or for national office.

Nevertheless, he was wise to quell speculation the other day about his political plans. In politics, timing is often the decisive factor. The year 1968 is not going to be Mr. Lindsay's except in the off-chance that Governor Romney, if nominated, selects him as his running mate.

Furthermore, Mr. Lindsay has a job to do. He has yet to prove himself fully as Mayor. He has made a strong start and shown impressive qualities of executive leadership, but it would be premature for him to move on . . .

I showed him the editorial. He read it, and laughed. "I remember it. I liked that editorial. It was a very shrewd one. But they don't know and I don't know at this moment whether I'm even going to run again for mayor. It's hard to make people believe that after this kind of job, you might want to get the hell out of public service and do something useful in the outside world. The options, it seems to me, are superb. There's your terrible racket—writing. I'd like to try that. I don't think I could succeed in it as a full-time occupation, but I'd like to see if I could; and if I did try, I'd like to do it abroad for a while. Also there's always the law to go back to. I'd have to learn the tricks of the trade again, but I used to enjoy trying cases. And there's foundation work, and teaching, although university life has its drawbacks—and the more I see of it, the more of those drawbacks I see. Especially in administration. I can think of nothing more aggravating than being Mayor of New York except perhaps being a college president. Another option I find intriguing is television work—news, running discussion programs, that sort of thing. Really, the variety of options is enormous."

"It's hard to believe though," I said, "that you won't run for a second term as Mayor, since you won't be able to make all the changes you want in the first four years."

The Mayor nodded in agreement. "Yes, four years isn't long enough. You can just about get things started in four years. You can just about get them going down the track. But that's not so small an accomplishment—not in this city." He smiled. "Assuming, of course, that they're going in the right direction down that track."

XI   I next saw the Mayor, unexpectedly, on the lower East Side, on a hot afternoon at the end of July. Two days before, the ghetto explosions which had been visited on so many other cities in the summer of 1967 had reached East Harlem. In comparison with Detroit and Newark, New York's explosion had been mild. But tension remained, and on Second Avenue and Third Street, a Puerto Rican friend of mine was saying, "If it starts down here, I'm ready. It gets dark, I stay at home with my gun. I don't care who comes in, they get it." We were standing on the sidewalk in front of his barbershop, and his eyes left mine when a black car stopped at the curb a few yards up and four men including the Mayor, in his shirt sleeves, got up. My friend gaped at the Mayor for a few seconds, smiled, and went back to his shop.

The Mayor, seeing me, waved, and I walked over. I asked him about East Harlem. His face hardened in anger. "We weren't getting to the kids. The agencies, the organizations weren't reaching them. Nobody's been talking to them. So we're finding ways to do that ourselves. The hell with the organizations. We're getting street people involved in setting up programs for the kids, and the kids are having a say in how they're run."

While we were talking, a small crowd had gathered, its

members wanting to tell the Mayor about malevolent land-lords or simply to confirm their actual nearness to the man they had seen on television by shaking his hand. A very old Puerto Rican woman tugged at the Mayor's sleeve. He bent down, accepted her good wishes, and was still smiling as he turned away until he caught sight of an ugly mound of debris in front of an empty store a few doors away. Two small children were playing in the filth, and Lindsay's face hardened again. He told an aide to have the Sanitation Department clean it up.

"You looked so angry just then," I said, "but you see that sort of thing all the time."

He shook his head, "Each time it's a fresh experience," he said, and walked off to an appointment.

The tension in the city continued, and a few weeks later, I accompanied the Mayor on one of his neighborhood tours. It was to begin at a public swimming pool in the Red Hook district of South Brooklyn. The Mayor was due by helicopter at 6 p.m., but he was late. A small, restless group of Puerto Rican boys, some in wet bathing suits, waited in a park near the swimming pool for the Mayor's descent. Also present were four policemen, several newspaper reporters, a still cameraman from the *Daily News* and a CBS man with a hand-held television camera. I asked one of the Mayor's aides how closely he followed his schedule on these tours. "You never know," the young man answered. "He often deviates. Whenever he sees any hint of action, or if he hears a fire engine, that's where he'll go."

Four Negroes in their late teens appeared, wearing neat blue jackets that identified them as members of the South Brooklyn Youth Council. In another park directly across the street, some twenty-five younger Negroes were assiduously involved in what appeared to be a military drill —without guns. Directing them was a bulky black man of about forty. I asked the Youth Council arrivals what was happening across the street. No one knew. I turned to a young white policeman. "Oh them, they're there every night. No one seems to know who they are or why they're there, but they don't bother nobody. I'd rather have them there than in the street."

One of the Youth Council staff members, tall and slight, began talking about his job. "We work with the kids, you know. Recreation, keeping them quiet, stopping fights. It's city money, you know. But it don't make it. I mean, we just got started in July and we're through in September. You know, this should be year-round. It's too hard trying to cool things just for a couple of months. It ain't easy, man. We got no protection. We can't carry nothing but our mouth."

At six thirty, some of the boys in the park shouted, and we all looked up at a blue-and-white police helicopter heading toward us. It appeared to be overshooting the park, but it swiftly banked and came to earth not far from where we were gathered. The Mayor, in gray pants and a short-sleeved white shirt, with no tie, jumped out. He saw the cameramen and grimaced. In what seemed an instant, a small reception party expanded into a swarm of children, teenagers, mothers, and poverty workers, with the Mayor at the center of a bulging parade to the swimming pool. But the parade scattered to a stop as the Mayor suddenly turned, found an opening in the crowd, and sprinted back to where the helicopter had landed. He had forgotten to shake the hands of the policemen who had been waiting. Just as he was about to be engulfed by the crowd again, the Mayor said to Harry O'Donnell, who had replaced Woody Klein as his press secretary, "Ask CBS to cool it—this is getting to be too much of a show."

"The point of these trips," O'Donnell said to me as the Mayor moved away, "is for him to find out what's happening in the neighborhoods. If there's too much press, they get in the way of his finding out."

As the parade resumed, the Mayor, almost automatically

shaking hands and signing autographs, listened attentively to an account of the neighborhood and its problems he was being given by a tall Negro, who was later identified for me as a senior staff member of the South Brooklyn Youth Council. At the pool, Buster Crabbe had just presented the first of what was to be a series of demonstrations in ghetto neighborhoods throughout the city. Sidney Davidoff, who had become an Assistant to the Mayor since I'd seen him last, was explaining Crabbe's function to several women of the community. "He says he can teach any kid to swim in a few minutes—at least give him a few strokes. You see, Crabbe believes you can get a lot of inhibitions and frustrations out through athletics."

An obviously frustrated blond young man in his mid-twenties had been trying to elbow his way through to talk to the Mayor. Acknowledging his defeat, he directed his complaint to Davidoff. "I'm Peter Hughes, of the South Brooklyn Community Progress Center. Look, it's very clear to us that because there have been no disturbances here yet, Red Hook has been put at the bottom of the list for this summer. But you have to realize this is a worse ghetto than Harlem in some respects. We have practically none of the recreation or entertainment facilities Harlem has. And the people here—ask anybody—have to walk half a mile to get to the subway. There's only one good bus route, and that just skirts the area. We've got only four working traffic lights, and there's a terrible sanitation problem with some of the houses—toilets backing up. The streets aren't cleaned nearly as often as they ought to be, and we even have electricity lines running overground."

Davidoff promised to see what could be done, and I asked Hughes whether the neighborhood had been organizing itself to protest. "That's just the problem," he said. "It's hard to get any kind of organization going. These people don't know how to organize around a problem. They don't know how to bitch, and that's why they're at the bottom of the list."

I worked my way back into the crowd and caught up with the Mayor as he was leaving the pool. Looking up from a conversation with a teen-ager, he saw the *Daily News* camera pointed straight at him. "Damn these cameras," he muttered.

With his arm around the shoulders of his adviser from the Youth Council, the Mayor walked on to a nearby housing project, listening to a list of the neighborhood's needs, including more sprinklers for hydrants and more measures to combat drug addiction in the neighborhood. Meanwhile, another worker from the Youth Council was telling me, "Since they built the Brooklyn-Queens Expressway, this neighborhood is cut off from the rest of Brooklyn. No movies, no market to speak of. I tell you, the community feels nobody thinks about it anymore, that it wouldn't matter what happened to us here. Him coming in here, that's a good thing. It gives them a little hope."

"How long can the hope last?" I asked.

He shrugged. "Well, now, that's another thing."

The housing project, built in 1939, looked worn but not at all squalid from the outside. Seeing a thoroughly demolished automobile in front of one of the buildings, Lindsay told an aide to have it removed. As he accelerated his walking pace, on the far side of the crowd four scowling Negro teen-agers stood, shouting, "Hey, Mayor, this may not look like it, but this is a slum too. We need new windows and new—" Whatever else was needed faded out of hearing as the Mayor and the crowd surged ahead.

From the Negro and Puerto Rican section of Red Hook, we moved on by car to Park Slope, a largely Italian enclave, consisting in the main of well-kept stores and two- and three-family houses. The Mayor got out, and in the first three blocks of his walk, the Mayor was noticed only by one man who stopped, stared, did a double take, and managed a stunned "Hello" before the Mayor's party had passed. Lindsay was being briefed on the tensions between the young in Park Slope and Negro adolescents in adjacent areas. "There are Negro kids who come to school here," the adviser from the Youth Council was saying, "and they go into this neighborhood in a group. They have to. To protect themselves."

"What are the churches doing?" the Mayor asked.

"They try different things to bring the different elements together, but somehow they don't do too good a job."

By now, we were at the center of another parade. Park Slope had awakened to the presence of the city's chief executive. Men yelled greetings from cars, elderly Italians stepped gingerly toward the Mayor from doorways and had their hands shaken, and children skipped alongside the swelling procession like the second line in a vintage New Orleans funeral parade. Seeing a park, Carroll Park, the Mayor strode in, and was guided by a group of men to the area in which they play boccie. "The dirt is no good, it's too dusty," he was told. "And we need lights, for at night." The Mayor nodded to an aide who made a note about better dirt and lights.

I asked the black adviser from the South Brooklyn Youth Council, "Is this park kind of exclusive?"

He looked at me and smiled coldly. "*I* wouldn't come in here all by myself."

"How about some more parks, Mr. Mayor?" one of the boccie players called after Lindsay as he moved out to the street. A short, swarthy teen-ager, with dark glasses and long hair, carrying a half-full quart of beer, stepped in front of him. Lindsay grinned down. "A Brooklyn hippie!"

"Yeah. The difference between us and them Greenwich Village hippies is they smoke pot and we drink beer. Have some of my beer, Mr. Mayor."

Lindsay took the bottle, saw the *Daily News* photographer, looked hard at him, and said, "No shot—okay?" The photographer nodded, and the Mayor of New York took a swig from the Brooklyn hippie's bottle.

As we continued walking, I asked the Mayor, "Don't these neighborhoods eventually blur in your mind?"

He thought about the question, and said, "I've got them pretty well sorted out. Once in a while, Davidoff will mention a particular intersection and I have to do some digging, but I come out with it. I know the city now—just about all of it."

As the Mayor stopped to shake hands and talk with a group of middle-aged men in front of a bar, I told Davidoff about the Mayor's comment a few weeks before that East Harlem had erupted at least partly because no meaningful contact had been made with many of the young people in the streets. "That's right," Davidoff said briskly. "The official anti-poverty groups—and not only in East Harlem—had not been making contact with the most rootless of the young, because these kids are not part of the community structure. That's why we've been focusing this summer on sixteen satellite centers around the city. They're satellites of Youth Board offices but they work pretty much on their own. The money comes from O.E.O. and some private corporations, but the policy is made by the indigenous young people themselves under the guidance of supervisors who also live there, or used to. The supervisors don't necessarily have social-work degrees. In fact, most don't. The kids in these centers decide what sports equipment they need, what programs they want, what trips they want to take. And as for jobs, the centers refer some to the Neighborhood Youth Corps and try to get others work elsewhere in the community. The mistake we made in East Harlem was that we'd figured any trouble would come in border areas. Therefore, the satellite center there was at 119th Street, where Puerto Ricans and Negroes come together. But the disturbance was entirely within the Puerto Rican area, so two days after it happened, we had an emergency satellite center on 112th Street. Through that, we're reaching a much broader base among the kids."

"How long do the centers operate?" I asked.

"Well, we didn't get any of them going until July 10. Bureaucratic procedures—the courier between Washington and New York seemed to have got lost. I don't know where we'll get the money after the summer, but somehow we'll keep at least some of these centers open through the winter. We've got to."

I caught up with the Mayor again. Walking faster, with youngsters rushing up to pat him on the back, he was stopped by an old woman who grabbed his hand. A younger woman with her said, "You really turn the kids on, Mr. Lindsay."

"They're the brightest of the crowd," the Mayor said. "They really know what's going on."

A man from *The New York Times* broke in. "Mr. Mayor, do you really think these walks will continue to keep the city cool?"

Lindsay sighed. "I don't know. I really don't know. I'd have to be a bigger fool than I usually am to make predictions about that. Obviously, the thing to do is to rebuild the city the way it ought to be rebuilt."

"Hey!" A storekeeper rushed out into the street. "Hey, it's the Mayor! How about that?"

Lindsay grinned, waved, and kept walking.

XII For the rest of the summer of 1967, there was peace in the streets, but a fierce labor-relations conflict between the United Federation of Teachers and the Board of Education prevented the city's schools from opening according to schedule, a week after Labor Day. Midway through the second week of that battle, a nonstop, twenty-six-hour bargaining session at Gracie Mansion appeared—mistakenly, as it turned out—to have settled the dispute. On the following Saturday, which was the first day of fall, I went to see the Mayor at the Mansion.

Except for the policeman who took me to a downstairs conference room in the Annex, the Mansion seemed deserted. A few minutes after I arrived, the Mayor, in a short-sleeved blue sports shirt and gray slacks, came into the room. At the door, he turned around for a moment to say good-bye to an assistant. "Stay loose," he said. The Mayor then led the way to his office on the same floor. I mentioned how quiet it was, and the Mayor grinned. "Yes, it's great. I got the teachers out and the Board out, and I sent the family away, and now I can get some work done." He sat down behind his desk, stretched his legs, and ran a hand through his hair. "Although," he continued, "the place may get crowded again. Snags have developed in getting the oral agreement into a written contract."

I asked him if, during the long, tense negotiations earlier in the week, he had looked back at all to his stormy initiation into municipal labor wars—the transit strike with which his administration had begun. I reminded him that at the time he had been accused of being unnecessarily rigid, and also of being ignorant of such elementary knowledge of labor relations as the difference between mediation and arbitration.

The Mayor shook his head in exasperation. "I don't know where that one started. Of course, I knew the difference. I took a course in labor law in law school, and as a lawyer, I'd been involved in some labor cases. Anyway, the transit negotiations and what's been going on here this week are not comparable. I mean in terms of the issues, the union's internal politics, and the kinds of mediators and their roles. Besides, the transit dispute was very unfamiliar and difficult

terrain for me. I didn't know anyone involved that well. I
do now. All of the transit people, on both sides. And I've
been meeting with them since early August. That's why I
feel more comfortable about the renegotiation of the transit
contract later this year.

"In the school situation, the issues and the people were
already quite familiar to me. And in the past year and a
half, I'd learned more about my own capacities in this sort
of conflict. The other day I was telling a city official who's
going to have to deal with a municipal union soon, 'I'm a bad
guy to deal with unions when I get angry because then I
become pompous and get their backs up. And I've got news
for you—you're worse than I am.' That shook him up.
'Nobody ever said that to me before,' he told me. 'Well,'
I said, 'it's the kind of thing your best friends won't tell
you.' Actually sometimes I get pompous deliberately."

I asked him what he meant by "pompous."

He laughed. "You know, when I lecture them about the
public interest and insist that the needs of eight million New
Yorkers should transcend narrow self-interest. They don't
like it at all, but sometimes it has to be done. However, if
you're doing it deliberately, your timing has to be right. It
can be especially useful during a first lock-in session—
when you've gotten them all together with the understanding
that no one can leave. Then I can crack heads on both sides,
and when I leave the room, they're all mad at me and it's
easier for the mediators to be the nice guys who'll smooth
things over. But you can't do that sort of thing after exhaus-
tion sets in."

I had heard, I told the Mayor, that when Albert Shanker,
president of the teachers' union, interrupted one such speech
by shouting, "How much longer do I have to sit and listen
to this lecture?" Lindsay answered sharply, "This is the
Mayor's house and I'll thank you to keep a civil tongue in
your head."

The Mayor smiled. "That's right, that's what happened.

But you have to be firm with both sides. Later that night, Giardino, the president of the Board of Education, was on his way out to make a television appearance. I pulled him in here, called Channel 13 myself, and told the producer Giardino wouldn't be there."

The phone rang, and Lindsay questioned the caller, Superintendent of Schools Bernard Donovan, about the possibilities of getting talks going over the weekend to clear up the new complications. When he hung up, I asked him, now that he was almost midway through his first term, how disturbed he was at the number of top-level aides who had already left his administration—Deputy Mayor Robert Price, Parks Commissioner Thomas Hoving, Buildings Commissioner Charles Moerdler, Human Resources Administrator Mitchell Sviridoff, and, more recently, Walter Washington, the chairman of the City Housing Authority, who had returned to Washington to head that city's new municipal government.

"No," Lindsay said, "I'm not disturbed. That kind of turnover is normal, particularly as this city becomes a place where talent in handling urban affairs is developed. The more we get recognized as a city which is learning how to deal with its problems, the more often we'll get raided. Take Walter Washington. One reason he came here was that he'd been turned down by the White House for that job in Washington. But since he started moving around here, he became a candidate again. I'm not saying that's the only reason the White House changed its mind, but his visibility in New York may well have been a factor. Sure, some people go. But suddenly, other people you want and never thought you could get, become available. I'm not worried about keeping a good team together for the next two years."

I asked the Mayor about a departed member of the team, Robert Price. "Many Lindsay-watchers," I said, "consider his leaving particularly significant because up to then, there had been a widely held assumption that Price's capacity for

making quick, clear decisions was essential to your administration. With him gone, it's become clear you're able to
make your own decisions."

"I've heard that said, of course, about my having been
very dependent on Bob. But nobody seems to know that
there was increasing disagreement between us—on how you
pick people for the administration, on policy, on how you
run a government. Bob tends to be a fixer. I don't mean
that pejoratively. I mean he looks for ways to manipulate
problems so that they'll be smoothed over for a time. That's
good in the short run, but it's not the way to build a whole
new structure of government. You see, there *is* a difference
between government and politics. Sure, they're intertwined,
but government can't be *all* politics. It can't entirely be a
matter of keeping yourself in the clear. Occasionally you
have to take stands on pure, lofty principles even though
you know the stands are just wrong politically. The Civilian
Review Board was an example of that. So was the city income tax. There were ways in which we could have patched
up the city's fiscal problems for a year or so without the
income tax, but they wouldn't have rung true. Not for the
long run.

"I haven't taken any popularity polls, but according to
what my own antennae tell me as I move about, I think
we've come a considerable way. I still get heckled and
screamed at in middle-class white areas because of my plans
to scatter public housing in those neighborhoods, and for
other reasons, but it isn't as intense and violent as it was.
Reaction in the ghettos is good, but there's also a great deal
of skepticism there. And with damn good reason. They
want us to *show* them something's happening. Last Thursday, I sent everybody on the City Planning Commission and
all the building guys to Brownsville, which is one of the sites
we've selected for a Model Cities program. I made them stomp
around, building by building, block by block, so that they'll
really be prepared for next Tuesday's cabinet meeting which

will be entirely about Brownsville. Which buildings should be coming down *now?* How fast can we move on our own Model Cities financial commitment—even before we get any federal money—to put up some low-income housing there fast? The trouble is speed won't help if it's just imposed. We've got to have the participation of the people in the area, and that takes time. But, with the amount of pressure I'm putting on my departments, we are going to show visible change in the next two years in Brooklyn and the Bronx and Harlem."

The Mayor stopped, frowned, and went on. "I say this cautiously, though. There shouldn't be any more talk. It's time to *do* things. People need to *see* change."

I had noticed in recent days, I told the Mayor, an acceleration in his administration's use of systems-analysis techniques in making policy decisions. A long-term contract with the Rand Corporation to strengthen the city's planning and budgeting processes had been announced, and that morning's *Times* had reported the setting up of a city "war room" for which wall charts, known as issue maps, would be prepared with the assistance of computers and would list the objectives, the available resources and alternative ways of using those resources in respect to at least a hundred key problems about which the Mayor requires as accurate and complete information as he can get before he makes a decision.

According to the *Times,* an official of the company that constructed the first issue map—one on air pollution—had said that until now the Mayor's basic sources of information had been *"The New York Times,* New York *Post, Daily News,* pressure groups, and unsystematized reports from commissioners."

I asked the Mayor's reaction to that assessment. He banged his hand on the desk. "I'm outraged over the damned thing, and I've gotten the word to him that if he makes any other damn fool statements like that, the whole thing's off.

Sure, it's a pretty good program, and Rand will be of help, but these are tools, like any other tools. I don't care how good the war room is, and how many issue maps we get up. I'll still be the one who has to make the decisions. The whole thing reminds me of when I started my first year at Yale Law School, in the summer of 1946. It was right after the war, and everything was being doubled up. The faculty machine, however, had not been geared to that kind of pace, and so the first team of professors was in Europe or around the country on exchanges. For us, they put in a second team. I was disappointed, and in one course—a required course on research—I was appalled. It was the goddamnedest experience I'd ever been through. The teacher spent the summer on the most elaborate system you ever saw—a big sort of model of a book, with wires and pulleys and arrows and cards in eight different colors. We had to take each problem apart and assign a different color to every part of it. All research had to be done on specified color lines. Toward the end of the course, I was almost ready to quit in boredom and despair. And then, the last week of summer, the man who normally taught the course came back. In his first hour with us, he put on a great show. He picked up all this stuff and went through the whole routine. It wasn't until he was well into it that a few of us caught on to the fact that it was a performance like Robert Benchley's treasurer's report. Gradually, he had gotten the whole thing so screwed up that he was all tangled up in cords of different colors, some of them sticking out of his pockets, others under his feet, and still more clutched in his fists. When the bell rang, he took the whole thing—the book, the wires, the cards—and dumped it on the floor. From an inside coat pocket he took out a batch of crumpled papers and said to us, 'I use the backs of envelopes myself.' That restored my faith."

Laughing, the Mayor rose. He had to change into his tennis clothes, he said, because he had an appointment at twelve o'clock with Fred Botur, whom he calls Tennis Consultant to the Mayor, at Botur's West Park Racquet Club on Columbus Avenue at Ninety-seventh Street. As we walked out of the office, he reverted to the subject of system analysis. "Of course, in a big show like this, you need all the data you can get," the Mayor said. "In the Police Department, for example, after a few months of systems-analysis, tied in with budget processes, we got twenty-five hundred more cops on the streets. But no matter how much data I get, I'm always the one who has to follow through, and there are some decisions I simply have to make by using my antennae."

"What about the statement that the war-room planner made about the inadequacy of your present sources of information? How are you going to answer press questions on that?"

The Mayor looked at me, thought for a while, and said, "I'll say I pulled this fellow out of a computer and I may have to stuff him back in."

After the Mayor had changed into tennis whites, he headed for his car carrying a business suit on a hanger. I rode along with him to the courts. During most of the ride, he was talking on the telephone to Jason Nathan, the Housing and Development Administrator, about plans that several insurance companies were making to invest in the rehabilitation of ghetto neighborhoods in the city. As we got out of the car, I asked the Mayor's appraisal of Charles Percy, the junior Senator from Illinois, who had developed an ambitious national low-income housing plan and who appeared at the time to be a long-shot possibility for a place on the 1968 Republican ticket.

"Oh, he certainly has substance," said Lindsay. "Of course, he's a bit of a Boy Scout, but aren't we all?"

Still grinning, the Mayor began to warm up with Botur. I stayed a while and watched as Botur, with easy precision, placed shots to develop the Mayor's ground strokes. The Mayor plays intensely, hitting and running hard. "Just relax—easy, easy," Botur said as the Mayor slammed the ball into the net. "Under the ball, under the ball, get your racket back." As the Mayor started to serve, a girl came on court. There was a telephone call from the Superintendent of Schools. Botur waited for the Mayor to return. When he did, the Mayor ran Botur back to the baseline with a furious forehand drive.

The Mayor:
Continuing

I   The citizens of New York City are rightly credited with
    unusual resiliency—as is their Mayor—but on certain
days the city seems finally to be escaping from us all in a
slide toward irredeemable disintegration. It is a measure of
the turbulence of John V. Lindsay's first term that a sizable
number of such days can be cited. I expect that the citizens
would differ widely among themselves if asked to select the
one day on which each felt most deeply pessimistic concerning the future of the city. My own choice, in retrospect, is
a cold Friday in February 1968, the third year of the Lindsay
administration.

The Uniformed Sanitation Men's Association had been
on strike for seven days, and 70,000 tons of garbage—in
mounds, in dunes, in rotting drifts—were on the streets. At
a six o'clock City Hall meeting the morning before, the
Board of Health declared the first city-wide health emergency since 1945. Fires originating in refuse were up seven
hundred per cent from the normal rate; the rat population
was presumed to be on the rise; and there was danger that
garbage backing up in the sewers could lead to the spread of
typhoid fever, dysentery, and hepatitis.

The strike had begun a week before at a rally of sanitation workers in front of City Hall. The union's previous
one-year contract having expired seven months before, the
head of the union, John DeLury, had finally agreed to a
retroactive proposal recommended by two special mediators
whom the Mayor had appointed. But as has often happened
since in the city's labor relations with its municipal employees, the rank and file vehemently disagreed with its
leadership. At the rally, after ducking an egg thrown by a

dues payer, Mr. DeLury retained his leadership by following his members, urging them on to a strike they had already decided to undertake. DeLury was jailed five days later for violating a court order which had enjoined the strike under the no-strike provisions of the Taylor Law, passed by the state legislature in 1967 at the strong behest of Governor Nelson Rockefeller who then proclaimed the measure to be a national model for harmonious civil-service labor relations.

The Mayor refused to continue negotiations while the union was on strike. To do so, he said, would be yielding to "blackmail." And in the kind of language that has given him the reputation of being at best ingenuous in his relationships with organized labor—and at worst haughtily insensitive to the rules of the game—the Mayor also declared: "Now is the time, and here is the place, for the city to determine what it is made of; whether it will bow to unlawful force or whether it will resist with all the strength and courage that eight million people can find within themselves." As part of the resistance, he asked the Governor to call out the National Guard to clean the streets. "I told him," Lindsay later said to me, "that it would have helped the city and possibly the country if the people in the slums could have seen the men of the National Guard—*their* National Guard, by the way —working constructively with their hands instead of patrolling the streets with rifles at the ready."

His vision of a calming, cleansing army in fatigues was not nearly so persuasive to the Governor as the word from the chieftains of New York City's Central Labor Council— which represents 1,200,000 union men—that bringing in the National Guard would be considered strike-breaking and would lead in turn to a general strike in the city. Rejecting the Mayor's plan, the Governor bypassed him entirely, appointing his own five-man panel to work out a settlement, and releasing DeLury from jail to join the conferences it called. "My God," one of the authors of the Taylor Law said at the time, "this is just the thing we all had the horrors about. This is the Governor's law; he wanted it; now it's going to be emasculated."

With all this in mind, I felt for the first time the next morning, Friday, that John Lindsay had probably made a mistake, that he should not have run for mayor, that the highest office in the City of New York was no place for a man I had come to consider, not pejoratively, the last Puritan in politics. An editorial writer in that day's *New York Times* had observed in furious gloom that the Governor had cut "the ground out from under the Mayor." Yielding to an impulse, I called Bob Laird, an assistant press secretary to the Mayor. "For what it's worth," I said to Laird, "tell the Mayor I think he's right." I wasn't that sure he was right in asking for the National Guard, but I respected his principled stubborness, hoping at the same time that my building was not vulnerable to rats.

"How'd you like to inspect some garbage?" Laird asked. He gave me the itinerary of the Mayor's tour of the city's squalor, and I decided to join the expedition at a point on the Lower East Side.

On Ninth Street near First Avenue, I was walking behind two Puerto Ricans in their late teens. On our left was a boarded-up building. "You know how long this building has been shut?" one said to his friend. "Since I was ten years old." They turned north on First, and I went on east to Avenue D, passing smoldering trash cans and trying to avoid the crusts of bread and other less identifiable objects being blown against my feet by a sharp, hard wind.

Third Street and Avenue D was a field of garbage into which the Mayor, gaunt, grim, hatless, hands jammed into his overcoat pockets, stepped from his black official car. I had never before—nor have I since—seen him look so burnt out. He had had no more than three hours sleep in the past two days, his press secretary, Harry O'Donnell, told me. But the

Mayor was more than tired. "He finally got into bed at five this morning," O'Donnell continued, "but he couldn't sleep. He just couldn't stop thinking about this thing."

"How do you figure Rockefeller?" one of the Mayor's young aides asked me. "Does he really think he's going to get the Republican nomination *this* way? George Meany and Harry Van Arsdale can't help him there."

I went up to the Mayor who acknowledged my mumbled expression of nonspecific support by patting me on the arm. "Were you surprised at Rockefeller rejecting your plan?" I asked.

"No, not really," the Mayor said. "I tried to help him out of a problem; he says I put a problem on him." The Mayor shrugged. "I'm afraid I'm screwing up someone's political plans."

Television cameramen, still photographers, and reporters were tramping in the garbage. "What's next?" a reporter asked. "Can you get federal help?"

The Mayor looked at him. "I can ask for paratroopers. How's that?" He stared at a fire in a trash basket as two girls squealed in recognition of his presence.

"Do you *have* a strategy?" I asked the Mayor.

"Up to a point, but in a situation like this, you have to make a lot of it up as you go along. You don't know what the other guy is going to do to you until it happens."

The "other guy" was plainly Rockefeller, not DeLury. We went off to Bedford-Stuyvesant and then to Long Island City. As the Mayor walked the streets during the latter stop, I fell in behind him with Barnard Collier of *The New York Times.* Collier had been based in Latin America for several years until being reassigned to New York a few months before. "You know," he said, "if you look at this as a foreign city, you can live here. But if it's yours *forever*—" He grimaced.

The Mayor had stopped in front of a fallen garbage can from which an astonishing quantity of refuse had spilled into the street. "Oh this is beautiful," he said to himself and put the can on its bottom again. He was called to his car to take a call from the Health Commissioner. Across the street was a burned shell of a car heaped with garbage.

"We've got to get a photographer up here," a reporter made a note on his pad, "so everybody will see *more*. Just like they see more death in Vietnam. But nothing changes."

The walk resumed up a hill, and there was no way to step around the garbage. It was a question of trying to pick the least repellent path. The Mayor, who had seemed to be in a sort of trance for a few minutes, suddenly said to me, "It's the seventeenth century that most interests me in English literature. The people of that time walked through this, and worse than this all the time, and they produced a great literature. They were better people too than we are."

He moved ahead. A photographer was speculating, "What if he calls on LBJ for help? That would be a whole new ball game, right? He'd be breaking all the rules—party loyalty, the whole bit."

Half an hour later we were in a shopping section in the Bronx. A husky man in his fifties, his face red and puffed out in anger, yelled at the Mayor: "You big stiff! What are you walking around for? You don't know what the hell you're walking around for!" The Mayor gave no sign of having heard the commentary.

Around a corner, a large group of youngsters were lined up in front of a theater, the titles on its marquee in Spanish. "Hey," one of the children shouted, "is that Bobby Kennedy?" For they first time that morning, the Mayor smiled.

"Look at him," a woman poked a boy on the shoulder. "That's the Mayor. You may never see him again."

"And if he doesn't," the man with her said, "so what?"

A Fire Department car sped around the corner, stopped, and first Deputy Fire Commissioner James Ward got out. The burly Sid Davidoff, an assistant to the Mayor, pushed the crowd of reporters and neighborhood people back so that the Mayor and Ward could confer. "It's not only that this guy makes himself so visible—Collier of the *Times* nodded in Lindsay's direction—"but he's so vulnerable. Anybody can shoot him from a rooftop."

By early afternoon we were in central Harlem. The Mayor, in front, alone, walked quickly through a few blocks. "What's the point to all this?" a photographer said. "He's like a zombie, and he's going so fast he can't get any feedback from the people."

"The big mistake he made," a woman reporter broke in, "was not taking a shovel in his hand the day after the strike began. The people would have followed him." We all looked at her, I with a certain amount of awe.

Several men at the corner of 127th Street and Seventh Avenue were chanting, "Get the garbage out of here! Straighten out the mess! Get the garbage out of here!" The Mayor walked past without acknowledgment.

Half a block later, he suddenly turned and snapped at us. "The trouble with you reporters is that you're white. One night here last summer, I had to tell the press to fade because they were all white that time too."

"Does that intimidate you?" Collier asked.

The Mayor frowned. "No, it doesn't intimidate me. What does that mean? But it keeps reminding me of all that's wrong in this country and of what should be in that report by the Commission on Civil Disorders. That's going to be a damned strong report."

(When the *Report of the National Advisory Commission on Civil Disorders,* John V. Lindsay, Vice Chairman, was released in the spring, I turned first to the section on the press: "The journalistic profession has been shockingly backward in seeking out, hiring, training, and promoting Negroes. Fewer than 5 per cent of the people employed by the news business in editorial jobs in the United States today are Negroes. Fewer than 1 per cent of editors and supervisors are Negroes, and most of them work for Negro-owned organizations. The lines of various news organizations to the militant blacks are, by the admission of the newsmen themselves, almost nonexistent.")

"How about that?" a reporter said as the angry Mayor strode ahead. "Maybe he ought to focus on getting some black governors."

Two Negroes in their thirties came up and asked for the Mayor's autograph. "You realize," he told them as he signed, "that you're the only two people in New York who want this."

"Stick with it!" an old black man shouted at him. A boy, about thirteen, stood in front of us, shaking his head. "Are those cats the National Guard?" he asked, pointing to the Mayor's party.

The Mayor roared. As a group of people moved toward him to shake his hand, saying "Welcome, welcome," the Mayor, noticeably thawed, straightened his shoulders.

"Okay," he said, "I'm recovered now. Let's go!" He spoke to an aide about getting more information on the fires breaking out around the city. "That's what I'm most concerned about right now," he said to me. "Whole blocks of buildings could go up."

The tour was at an end. As the press surrounded him, the Mayor gave his conclusions: "It's as bad as I thought it was. And the people have a remarkable amount of fortitude."

"I still say"—the photographer watched the Mayor get into his car—"how does he know? He didn't respond to anybody unless they came up to him, and then it was only a smile or a wave. There was no real attempt to hear what anybody had to say."

"He knew what they had to say," the woman reporter answered. " 'Clean up the mess.' "

That night the Mayor was still out, checking on fires, winding up at the Fire Department's Communications Center at Central Park West and 79th Street. On Saturday, the Governor came to an agreement with the sanitation workers. They would go back to work and he would ask the legislature in a special message to authorize the state to take over the Sanitation Department. A few hours before he made the announcement, Rockefeller called Lindsay and asked to meet with him. The Mayor, not wanting to appear at all involved in the Governor's next move, refused. "I am the Governor," Rockefeller said icily, "and I am inviting you to come." "I am the Mayor," Lindsay responded, as if in a morality play, and he hung up. After the Governor had made his public announcement, the Mayor publicly reacted: "I had hoped that the Governor would join me in combating the extortionist demands of the sanitation union. I deeply regret that he has chosen not to."

During the next few days, state legislators were barraged by telegrams, letters, and telephone calls supporting the Mayor's stand against what he called "capitulation." When the Governor asked to address the legislature on Monday, that body refused and by Wednesday it was clear the Governor would not be given emergency powers over the city's Sanitation Department. The conflict was finally resolved when both the city and the union agreed to abide by the recommendations of Vincent D. McDonnell, chairman of the State Mediation Board. On February 29, the sanitation workers agreed to a contract giving them a somewhat higher wage package than the city had been willing to offer earlier, but in turn the duration of the new contract—going back retroactively to the end of the old one—was extended.

II   In the fall of 1968, John DeLury and the sanitation workers were negotiating with the city again, along with the Uniformed Fire Fighters Association and the Patrolmen's Benevolent Association. At a particularly tangled point in the simultaneous contract deliberations with the three unions, former United Nations Ambassador Arthur Goldberg was asked by the Mayor to mediate. "It was quite a time," a man who had been present before and during Mr. Goldberg's ministrations told me. "At first, contrary to all you hear, John was getting along fine with Mike Maye of the firemen, John Cassese of the P.B.A., and DeLury. I mean on a personal basis. Why, DeLury even told him at one point how amazed he was that the Mayor knew in such detail how rough and hazardous a sanitation man's job is. 'With all that you have to do,' DeLury said, 'I didn't think you'd have the time, let alone the inclination, to find out.' And there was genuine bargaining going on. But then the complications did thicken, and it was smart of John to call Goldberg in. Goldberg really had things moving until one day John couldn't resist the old call to the civic colors. He started to make a speech during a bargaining session about the need to keep the interests of the city as a whole paramount. You know, we should all think in larger terms than our own narrow interests. Well, the room got very cold indeed. Goldberg asked John if he could have a word with him outside. In the corridor, Goldberg told the Mayor that if he came back into that room again, he could find another negotiator. John stayed away. Fortunately Nelson wasn't involved in that one."

The Governor did engage in another duel with the Mayor that year, but it concerned the naming of a successor to the late Robert Kennedy rather than labor negotiations. On a Wednesday afternoon in mid-June, two weeks after the assassination of Senator Kennedy, I had an appointment with the Mayor at Gracie Mansion. The press had been quoting the Governor as saying the Mayor was one of the men being considered for the Senate. The two had spoken on the telephone about it twice, the Governor told the *Times,* and once at a face-to-face meeting the previous Sunday. The Mayor's only comment to the press had been: "The question is not before me. I've received no offer. There's nothing to accept or reject."

The Sunday meeting, I learned, had begun with the Governor asking, "Tell me why I should appoint you to the Senate, John."

"Nelson, you're starting wrong," the Mayor answered. "You're inviting job applications. I don't do business that way. The stakes are high; we're grown up, we're not children. Are you making me an offer?"

"I've told you that you're my first choice."

"Then that's an offer."

"No it isn't."

"Okay. That's the end of the conversation on this subject. We'll tell the press no offer has been made."

Before going to see the Mayor, I asked one of his assistants at City Hall if he had any additional information. "First," the aide said, "Rockefeller obviously wants to wait until after the Republican Convention—if he can get away with it. Anybody he chooses now, he figures, will alienate some section of the Republican Party. He's in a real spot about John. As John told Rockefeller from the very beginning, 'You're crazy if you think you can hide the fact that you've thought about me in terms of the senatorship.' That was just as obvious to the Governor, but Rockefeller doesn't want to make an offer, not only because of the convention but also because he's afraid that if he's finally forced by public opinion to ask John, he'll be turned down. What he'd like John to do is make a statement taking himself out of it entirely. But John wants to keep him on the hook."

A few hours later, approaching Gracie Mansion, I forgot for a time the jousting between the Governor and the Mayor in my curiosity about the effect of the assassination on security arrangements at the Mansion. I had expected to find a considerable force of police there, but there was only one officer at the entrance gate, just inside of which John Lindsay, Jr., was playing with several friends. At issue was the siege of a fort by a large army of tin soldiers with a cannon in reserve. The policeman, having checked my name on a list, motioned me through without a search. I was surprised. Waiting in a room on the first floor, I looked out the window at Carl Schurz Park. Just a few feet away people were walking past or sitting on benches. A telescopic lens wouldn't have been at all necessary. The only sound in the room was that of the air being cooled. A child's drum set was stationed underneath a nineteenth-century painting of the bay of the City of New York as seen from Weehawken. A water pistol lay on one chair and a Buffalo Bill six-shooter on another.

The Mayor strode in, shook hands, and told me to follow him downstairs to his office. I said I'd expected an armed camp and that he seemed quite casual about his safety. "Oh" —he waved the question away—"that's nonsense, the idea that you can prevent yourself from being killed. I travel with one guy, and he's useful to have for a number of reasons, few of them having to do with safety. Like a guy asks me for a job, I point to the detective and say he's my assistant who'll take down the information."

When we settled down in his office, I asked the Mayor about the speculation concerning the successor to Robert Kennedy. "The thing is," the Mayor said, "Nelson doesn't realize that if he did offer it to me and I turned it down, that wouldn't hurt him or the man who does eventually accept the appointment. My answer would be that I have to support the mayoring business, that the action is here. Sure, I'd turn it down. I've told Nelson that in power, complexity, and responsibility, my job dwarfs even his and that he ought to keep that in mind. But he still thinks I might accept, and that makes him fearful. I know what he's thinking. 'If I do make you a senator, would you still come up to New York this summer and walk through the ghettos?' He's afraid there might be a riot while he's running for President and he wants me in the city to cool it for him. That's just an illusion he has—that my presence can guarantee quiet. He doesn't know the problems; he really doesn't. I can't prove it but I'm sure he hasn't read this," the Mayor picked up from his desk a paperback edition of the *Report of the National Advisory Commission on Civil Disorders*. "I'll grant him that he has reason for anxiety, precisely because he doesn't know the problems. He could make a mistake. He could use not enough force or too much. Anyway, what I finally said to him Sunday was: 'Nelson, for whatever reason —whether it's for your own good or the good of the party or whatever—make up your mind and come to a decision.' "

There was nothing more to be said about the Senate appointment, and since he was definitely going to finish out his first term, I asked the Mayor about the cumulative effects on him of his job so far. "When you began," I said, "some people on your staff were concerned that in order to survive all the pressures, you'd have to develop layer upon layer of toughness until you'd eventually lose most of your sensitivity."

The Mayor looked at me solemnly. "It hasn't happened." Then, unable to suppress a smile, he added, "Except that I don't trust anybody. I'm not counting Mary, of course, but otherwise there are very few people I fully trust. And I'm not entirely sure about them." He was no longer smiling. "This game is so big, the stakes are so high, that ninety-nine and nine tenths per cent of the people out there," he pointed vaguely beyond the confines of his basement office, "are going to look after their own skins first. There are very, very few who will walk over the cliff with you. The rest go for themselves."

"Who would walk over the cliff with you?"

"That's a tough one." The Mayor thought for some time. "Harvey Rothenberg, Don Elliott, Fred Hayes. Mitch Ginsberg—he's great. And Harry O'Donnell would."

He frowned as he considered how small the number of absolute loyalists appeared to be. The frown deepened when I turned the conversation to the police. I had written him a rather contentious letter about what I had considered to be police rioting at Columbia University that spring, and I'd listed other instances of gratuitous police violence at peace demonstrations in previous months. "What you don't realize"—the Mayor drummed his fingers on his desk—"is that my job is to keep perfecting that institution and to keep reasonable control over it. Not to overthrow it. You remember the movie in which Bob Hope played Jimmy Walker? There was a scene in it with what looked like twenty-five thousand cops in front of the Mayor and Walker's line was: 'I don't know if I'm running them or they're running me.' You can't move that monolith overnight. You do it by constant pressure—push, push, push. The Police Commissioner has his problems, and I give him more every day in private conversations, in private notes. Your eyes would pop if you saw some of our exchanges. He'll curse me out, and I'll come back to him with more. Sure, he gets his back up, but he comes around. Like he'll bridle at the young Turks occasionally—Jay Kriegel of this office, for one—but the next day he'll call up Kriegel and say, 'Let's go out for a drink.' I greatly admire that man. Howard Leary has been good for the city. What's come out of all this is that Howard has made some excellent appointments, and there has been a definite move in that department toward being more responsive to particular sensitivities in particular places in the city. I'd say that gradually we've gotten on top of the police problem.

"It's easy for you to write a letter," the Mayor continued, "but I have to pick my battlegrounds on this whole subject of the police. In the long run, what's most important is the quality of the new leadership and the increased productivity of the department. As you know, we've been trying to make this damn government work, trying to make it more flexible by the use of modern management techniques. And so far this approach is working best in the Police Department, of all places. Our next step, by the way, is to make clear that *we* are in charge if the State National Guard ever has to be called in. Leary and I have been having a big fight about that with the Governor's people."

"Have you won?"

The Mayor grinned. "Let's say we haven't lost yet."

The Mayor took a telephone call. He was being asked about the job qualifications of an official who had recently left the Lindsay administration. The applicant was being considered for an executive position in a private agency working with community-action groups. "He'd be just right for you." The Mayor leaned back and put a foot on the desk. "He only went out of the other job because he was the wrong color. At that place, at that time, you had to be black for that job. He's good because he can make decisions. You need some arbitrariness in this community-action field once in a while. Christ, you get so many power groups banging into each other, with some of them trying to stop *any* decision. He showed here that while he believes in the maximum feasible participation of the poor, he's also convinced that there comes a point when the government simply has to act. I also like him because he took a chance coming into this administration. He's not of my party, he comes from a different world, and I know he took it on with a great deal of hesitation because he didn't know me well. He thought, 'What the hell am I doing with a Republican mayor? But we worked well together, I think. He was just the wrong color for where he wound up, that's all. He's your man."

With the call over, and a signal from the Mayor's appointments secretary that I didn't have much time left, I asked the Mayor about a news report that the day before, he and Carl Stokes of Cleveland had persuaded the United States Conference of Mayors, meeting in Chicago, to form a lobbying committee for a federal annual guaranteed income for the poor. "Yes," the Mayor said, "it took some doing but that's the direction in which we have to go. The whole welfare apparatus is falling apart. All that bureaucracy and red tape, and you can't live in dignity or decency under it. Meanwhile the middle class is getting increasingly fed up with paying taxes for something that isn't productive and that isn't getting us anywhere. The federal government has to take the responsibility for income supplements, and within a greatly simplified administrative structure. But for that to happen, we'll need a greatly changed Congress."

"How are we going to get that?"

"The young people in this country are going to have to accomplish that. It's one thing to get all fired up about Gene McCarthy and swarm into New Hampshire for him from all over the country. But they've got to focus that energy into working in their own communities for *ideas* like the guaranteed income. Up to now, as with McCarthy and Bobby Kennedy, ideas have been translated into personalities. But now the ideas themselves have to take on personalities. You just can't bring change through building up single men any more. People have to start thinking about and working for fundamental issues."

"Do you think it's conceivable," I asked, "that we can get that different a Congress within the next ten years?"

The Mayor raised his eyebrows. "Just barely," he said.

III   I did not see the Mayor again until after the Republican and Democratic conventions. His role in Miami had been subject to diverse interpretations, many of them quite critical of the Mayor. After initial reports, for instance, that he might be willing, if asked, to accept the Vice-Presidential nomination on a Nixon ticket, there was considerable dismay both among members of his staff back in the city and among the citizenry at large. "I can't believe it," I told myself, "but still—" And a high-school junior wrote him a letter that *The New York Times* printed in part: "You will probably never see this letter. Still, I felt that I must do something to show my pure and utter disgust that you, a man I held in such high esteem, would even consider running with Mr. Nixon. . . . Assuredly you will disenchant many of your young and idealistic supporters. . . . What we need in this country are statesmen. People who will place personal integrity above personal ambition. We no longer need you."

When Spiro Agnew turned out to be the chosen one, the Mayor's agreement to make a seconding speech for his nomination was regarded by many liberal Republicans and independent voters to be one of the least luminous moments of his career. One newspaperman, Jimmy Breslin, went so far as to proclaim: "The thing that allowed John Lindsay to get up and second Spiro Agnew is the thing that is the matter with the country." And the defeated contender for the Presidential nomination, Nelson Rockefeller, when asked if he disapproved the Mayor's decision to second Agnew, said on television with a certain degree of merriment, "No, there was great pressure on him to be regular, and, besides, he's looking toward 1972."

The sensible course, it seemed to me, was to ask the Mayor himself about the events and the pressures in Miami. In the ten years I've known him, I've found the Mayor to be unusually, even irrepressibly candid. At times he has asked that some of what he has said be off the record, but he has seldom evaded a question.

On the afternoon of the first Wednesday in September, I arrived at Gracie Mansion where I noticed more policemen than had been there during any of my previous visits. Four were stationed at the front gate, two of them with walkie-talkies, and when I walked to the porch in back of the Mansion, I saw two more patrolling the grounds. Sitting on the porch, looking at the first fall leaves near the flower beds, a red hula hoop on the grass, and a squirrel monitoring the policemen, I thought the Mayor lucky to have this retreat, if he ever had time to use it. Except for the rather crowded East River and the police, the ambience was that of a country house. But a sudden, particularly noisome smell from some polluted source destroyed that feeling. The smell gradually disappeared, a dog was chasing the squirrel, and the Mayor came onto the porch.

Lean and tanned, he answered my question about Miami briskly. "There was no mystery about what happened there. Sure, I was under terrific pressure to go for the Vice-Presidency from liberal governors, senators and congressmen up for election this year. They were very worried about their chances on a Nixon ticket and they thought I could help if I was part of it. But I kept telling them I didn't want the job. From the very beginning, my strategy was to make myself as unavailable as possible without becoming obnoxiously obvious about it. And there did seem to be a possibility Nixon might ask me. I was talking to Herbert Brownell at the start of the convention. He was absolutely cold-blooded about it. 'Nixon may turn to you,' he said. 'It would be the smartest thing for him to do politically. And if he does, only you and Mary can decide what the answer will be.' Well, I didn't want it to get to that point. Accordingly, that speech of mine introducing Dan Evans of Washington as the keynoter was specifically designed to put everyone on notice where I stand and thereby keep me off the ticket. I not only came on strong about Vietnam—the phrase was 'deadly folly'—but also about black demands. One paragraph in particular was not about to get me on that ticket."

In a folder of Miami material I'd brought with me was the Mayor's keynote speech. He pointed out the paragraph: "Others of our citizens are prisoners, too—not just of fear, but of that persistent injustice which denies their decency. These black Americans have told us that they are unwilling to accept this indecency as their legacy; that generations of unfilled pledges are enough; that generations of welfare dependency are enough; that another generation of ruined lives is too much."

It didn't seem that strong a statement to me, but remembering the Republican convention, I saw his point. That paragraph hardly reflected the convictions—let alone the order of priorities—of the majority of the delegates.

"As it happened," the Mayor continued, "I got black-balled, I'm told, early in the game in the talks about the Vice-Presidency after Nixon was nominated. It was my stand on Vietnam they landed on. Okay, then he announced it was Agnew. As soon as I heard that, I called Nelson and we chatted about it. 'As sure as I'm sitting here,' I told him, 'I'm going to get a call tonight. I don't know whether it'll be to nominate him or second him.' Nelson said that if I was going to discourage last-minute attempts on my behalf for the Vice-Presidency on the floor, I had no particular choice in the matter. As for himself, he was going to ask the New York State delegation to support the man Nixon wanted because he didn't want to look like a spoiler, a sore loser. And also because if *he'd* been nominated, he would have demanded the same right to pick his own man. It all made sense to me. I was certainly not going to encourage any last-minute battle for *me* that night, and I was certainly going to support the ticket. So it seemed consistent to do what I was finally asked—second Nixon's choice."

"That was some seconding speech," I said. "As I recall, you only mentioned Agnew's name twice."

Mary Lindsay had come onto the porch with a tray of soft drinks. She smiled. "Kathy says you didn't mention his name once."

The Mayor grinned and made no comment.

"So you feel you came out of Miami okay?" I asked.

"Yes, on balance. I'm not running in 1968, which I didn't want to do, and I'm free to say what I have to about the war and the cities. I certainly wouldn't have enjoyed being the Vice-Presidential nominee. First of all, I would have been under some restraint. Secondly, the press would have kept looking for the slightest deviations between Nixon and me and would have blown each one way up. So if Nixon lost, who'd be to blame? Me. You know, Dewey talked himself into believing that the real reason he lost in 1948 was Earl Warren being on the ticket. Also, it wouldn't have been a joy for Nixon either if I'd been running with him. Deviations between us *would* have been inevitable. And if you're the candidate for the Presidency, it's tough to pick up the newspapers and see that your running mate is on another tangent entirely. He would have been on his heels every day—defending, explaining."

"Tell me," I said, "what if Nixon had asked you?"

"If the crunch had come," the Mayor answered, "I would have made a deal with him. He would have had to let me say exactly what I think is needed concerning Vietnam and the cities. But," the Mayor said with visible relief, "it never came near that."

"It's worked out so that your standing in the party hasn't been hurt," I said. "But I wonder if you'll ever have a real chance at the Republican nomination for the Presidency." I read the Mayor part of a column Clayton Fritchey had written shortly after the Miami convention: "Lindsay is simply too outspoken, too sophisticated, too liberal, too intellectually and morally impatient for a party which, while possibly moving toward moderation, is still moving slowly. It is doubtful if Lindsay will ever have a better chance nationally than he had last week, and nothing came of it."

The Mayor had no immediate reaction. He looked out at the East River, and then shrugged. "You never know what's going to happen," he said. "Who would have been able to foresee a Republican convention, four years after the Goldwater nomination, applauding the kind of speech I made introducing Dan Evans? Actually I was surprised that the response to me that night was so good, particularly since I followed Goldwater himself. They had themselves a little orgy for him, but most of it, of course, was sentiment. It happens to anyone who's run on a national ticket. But in answer to Fritchey, I say again that anything can happen. I still do think in any case, that if a liberal Republican is serious about running nationally in the years ahead, he's going to have to go into the primaries and be very candid about bringing the issues to the people. I've always done that. I've had to; I've never had any organizational support. I made clear where I stood and told the Republican Party to come along with me."

With regard to the more immediate future, I asked the Mayor if he had decided whether or not to run for re-election in 1969. "I can put that one off for several months. I haven't had any long talks with Mare about it."

"Whom else do you consult with about political decisions these days?"

"Herb Brownell. He has very good judgment, completely dispassionate. Of my brothers, Rod has never enjoyed the political ambience that much. George is a good combination of practicality and idealism. And Dave is especially useful. He's a natural-born politician. And increasingly I've been consulting with the Mayor's cabinet on purely political questions and on issues that have political overtones. I used to be quite diffident about bringing up that kind of question at one of those eight a.m. meetings, but now it's no problem. We occasionally talk about the political effects of certain moves, the right timing, the political relationships between the state and the city, and of how we can get the things we need for the city no matter who's elected President.

"In and out of the cabinet," the Mayor continued, "we've developed a good, mostly young team with marvelous political acumen. Bob Sweet is chief of staff and the team also includes Lee Rankin, and several assistants to the mayor —Jay Kriegel, Lew Feldstein, Peter Goldmark. I've recently added Jeff Greenfield, who was an assistant to Bobby Kennedy, and there's Peter Tufo, who runs our Washington Office." An aide, who had been standing in the door for a few minutes, signaled the Mayor that a phone call was waiting for him. "And we're about to add a new guy," the Mayor said as he rose. "Gordon Davis, from the Bureau of the Budget. And of course, there's Harry O'Donnell. He's in on all the political decisions. It's a very useful team. I don't hesitate to bounce really sticky questions off them, and they appreciate being asked."

"About that team," the aide said when the Mayor had left, "I'll give you an example of how it works. There's trouble in the Patrolmen's Benevolent Association, and it's going to get worse. Inside the organization, there's a growing group to the right of John Cassese, head of the P.B.A., and Norman Frank, its public relations strategist. In trying to accommodate it, Cassese has been charging that it's City Hall policy, implemented through the cops' superior officers, to tell policemen to go easy on looters and demonstrators. Then, if you remember, Cassese publicly told his membership to disregard any such orders from superior officers. Well, Leary can handle that kind of thing"—the aide smiled—"providing the team of Rankin, Goldmark, Kriegel, and Lindsay are there to give him the proper help. Did you read that statement Leary made on August 15, the one that was sent over the police teletype to every unit in the department. The press carried it. It was a hell of a fine statement, and it was drafted by Rankin, Kriegel, Goldmark, and Lindsay. Leary accepted it."

(The aide later sent me the statement; it was indeed a model of hard-edge clarity:

> The members of the Police Department are charged with the duty of enforcing the law and maintaining order. This has been and will continue to be the clear policy of this Department.
>
> The Police Commissioner has the duty to run the Police

Department, which is also according to law. The Commissioner alone has the lawful authority to direct the operations, administration, and discipline of the Department.

Any member of the Department who has been instructed not to enforce the law is hereby directed to provide full information and a detailed report to the Commissioner. It is the duty of every member of the Department to report in writing immediately to the Commissioner any such instruction.

Every member of the Police Department will adhere to the policies of the Department and will follow the Department's military chain of command as set forth in the Rules and Procedures. Any member of the Department who fails to respond to the orders of a superior officer will be promptly subjected to disciplinary action.

This Department will continue to enforce the law and to be run according to the law.

"Before that went out," the Mayor's aide said, "Cassese announced that the P.B.A. was going to issue its own guidelines on law enforcement to its members. This statement stopped that."

The Mayor returned. I asked him if he had done any more thinking about the violence at Columbia earlier in the year and about how to avoid more in the fall and winter. "Mitch Ginsberg has been my rabbi on that," the Mayor answered. "He was associate dean of the School of Social Work there, you know. Oh, there's been an awful lot of conversation about it and messages back and forth. Mitch feels it's not a good idea for me to pull in Columbia to Gracie Mansion and read the riot act. Like 'There's more to be done and you haven't done it.' Pronunciamentos have little importance, and besides that approach just wouldn't work in this case. Columbia has to figure out its own destiny as a private institution."

"Do you think it will?"

"Probably not."

John Lindsay, Jr., was now on the porch. "Could you come here for a second?" he asked his father. "I can't get

the kickstand up on my bike." The Mayor solved the problem.

"I'm still bothered by what happened at Columbia,"
I said as John Lindsay, Jr., left. "Do you think Leary learned
anything from that police riot? I haven't seen any strong
statements from him condemning what the department re-
luctantly calls 'excessive use of force.' "

"Yes," said the Mayor, "I think he learned some important things. He learned a lot more about his own police
force. He knows more about their strengths and weaknesses
now. He knows which commands are better than others.
And increasingly, he knows who's good and who isn't in the
ranks. He knows more and more of them by name. Leary
has been continually gaining more knowledge and confidence. And he doesn't do it by being one of the boys. That's
not his nature. He's a lone wolf. He really needed that added
confidence. I'd read the stuff in the papers, but it took me
quite a while to realize how deep the impression in the
Police Department was that Leary wouldn't last, that they'd
get him somehow."

"They?"

"The Establishment in the department. All down the
line the prediction was that they'd either so corner him that
he'd be wrapped in cotton, stuffed like a mummy, or they'd
force him out. By golly, the guy has overcome all those attempts, and he's won the respect of the force. Also," the
Mayor continued, "I think that what happened in Chicago
during the Democratic convention had a profound impact
on Howard. It reaffirmed, but very deeply, what he already
knows—you can never let the cops go for themselves. It's
like war; you can't leave it to the generals. Another thing.
What happens here in the Police Department has more ram-
ifications than you might imagine. When he was Home
Minister, Roy Jenkins, who's now British Chancellor of the
Exchequer, used to come here quite often. And twice we
had long talks about the police system, hiring problems, the

Civilian Review Board, brutality, the handling of hippies and demonstrators. They're in the same bag we're in, and he was very interested in what we were doing."

Standing at the entrance to the porch was a visitor, J. Robert Schaetzel, United States Ambassador to the European Economic Community. The Ambassador appeared to be in his mid-fifties. Tall, self-assured, he was in bearing and dress the very model of the career diplomat. My time was up, and I rose to leave. "You don't have to," the Mayor said. "Stay and have a drink." Mary Lindsay had appeared again, and asked what we wanted.

"I heard what you were saying about Chicago, John," the Ambassador said. "But it seems to me that a lot of us in this country forget that cops are people too. They're bound to respond when they're provoked."

The Mayor looked toward the river, and said softly, "But it's the cops who have guns."

The Ambassador, a bit uncomfortable, switched the subject. "I saw George Ball the other day. He said, 'I don't know who the next President will be, but I know his name —Mendès-France. Whoever he is, he'll have to get us out of Vietnam.'" The Mayor nodded in agreement.

"The main reason I came back for a while," the Ambassador went on, "is to assemble answers to some of the questions Europeans are going to be asking me once the campaign is over. The primary question is whether America is going to overreact to the Russian invasion of Czechoslovakia and its aftermath. Will it say, 'Screw Europe; they're a bunch of slobs'? And sophisticated Europeans also fear that if America does say 'To hell with Europe,' it will go over their heads and make deals at *their* expense with Russia."

"There's always been that fear," the Mayor said. "That's why De Gaulle insists on having a *force de frappe*. That's why the other countries there want to have a mobile atomic European force."

"And what happened in Czechoslovakia," the Ambassador broke in, "intensified that fear. A number of European ambassadors in Washington told me they were greatly disturbed by the ambiguity of our reaction to the invasion. To them we appeared to be more concerned about our relationship with Russia than with what was being done to Czechoslovakia."

"I understand how they feel," the Mayor said, "but they can't really have expected us to take unilateral action on that any more than we did when the Russian tanks went into Hungary. I'll tell you what I think is going to happen, and it will reassure Europeans more than anything else because they'll be the driving force. The one positive result of the invasion of Czechoslovakia is that it now provides a focus for NATO to reassemble itself."

"To do what by reassembling?" the Ambassador asked.

"To do what you and I used to talk about when I was on the NATO Parliamentarians' Committee. To broaden its base, to get away from the notion that military alliances last forever, to get an economic footing under itself, and to bring in new institutional frameworks that will gather in the neutrals. The old Jean Monnet theory was to create an organic framework in the Atlantic community that would capitalize on the natural tendencies of nations in a given area to link together—militarily, economically, socially, culturally, politically. Obviously there's a lot more to be done in that direction, and it seems to me that for Europe, the answer to the Russian invasion is to get itself together. And after the election here, whoever is President can help once we're no longer bogged down in Vietnam. That's part of the sadness of these last years—so little moved forward *anywhere* because of that morass."

They began to talk about the Presidential candidates, and the Ambassador chuckled. "I meant to tell you. John McCloy told me Tom Finletter had made a fool of himself raising money for McCarthy."

The Ambassador had expected agreement, but Lindsay

said seriously, "I don't agree with that at all. My brother Dave gave McCarthy five hundred dollars, and he's a solid Republican. He's a more regular Republican than I am."

"Well," the Ambassador remained jocular, "whatever your views of the club you used to belong to, I myself take the judgment of the best men in Congress about McCarthy. They don't take him seriously. They figure he'd make a good professor somewhere, but he's not Presidential material."

"I don't agree with that either," the Mayor answered. "The best men in Congress didn't take Jack Kennedy seriously either when he was a senator."

"But I do see in the papers," the Ambassador moved to the other party, "that now the conventions are over, you're going to be a heavy campaigner for the Nixon ticket."

The Mayor was annoyed, not at the Ambassador, but at the press. "You've been reading fiction. That was in the *Times*. They got that from Nixon headquarters. Since when are the Nixon people running *my* schedule? No, whatever campaigning time I do take will be mostly for friends of mine in trouble in marginal districts. They're in trouble for good reason—they're damn good liberal Republicans."

"Do you think Javits is in trouble?"

"No, not at all. Hey, did you see him pulling down his underdrawers on television during the convention? He forgot the cardinal rule. Once you're on the floor, you've got to act as if you're on television every second." The Mayor rose, and laughing, did an imitation of the Senator adjusting his underwear.

"Well," the Ambassador rose, "will I see you in Brussels in the fall?"

"I'm thinking of it, but I've got to look at the money situation. My wife has a short leash on me. She likes to travel too, especially to Europe, so Mare would come along. But on the other hand, we rented a place this summer and paid too much for it. And thirdly, the kids all want to go to Aspen this winter."

With the Mayor weighing his economic options, the Ambassador and I left. At the front door, as the Ambassador walked ahead, Harvey Rothenberg, the Mayor's appointments secretary, stopped me. "Remember what I said on my first day in this job?" he said. "That if this was a business, I'd sell it. Well, I wouldn't sell it this year."

IV   The Mayor never did get to Brussels, nor was he able to spend much time campaigning for his friends, because by the fall of his third year in office, New York City seemed to be disintegrating to such a degree that I expected Rothenberg might again be eager to sell. An intensifying conflict between the United Federation of Teachers, headed by Albert Shanker, and the local school governing board of Ocean Hill–Brownsville in Brooklyn (one of three vaguely empowered experimental school districts in the city) had led to a series of city-wide U.F.T. strikes, with more than a million children out of school. The original dispute had centered on the local board's attempt to transfer out of its district a group of union teachers it charged with being detrimental to its attempt to transform the schools of Ocean Hill–Brownsville. The union claimed the teachers were being denied due process and that it had to use its city-wide power to protect them.

By October, the struggle had split the city. Black and Puerto Rican groups accused the U.F.T. of trying to destroy any possibility that failing ghetto schools could be made accountable to the communities they purportedly served.

The U.F.T., on the other hand, charging that "Nazi" and "vigilante" tactics were on the rise among its opponents, circulated huge quantities of leaflets of dubious origin intended to prove that anti-Semitism in particular was an inevitable corollary of the kind of local control exemplified by Ocean Hill–Brownsville.

Meanwhile police and firemen were threatening "job actions" (newsspeak for work delays) if their new contractual demands were not met by the city. And among many other unhappy groups, welfare clients were sitting in at and otherwise disrupting welfare centers out of an accumulation of grievances. While most public attention was focused on the confrontation over the schools, slightly deflected on occasion by anxiety that the police and firemen might really be serious, the intermittent rebellions by welfare recipients were more a source of annoyance than concern among those of the citizenry who considered themselves responsible if beleaguered taxpayers. Yet I realized with some degree of shock that fall—although I had seen the projected statistics before —how large the welfare population had become. More than ten per cent of all the people in the city were already on relief, the number having doubled from 1965 to 1968. And the Mayor was predicting that by June 1969 one New Yorker in every eight—one million persons—would be receiving welfare payment. As it turned out, that figure was reached six months earlier.

The man who had been in charge—from February 1966 to December 1967—of what used to be called the Department of Welfare (now renamed euphemistically the Department of Social Services) was Mitchell Ginsberg. His responsibilities and worries had manifoldly increased in the third year of the Mayor's term, since he now served as administrator of the Human Resources Administration which oversaw many programs, including welfare. I had talked with him from time to time and had been impressed by the quality and clarity of his intelligence, his wry resiliency, and his fundamentally humanity. "Mitch's problem," one of his assistants had said, "is that he can't turn his mind off the city when he leaves his office. The job is with him all the time, and Jesus, what a job!"

Mitchell Ginsberg and I met for dinner in early October. He preferred not to take time out during the day for interviews, but since he did have to eat, a conversation at Casey's in Greenwich Village seemed to him a pleasantly functional way to meet my request. I have never seen Ginsberg when he didn't look tired, but the low-key atmosphere appeared to relax him as he leaned heavily against the back of a booth. I was going to start by talking about welfare, but the school strike was very much on Ginsberg's mind as were the tensions between Jews and Negroes it had exacerbated. "Trying to do something about those tensions has been one of my jobs for the past six months, from before the strike," Ginsberg said. "Sometimes with the Mayor, and sometimes by myself, I've been meeting with representatives of Jewish organizations. There's been a feeling among some of them for quite a while that the Mayor primarily looks out for the interests of the blacks. That concern was revived—and it's connected, of course, to fears of anti-Semitism—after the assassination of Martin Luther King. There has been growing criticism by Jewish groups of what they considered police restraint in dealing with looters during the immediate aftermath of King's death. They've emphasized that it was Jewish shopkeepers in Harlem who were hit hardest. So those anxieties fed right into the controversy about the schools—blacks and Puerto Ricans against a largely Jewish union. I've met with the leadership of the New York Board of Rabbis and its lay advisory groups as well as with other solid groups of citizens who keep on stressing that the Mayor has over-identified with the blacks and has not expressed himself clearly or forcibly enough about the needs of Jewish New Yorkers. 'This is the way it started in Germany,' they say, 'and we are not going to let it happen here.'

"In talking with them at first," Ginsberg continued, "I tried to present the school situation on its own terms. I pointed out that many of them came from suburban communities where locally elected boards do indeed have control of the schools. That approach had some impact. At another meeting, with the Mayor present, I also suggested that they should be *for* some things. They hadn't supported the poverty program as firmly as they might have. And the Mayor added that they also hadn't spoken up for a bigger budget or for a police civilian review board. That was a rather unsatisfactory meeting. There have been others since; none of them has gone particularly well; and the Mayor is taking these complaints more and more seriously. As his advisers tell him to. The membership of those groups represent a very significant part of the population and there's no doubt of the depth of their concern. You find it everywhere. You don't need to learn about it from representatives of organizations. And so, in the last month, the Mayor has been giving more weight to that concern, a degree of weight that reflects itself subtly in the way he's been approaching the Ocean Hill–Brownsville situation."

"Maybe not so subtly," I said. It was my feeling that the Mayor could have been much more forceful from the very start of the conflict in publicly clarifying the issues—the failure of the schools in the ghettos and the intransigency of the United Federation of Teachers.

Ginsberg looked at me and smiled. "I know, you're a supporter of Ocean Hill–Brownsville. But it's the Mayor's intent to be the bridge between various groups. That, however, is getting to be more and more difficult. At this moment, I don't know how it's going to come out. As for him, there's no question he's been badly damaged politically, but there have been times before when he's been hurt for the moment and then eventually winds up having gained. It's never been as rough as this, though."

I knew Ginsberg had been present at many of the negotiating sessions at City Hall during the teachers' strikes and in the course of other impasses with labor unions. "Aside from all the bitterness in this one," I asked, "is it becoming easier for the Mayor to deal with labor people?"

"He's much better in negotiations than he used to be," Ginsberg said. "Oh, he still has troubles with the typical labor leader. When John says, 'The city belongs to all of us,' they look at him as if he's crazy. 'What's that got to do with it? How much money do we get?' When he talks like that, they think he's trying to put something over on them. But he means it. He really does. He believes everybody has a stake in everything that happens in New York. So in that sense, he and the average labor guy continue to talk a different language. My guess is that in the past three years, the Mayor hasn't had an informal drink with a labor leader. It's hard for both him and them to get together on those terms. But I will say that he lectures them less than he used to, and they are not by any means unaware that labor unions have done very well under Lindsay."

Ginsberg suddenly laughed. "I was just thinking. You always have that foundation of the Puritan in him, even as he does get more skillful in dealing with labor people. Two of the top negotiators, Vincent McDonnell and Harold Israelson, have told me how increasingly effective the Mayor is during contract talks, but at the same time they mentioned coming to him during those simultaneous negotiations between the policemen, firemen, and sanitation workers. 'Well, we've got something for you,' they said. 'I assume,' the Mayor responded, 'that you've been protecting the people's interests.' They stopped dead in their tracks. 'What does that mean? We're talking about a settlement.' He wasn't trying to put them on, you know. That's his job—protecting the public interest. He still uses the term 'power brokers' to describe those concerned only with their own interests. I remember the day he was trying to get me to take the job as welfare commissioner, he told me of an exchange he'd had with the late Mike Quill of the sanitation workers. 'It's your city as much as mine,' he'd said to Quill. 'Actually it's more important to you. I can go to the Sorbonne or someplace, but you've got to stay here. That's why you've got to give a little.' Quill thought he was crazy too. I would say," Ginsberg added drily, "that a primary source of disappointment to the Mayor the longer he stays in office, is his recognition that there are a lot of people who do not agree with him about the primacy of the public interest."

"You mentioned the Puritan in him. In what other ways does that quality manifest itself?"

"By the way," Ginsberg said, "I don't know if he takes that kindly to the term. After the mess of that sanitation men's strike last February, the Mayor said rather hopefully, 'Well, now they can't call me "Mr. Clean" any more.' But basically he *is* a Puritan. There's his whole attitude toward women, for another example. He really thinks women ought to be in the home. Look at how few women are high up in his administration. And the only woman commissioner—Marta Valle, Commissioner of the Youth Service Agency—was appointed by me. Not that he doesn't like women, mind you. But he's an old-fashioned guy. They ought to look nice and cook well. And maybe they ought to have key secretarial posts. There are a lot of good-looking Girl Fridays in his administration. But he distrusts women in relatively high office. He was talking about it the other day. 'They'll make their judgments on the basis of emotion,' he said. 'They don't think like men!' Yes, he's an old-fashioned man in many ways.

"Especially," Ginsberg emphasized approvingly, "with regard to his sense of ethics. He's the honest Puritan, and in this day and age, I find that refreshing. You and I grew up in Boston," Ginsberg said to me, "and as you remember, it was the real Yankees who were especially strong on civil rights and liberties. They respect the integrity of others as well as their own. He's like that. There's a New England thing about him. There's a stubbornness there and, I suppose, a certain stiffness too. I expect there are very few people he relaxes with."

"Are you one of them, would you say?"

"Not in that sense, I think. He trusts me more as a professional. There are certain things he can expect of me."

"How does he suffer disagreement?"

"He's certainly never tried to prevent me from disagreeing with him. He's never cut me off in any way at all. Sure, sometimes he's been angry with me, to put it mildly. When we disagree with particular sharpness and he gets really angry, I'm likely to have very little to do with what's going on for a week or so. You might say that at those times he values my opinion from a distance. But that never lasts long. It seems to me that what he does suffer from is not having *enough* people around him who'll disagree. Some of them are so committed to him they'll go along whether they agree with him or not."

Ginsberg smiled. "Maybe I'm *expected* to disagree because I'm a Democrat, and known to be. He's never raised the question of my politics but there was a period, I think, during which he felt my first loyalty was to Bobby Kennedy rather than to him. And there are certainly people around him who are still convinced no Democrat would be interested in the Mayor's political future. That's simply not true in my case. I'd like to see him President eventually. The only reason I took this job is Lindsay. I wouldn't have taken it under anyone else. And my judgment of him was right. He's supported me on programs that do not win votes. Like when I stopped what used to be called 'midnight raids'—sudden visits to the homes of women on welfare to see if there really was a man in the house. And he backed me on the 'statement-of-need' experiment we started in April 1967 in welfare districts covering parts of East Harlem and Bedford-Stuyvesant. The concept is that people simply declare their need for public assistance, and instead of running an intensive investigation of each applicant, we accept that declaration. Then, as Internal Revenue does with income-tax returns, we audit ten per cent of the applications at random. We save time and paperwork; we free caseworkers from being detectives; the dignity of the applicant is respected; and, as we've discovered, the percentage of ineligibles discovered by the audits is about the same as it was under the old system. But this approach—which has led to me being called 'Giveaway Ginsberg' in certain circles—is hardly a vote-getter. The welfare establishment told me I didn't have a chance of getting it approved and working. But all the Mayor asked me was, 'Mitch, do you really think it's a good move?' I said it was, and he told me to go ahead.

"I'll give you another example of why I respect the Mayor so much. Last summer, I was asked to testify before both the Democratic and Republican platform committees. By chance, a man in the administration who is very close to the Mayor and is in charge of his political destiny, heard about it. He asked me rather firmly not to testify. 'The identification with a flaming liberal like you,' I was told, 'can't do anything but hurt the Mayor politically.' I pointed out that I had already told the Mayor of the invitation and that his reaction had been, 'Great, lay it on them.' 'Ah,' this political tactician said, '*he'll* say that, but I don't.' Well, the next day the Mayor told me, 'I don't know what you're going to say and I don't want to see your testimony in advance. But after you testify, if you're asked, tell them the Mayor agrees with you completely.' 'But your political man says I'm not to go.' 'Listen to me carefully,' the Mayor said. 'To hell with that. You go ahead and do what you have to do.' It's that kind of thing which keeps me in the administration."

I later found out the political tactician was Deputy Mayor Robert Sweet. That evening, I went on to ask Ginsberg, "When he's no longer Mayor—and his first term could be his last—what do you think he'll have left that may have lasting effect? How will we remember he's been here?"

Ginsberg waited some seconds before answering. "Providing he's not entirely torn apart by this school thing and what comes out of it, I think he'll have left strong reminders of his presence. For one thing, he'll have left a spirit, a style that's very different from what characterized the mayoralty before him. I think style is important because it carries other meanings as well. I remember being at Gracie Mansion one evening around nine thirty in the summer of 1967. The Mayor kept getting telephone reports of disturbances in Bedford-Stuyvesant. As they increased in frequency, the Mayor got more and more uneasy. Finally he said, 'Come on, Mitch, let's go.' We went in an unmarked car and came to a precinct with a crowd outside. The people there were furious about an incident of what they were convinced was police brutality, and I had a strong feeling they would have torn the Mayor apart if they could have gotten at him. Leary and Chief Inspector Garelik were inside. We stayed in the precinct for an hour and a half, the tension building, large numbers of police being deployed outside. Word came that a group of the protesters was demanding to see the Mayor. A discussion started as to whether he should meet with them, and the Mayor cut through it. 'Sure I will.' Eight of them came in, with fezzes and African dress, and all of that. For an hour and a half the Mayor took a terrific tongue-lashing with great patience—a quality he doesn't always have. He didn't *do* anything; he just listened and showed very clearly that he was concerned. Then they left, and the antagonism in the crowd outside dissipated.

"I've seen that sort of thing happen with him at other times. Now that Bobby Kennedy is dead, nobody in American political life comes close to the Mayor in his ability to make himself believable in the ghettos. And it's more than the concern he shows. Here's this Ivy League, Puritan type,

and on the face of it, you'd say, 'What's the connection between him and the black poor?' But something's there, and
it gets across. Not only in New York but also in all those
cities he went through to do research for the Kerner Report.
So there'll be that element of style he'll have left when he
goes, and as a result, whoever takes his place will have to be
believable in the ghettos in his own way. What I mean is
that I can't imagine it possible for an ordinary mediocrity
to succeed him—the traditional politician who, whatever
his rhetoric, has the traditional attitude toward the ghettos.

"Nor," Ginsberg continued, "is Lindsay's legacy, if that's
the word, going to be only one of style. For better or worse,
he has consistently encouraged the idea of community people participating in affairs that directly concern them. Although he sometimes gets furious at the delays and conflicts
this causes, he really believes in it."

I mentioned that Charles Abrams, the housing expert
and city planner, had told me recently that he felt there was
a point at which too much community participation, and
its attendant delays until competing factions are accommo-
dated, can end up in hardly anything being accomplished.

"Sure, that's a problem," Ginsberg said. "But once you
start, you can't say we'll have them involved up to a point
and no farther. If you do that, you show you didn't mean
it in the first place. Whether he's Mayor for a second term
or not, community involvement in decision-making has taken
root in this city. Hell, we've financed welfare groups that
put pressure on the Welfare Department itself, and we've
turned over some sixty-two million dollars, including federal
funds, to the Council Against Poverty. That's the city's
policy-making body for the anti-poverty program, and the
largest single bloc in the Council consists of people elected
by the poor around the city to represent them. I don't control a dime of the funds allocated to the Council. No other
city in the country has given that degree of spending authority to a group outside the regular structure of city gov-

ernment. The Council decides priorities and allocates funds
to activities such as the organizing of parents around the
school decentralization issue and the forming of consumer
co-ops and credit unions. It also finances programs by which
tenants are informed of their rights against landlords and
of how to demand code enforcement from city agencies. And
on the school thing, the Council provides money to set up
courses instructing parents on how to act if they become
members of local boards. Now that's a lot more than just
talking about 'community involvement.' As a matter of fact,
when somebody urges me to try to see that a certain anti-
poverty project gets financed, I tell them that the most effective thing for me to do is to go before the Council Against
Poverty and attack that particular project. I'm the Establishment to them, and they're likely to do the opposite of what
I want.

"Certainly there's waste and inefficiency as people learn
to make decisions and implement them, but even at the
worst moments, the Mayor has never said, 'Take that authority away from them.' Every once in a while a community
group under the umbrella of the Council Against Poverty
will do or say something that antagonizes the City Council
and the Mayor will ask me about it. 'They had the right to
do that,' I tell him, and that's enough for him. People in
the poverty neighborhoods have become used to having a
say, and no successor of Lindsay is going to be able to turn
that all the way around.

"Another definite impact the Mayor has made," Ginsberg continued, "has been on the police. Leary is a Lindsay
product. The Mayor has taken a lot of time and effort with
him. Leary himself is a very able, interesting man, and he's
now in command of that force—so far as anyone can be. But
I am worried about what happens to the police after Lindsay
leaves. They may well slide back. The man after Lindsay is
likely to let them run their own show again because that's
the usual practice. And it's much easier. You know, this at-

tempt to make over the police has not been easy for Lind-say.

About a week ago, he was about as devastated as I've ever seen him. He'd gone to Queens for the wake of Henry Barnes, the Traffic Commissioner. There was a police guard there and the Mayor went up, as he always does, to shake hands with the police. But one cop said, 'No,' and turned away. That hostility goes all the way back to the Mayor's fight for the Civilian Review Board, but the incident shows how tense the force has become. The Mayor was really crushed. He kept talking about it in the car all the way back. 'Did you see that?' he said to Bernie, a detective with him. 'I'll get his number and crack down on him,' Bernie said. 'No,' the Mayor shook his head. 'He has a right not to shake my hand.' But that whole night he was in despair. Of course, he snapped back. He always does."

"Aside from that resiliency," I asked, "what about his capacity for intellectual growth? Bobby Kennedy, you re-member, called him a 'lightweight.' "

"I worried about that when I first met him. He's in-creasingly won my respect. I like him, but more than that, I respect the way he's developed and matured on this job. Two years ago, when I started working for the city, I was not impressed with the talk of his being potential Presi-dential material. I didn't think he was anywhere near ready. Not because I'm a Democrat and not because I think so highly of many who have become President. He just didn't seem to have the stature a President should have. I didn't think he was a subtle enough man nor did I think him knowledgeable enough in areas in which he should have been. Also he blew up too easily.

"Now, however, he is more subtle, although he still tends to see some things starkly. In terms of black and white. Well, that's a bad term now. I mean, for instance, he defines people as good guys and bad guys, and once he's put you in the latter category, it takes a lot to get out of it."

"You haven't indicated that much of a change in him in two years."

"I think particularly about his growth in knowledge-ability. He knows more about issues. He does his homework more conscientiously than he used to. He used to be more casual and sometimes made decisions without having explored a specific problem deeply enough. Now he sometimes does too much exploring. There'll be ten or fifteen people around him for hours on a problem, and he'll be pushed many different ways. But I should say that nobody makes decisions *for* him. Of course, he's influenced, but the final decision is not arrived at by consensus, and that I appreciate. It's made, moreover, on his own substantial knowledge of the situation. And as I've said, if he thinks something ought to be done, he'll go ahead even if he has nothing to gain politically and sometimes a lot to lose."

"Do you consider him an intellectual?"

"Well, the few times I discussed a welfare issue with John Kennedy or juvenile delinquency with Robert Kennedy, it was on a different level than such discussions might be with Lindsay. They were more intellectually curious than he is. Lindsay is much more pragmatic. He's primarily interested in what he needs to know to handle a current situation. But although he doesn't go into things with any great intellectual depth, if you provide him with that kind of analysis as a guide to action, he'll accept it if he has confidence in you personally. So he doesn't resist intellectual analysis.

"Although it's academic now," Ginsberg said, "I would say he does have the capacity to be President. Maybe it's not academic. Who can predict what'll happen in four years or eight years? Anyway, I don't know that being an intellectual is an essential quality for the Presidency. Lindsay cares, and that's important. He understands enough about people and about issues. He listens to others. And he has what a successful President most depends on—the ability to lead and inspire people. People need that in a President. They haven't had it under Johnson, and I don't think they're going to have it during the next four or eight years.

"It's not that I'm a hero-worshipper. Quite the opposite. And there have been times when I've been bitter and close to resigning, but then he talks about the enormous needs and problems of the city and convinces me again that this is the place to be. As a matter of fact, I did offer my resignation this week. There's been a fight in the administration about a certain program I'm going to start. I can't give you the details. There was a final meeting, and that political tactician I told you about headed the opposition. He wanted me to handle this program a certain way and I told him it was possible to do that but not with me as administrator. I left. Meanwhile the stories have been breaking about missing funds, about embezzlement, in H.R.A. Last night, at twelve o'clock, I was discouraged, exhausted, depressed, and there's a call from the Mayor: 'I'm going to Chicago, but I wanted you to know before I leave that in that policy argument, I back you completely.' That says something about a man. He goes against his political adviser, a man utterly devoted to him, and a man much more close to him in point of view than I am. I'm not even a close personal friend. But in this case, as in others, he somehow felt my program and my way of shaping it was right even though it isn't going to be politically popular. He may not have understood it completely, but he wants to do what's right. He's actually a man who believes in right and wrong."

Ginsberg ordered more coffee. "I'm not saying that doing the right thing is usually an easy, instant decision—for him or for me. That Willie Smith episode was a rough one." (The previous July, members of the Neighborhood Youth Corps had demonstrated in front of City Hall for funds to provide more summer jobs for young people in poverty areas. The demonstration became violent, with resultant damage to several cars and other property. Bystanders were roughed up, and fifty of the protesters had been arrested.

Willie Smith, director of the Neighborhood Youth Corps, a black man with strong roots in black communities in the city, was accused of helping to organize the demonstration. There had been strongly adverse reaction to the demonstration in white sections of the city and the Mayor, as he later told me, had been very disturbed.)

"It was clear to me," Ginsberg recalled, "that Smith had to be suspended. I had written evidence that he'd set up the demonstration. The night it happened I saw the Mayor. He asked me what I wanted to do, and I said I was going to suspend Smith. The political tactician was there and several other advisers to the Mayor. They disagreed vehemently with me. 'The black communities will blow up if you do that,' one of them said. So we all got into the Mayor's car, rode into Central Park, and talked for an hour and a half. I told the Mayor I didn't underestimate the dangers involved, but I couldn't let this pass by. If I did, there'd be more and more incidents like it. 'If you stand by this decision,' the Mayor told me, 'there may be riots and burning and killing. Again, what do you want to do?' 'I'm going to suspend him,' I said. Then I had a sleepless night. It's one thing to know what you have to do; it's another thing to fear what the consequences will be. I suspended Smith the next morning. That was a Thursday. By the following Wednesday, I had decided to put him back in again. Smith and I had discussed the matter, and he'd agreed that if the time came when he felt he had to engage in public action inconsistent with or contrary to city policy, he'd leave his job. He'd been doing a good job with the Youth Corps, and now that he'd made that pledge, there was no reason not to reinstate him.

"But now there was trouble again. The very advisers to the Mayor who had most strongly urged that Smith not be suspended were now insisting he not be unsuspended. It was too short a time, they said. Actually the Mayor gave the real reason: 'We've gotten a tremendous positive response nationally as well as locally by being firm. A very good response politically.' 'That may be,' I said, 'but the fair thing now is to put him back in.' Later that day I got a call from the Mayor. 'Mitch, all my advisers are against reinstating Smith. Do you still think it's a good idea?' 'Yes.' 'Okay. Go ahead and do it.'

"I should point out"—Ginsberg smiled slightly—"that although the Mayor did let me do what I thought best throughout that situation, I was also aware that I might have to pay if my decision turned out to be wrong. Right after I'd suspended Smith, the Mayor's political man came up to me. 'I want to tell you something,' he said. 'No,' I told him. 'Let me tell you what you were going to tell me. If this goes badly, the Mayor has to be free to reverse my decision and then fire me.' 'That's right.' I'm sure the Mayor didn't tell him to come to me and say that. I doubt he even knew it had happened. But this man was acting as the Mayor's political protector, and in that respect, he was right. Just as now if there are two or three more scandals in H.R.A., I would resign. Nobody will have to tell me to do it. It's all very nice that everybody knows I'm honest and nobody blames me for what happens. But ultimately, politically, I am responsible. I know that. Knowing it, however, is not going to make me so cautious that nothing can happen. In an agency like H.R.A., we have to take a certain amount of risks. We have to hire people who don't meet all the usual standards. We have to hire some people, for instance, with police records.

"If there are too many safeguards," Ginsberg emphasized, "the program can't work, and I won't have that. But I have to balance the risk-taking against the credibility of the programs. If enough wrongdoing takes place, the program will have been so discredited with the public that it would have to have a new head. The Mayor's loyalty to his people might make him resist my resigning, but I wouldn't let it. I would simply leave. Anyway"—Ginsberg looked at his watch—"Mike Sviridoff, who was my predecessor as head of H.R.A., was quite right. 'There is no way,' he used to say, 'of winning in this job. The question is how rapidly you lose.' "

"Do you feel that way about the welfare system as a whole?"

"Of course. Look at the figures. As of the fiscal year ending last June 30, welfare costs had risen to 26.6 per cent of the city's expense budget of 5.9 billion dollars—the largest single item on that budget. Education used to be. By contrast, five years ago, welfare costs accounted for 11 per cent of a 3-billion-dollar budget. Next year we're going to need more money; we're adding about twenty thousand to the rolls every month. You have to keep losing with the system as it now is. But that system has no future. It'll be out in ten or fifteen years. It won't disappear as fast as it should because of the conservative tide now running in the country. But for a variety of reasons and motivations many different kinds of groups have concluded that welfare just doesn't work. Nobody likes it—the taxpapers or the recipients. What we'll get instead in the long run is some form of guaranteed income—either in the way of a family allowance, which I'd prefer, or through some variation of the negative income tax. I prefer family allowances, payments on the basis of the number of children you have, because it eliminates the means test. And any means test is mean. Also we have considerable experience with family or child allowances. There are now sixty-two countries with some form of it. It just takes the United States longer to get into this kind of thing, but when this country is finally forced to scrap the old system, it is more likely to change to a plan that's tied in directly with children.

"In the short run, the answers are also clear. Whether they're politically viable is something else again. First there has to be a national standard of minimum welfare payments —the same in Mississippi, let's say, as here. And the federal government has to take over the full financing of those minimum standards. Second, everyone able and willing to work should be guaranteed a job. But for that to happen, we'll need federal subsidies for private employers who assume the responsibility for job training. If a man is worth only sixty percent of the going wage, the employer would pay that and the federal government would provide the rest. But it's unrealistic to expect private enterprise to do most of what's required to guarantee jobs. The main job development effort has to be in the public sector. It's perfectly evident that there are thousands and thousands of jobs which desperately need to be done, not just because they give work to the poor but also because all of us can use the services they would provide. You know what I mean. Jobs in hospitals, parks, welfare and health centers, and on and on. But cities can't pay for those added positions. Again you have to have federal subsidies. It all makes such sense. If the Federal government took over the costs of public assistance—there'll always be those who cannot work or need supplemental help even if there were guaranteed jobs—and if the federal government subsidized job development and training, then local governments would be free to make real improvements in health, education, and housing while also developing a broad network of public social services."

It was nearly ten, and Ginsberg still had some paperwork to do at home. "Yes," he said more to himself than to me as he put on his coat, "it all makes sense. But since when is that a guarantee of action? Especially now."

V   Throughout the fall, the conflict continued between the United Federation of Teachers and the Ocean Hill–Brownsville governing board. There were lengthy periods of negotiations at City Hall. An adviser to the Mayor, who was involved in nearly all of them, grew more and more depressed as the weeks went by. "Sure John has empathy with Ocean Hill–Brownsville," he said to me at one point. "There's no question he really understands their need to have the schools accountable. It's not just an intellectual conclusion on his part. He *feels* it. But he's a political being and so he can't go all the way with them. We sit and sit at those endless sessions. You have no idea how boring they are. People think we have a master plan, but most of the time we're in one place grumbling at each other and the teachers are somewhere else. Only occasionally are the Ocean Hill–Brownsville people called in. So the mediators go back and forth. They spend three or four hours with the teachers and then they tell us what's happened. What's happened is that the teachers work away at every little point until they've killed it. So we start again. There was one very long stretch of hours during which neither John nor I had any sleep at all. I remember at two in the morning we were watching *Petticoat Fever* on one of his television sets. That's a hell of a way to do business, isn't it?

"I know people like you blame Al Shanker for all this. But it's not a matter of a very militant head of a union pulling the rest of them along with him. There are people on his side who are in the negotiations because they're afraid *he'll* be too soft. The fear among those teachers and among the supervisors is really something. They say they're trying to protect the future of the union and the future of the system that got the supervisors where they are. But it's the past they're trying to protect and you can only do that for so long. What you see here, and what you're going to see in other institutions in this city, is the beginning of a shift of power. It won't happen peacefully. It never has. There'll be more tensions, more arrests, just plain more trouble. Those now in control will put up obstacles; the state legislature will; but in time the blacks and Puerto Ricans will get their share of power, as others have before them. Meanwhile

John says he's going to keep on trying to be the Mayor of all the people, and he just might come out with all the people against him.

"God knows," the Mayor's adviser continued, "I sympathize with John but sometimes, when he thinks he's being most pragmatic, he's wholly unrealistic. There was one bruising sixteen-hour session which ended with an agreement between the city and the U.F.T. The disputed teachers would be sent back to Ocean Hill–Brownsville with as many police as necessary to protect them and there'd also be teams of observers in the schools, including representatives of the union, to make sure the agreement was fully implemented. Sensible, right? There was one thing wrong. Nobody from Ocean Hill–Brownsville was there. They simply weren't part of the settlement. I fought against it to the end. 'They won't buy it,' I said. 'This is colonialism to them.' But the practical men around the Mayor insisted that Ocean Hill–Brownsville had to buy it. They still don't understand that the time is past when black communities go along and do what they're told. So they convinced the Mayor in the end. I lost, and the next morning there were the Mayor and Shanker smiling at each other in the *Times*. Of course the agreement broke down. The community felt humiliated and wouldn't stand for it. The next time I saw the Mayor, I told him, 'What did you expect?' He was furious at me. I should have kept my mouth shut."

During one stretch of time that fall the Ocean Hill–Brownsville experimental district appeared to be particularly vulnerable—a special session of the state legislature seemed imminent as a result of mounting pressure from white parents throughout the city who wanted the strike over and their children back in school. One evening in that period I went to the home of a young city planner with a highly responsible place in the city administration. He is black. Also present was his wife, who wears her hair Afro-style and also identifies herself as black, not Negro. She works for a private agency as an advocate for and with the poor in a Manhattan ghetto. Both have graduate degrees and are committed to working for change within "the system." They have friends, they told me, who have given up on the "system" but are accordingly alone with their anger in limbo.

The city planner and his wife had recently returned from a trip home, a large Eastern city. "There's a lot of division among black people there," he told me, "but in a deeper sense, they're united. They're moving in the same direction as black people in New York—toward getting power over their own institutions, like the schools. Of course, they're even more uptight there because if you're black and you're not subservient to the local political machine, you're locked out. Here at least black people have decent positions in the poverty program; militants can operate *within* the government. Look at the Council Against Poverty."

I was about to start asking him questions about his work with the Lindsay administration when a friend of his arrived. An urbane man in his fifties, the visitor projected considerable authority. From the initial conversation between him and the city planner, I assumed the newcomer worked in the same city agency as the young man but on a higher executive level. We all began talking about the school crisis. The city planner was worried. "This strike is going to be a near fatal blow to community control," he said. "That state legislature isn't going to go for anything real now."

The older man nodded but was more interested in discussing the Mayor's role during the teachers' strike. "He's been going this way and then that way, trying to walk the line."

The city planner kept trying to defend the Mayor. "What do you expect of him? He's a political animal. He's caught in a bind. If he goes with the teachers and the Jews, he alienates the blacks and Puerto Ricans. If he moves the other way, he's lost the white liberals."

"True," the visitor said. "But I wonder if he knows just how serious the situation is. I wonder if he knows that the people at the grass roots are ready to move if community control is threatened."

"Ready to move where?" the city planner's wife said bitterly. "Move to *what*? They could burn down all of Brownsville, and Shanker wouldn't have lost a bit of power. Let's be realistic. We are powerless."

"It's devastating, devastating." Her husband was pacing the room. "On the one hand, I'm with those black people who say, 'To hell with Lindsay's problems. We're not going to have any more of our children destroyed.' But on the other hand, if Lindsay doesn't have the support of liberal Jews to make basic structural changes in this city, he's locked in. He can't move. It's a bitch."

The conversation went on for some time. The older man never lost his aplomb. His anger at the United Federation of Teachers was intense but icily controlled. The young woman eventually grew silent but her husband, increasingly anguished, finally exploded. "These people are planning to put us in cages!" he shouted. Remembering that I was in the room, he turned to me, and said, "What I meant was that some of them are eager to put us in cages."

It was late, and I was reduced to abstract speculation. "What if the eight schools in Ocean Hill–Brownsville just dropped out of the school system and set up their own private complex with their own staff?"

"I've thought of that"—the city planner looked into his drink. "But they haven't the money, and nobody, not the Ford Foundation, nobody is going to give them that much money. No, I don't see any good way out of this for us. I do think Lindsay wants to do the right thing, but like I said, he's a political animal."

The visitor drove me home. "You know what the Mayor should have done, don't you?" he said as we moved downtown. "At the very beginning of that experiment, he should have made certain that the Board of Education set very clear guidelines for the district so that there would have been no questions as to what powers the local governing board had to transfer teachers out. All right, he didn't do that. The next thing he should have done, as soon as the U.F.T. went on strike, was to go on television as often as necessary to make the issues clear, to explain to everybody why those parents aren't going to stand still any more while the schools fail their kids. And he should have pointed out early, not late, that the U.F.T. was out to destroy that district."

"Would that approach have worked?"

"He couldn't be any worse off than he is now, but that's not what I'm talking about anyway. He would have done the right thing. That's what Lindsay's supposed to be all about, isn't he?" He laughed. "But then Lindsay is supposed to be a civil libertarian too. That's why George Wallace isn't going to speak at Shea Stadium." Still laughing, he dropped me off.

Wallace organizers had been negotiating for a rental of Shea Stadium with August Heckscher, Recreation and Cultural Affairs Administrator. After having made a ten-thousand-dollar deposit on the twenty-seven-thousand-dollar fee, they were suddenly told by Heckscher that the stadium was not available for "partisan rallies." I had been surprised because of the Mayor's strong record in Congress as a civil libertarian. I called one of his press aides when the decision was announced. The annoyed answer to my question was, "Does he have to take a position on *everything?*" I then asked a member of the cabinet if he knew what had happened. "I was there when it came up," he said. "Heckscher was all for giving Wallace the stadium, but Bob Sweet didn't think it was a good idea politically. John asked for a ruling from the Corporation Counsel. Well, Lee Rankin thought about it and came back with the conclusion that since no political rally had ever been held there, it was okay to remain consistent within that policy. John went along, which surprised me too. Then the State Supreme Court said Wallace *did* have a right to use the stadium, and the city appealed. By that point the Wallace people had switched the rally to Madison Square Garden. John made a bad decision, and he knows it. We were talking about something else the other day at Gracie Mansion; the Mayor suddenly turned to Sweet and Rankin and said, 'I disagree with you guys. We should have given them the stadium. I think we ought to drop out of the court case now.' But Rankin said we couldn't reverse ourselves at this point."

A few nights later I was at Gracie Mansion for a jam session. Jazz entrepreneur George Wein was about to send a group of prestigious musicians on a tour of Europe in alliance with the United States Travel Service, and the Mayor had agreed to act as host of a reception for the voyagers. I was standing at the door of the ballroom, listening to Gerry Mulligan and a rhythm section, when the Mayor walked by. He looked tired and thinner than the last time I'd seen him. I asked him about the refusal of Shea Stadium to Wallace. He grimaced. "We screwed it up. Somebody on the lower level made the wrong decision. I was surprised when Lee appealed it. That's error compounded. Well, this kind of thing happens once in a while."

I started to talk about the school dispute. The Mayor jammed his hands in his pockets and leaned against the wall. "I know where you stand," he said, "but there is *no* white support."

Disagreeing, I listed some of the city-wide groups being formed to support Ocean Hill–Brownsville.

"Not enough." The Mayor shook his head. "Not nearly enough."

"And support is growing in the press," I persisted.

"I know," he said wearily, "but they're late and it's all overshadowed anyway by this instant journalism day after day. The big play is always on whether there's going to be any violence. Look at how little they've run about what's actually going on inside those schools, the learning that's going on."

"But there have been a few articles on that," I said.

"Too late, not enough," the Mayor answered and walked away.

Dave Brubeck was in the hallway. "Hey." He came over. "I got a call from a woman who wanted my name in support of Humphrey. I said I'd give it if he promised to love his enemies and when elected, to turn around our resources so that we'll give to those in need. You know what she said? 'I'm sure Mr. Humphrey would subscribe to that.' Boy, politics!"

Gerry Mulligan was still playing. Hearing voices at the front door, I saw the black city planner and his wife coming in. I told him I wasn't sure I'd gotten the name of his guest the other night correctly. He gave it to me. "That's an impressive man," I said. "Just what does he do in the administration?"

"He's a driver," the city planner said coolly. "He drives commissioners around. Sure he's smart and he's damn articulate. But he's one of the brothers of his generation who said the hell with it early."

I listened to the rest of Gerry Mulligan's set. On the other side of the room, the Mayor, alone, was also listening, nodding his head. When Mulligan finished, I asked him how he felt being a sideman after all his years as leader of his own groups. He had recently joined Brubeck. "It's weird." Mulligan smiled. "I'm just for myself. No responsibilities. All I have to do is blow and enjoy myself. This way I can get down to basics. I like it fine." I told Mulligan he was a lucky man, and went home.

That Sunday night, on the Mayor's weekly television program on WNEW, a Puerto Rican girl asked, "Why is it that since you've become Mayor, we've had more strikes than ever before?"

"First of all," the Mayor answered, "here, as in all cities, there's a pile-up of unfinished business left over from previous administrations and previous ways of doing things. And furthermore, the city has no bargaining power. It's at the mercy of almost any powerful union. A private plant can close down. The city can't close down."

VI   The school situation was getting worse. On October 14, 1968, the United Federation of Teachers had called its third strike in six weeks because it claimed that eighty-three of its members were still in danger of being removed from their positions in Ocean Hill–Brownsville. The strike would not be ended, according to the union, until that experimental district had been dissolved. Meanwhile in Ocean Hill–Brownsville, where large numbers of police remained, the Board of Education had temporarily suspended the local governing board and its unit administrator, Rhody McCoy. The latter, however, remained in his office and continued to run the school district.

On the day the third U.F.T. strike began, I received a telephone call from William Strickland, a young black writer and activist who at one time had been head of the now-defunct Northern Student Movement. As usual, he spoke very softly and with great determination. He had been asked to set up a city-wide committee to meet with the Mayor to express support of Ocean Hill–Brownsville. Would I be on it? "But I don't represent anyone," I said. "That's all right. You're a citizen. You ought to be there." I had never been a member of a delegation to City Hall and thought the experience might be instructive.

Among those on our committee, I discovered, were two black legislators, State Senator Basil Paterson and Assem-

blyman Charles Rangel; a white assemblyman, Jerome
Kretchmer; Donald Harrington, minister of the Community
Church; Dr. Mamie Phipps Clark of the Northside Center
for Child Development; Aryeh Neier, executive director of
the New York Civil Liberties Union; Jesse Grey, who had
become best known for his leadership of rent strikes in
Harlem; David Dimkins of the One Hundred Black Men (a
group of civic officials and community leaders); the Reverend
Randy Nugent, executive director of MUST (Metropolitan
Urban Service Training Facility); Mrs. Edythe First of the
Citizens Committee for Children; and from the Public Education Association, Mrs. Angeline Pool and Mrs. Alvin Ba-
rach. Also to be with us was the Reverend C. Herbert Oliver,
chairman of the Ocean Hill–Brownsville governing board.

We met in the early afternoon at the MUST offices on
East Forty-ninth Street and agreed that on behalf of Ocean
Hill–Brownsville, the committee would request that the
Mayor immediately remove the police from that school dis-
trict and reinstate the local governing board and Rhody
McCoy. We would also request that the Mayor issue a state-
ment supporting community control of schools. "There's
one detail," Strickland said as the meeting ended. "Lindsay
won't be there. He and Leary are going to a hospital in East
New York to visit two cops who were shot by a sniper in
Brooklyn yesterday. So we're seeing Sweet."

Our appointment with the Deputy Mayor was for five
thirty. I arrived at City Hall a half an hour early to watch
a demonstration also supporting Ocean Hill–Brownsville.
Some five thousand people were filing past City Hall. The
majority was white, young, and good-humored. A black teen-
ager walked jauntily, holding up a sign:

> SEE SHANKER STRIKE
> STRIKE, SHANKER, STRIKE
> SEE TEACHERS FOLLOW
> FOLLOW, TEACHERS, FOLLOW

Several ranks behind, a white boy of about fourteen had his sign:

U.F.T. MATH

—TWO BLACKS + ONE PUERTO RICAN =

UNRULY MOB

The crowd began to jam into Murray Street, across from City Hall, to hear Rhody McCoy and other speakers. I was left at the barricades with several other committee members, police, and reporters. The black city planner came down the steps of the Hall. "You on City Hall detail?" I asked. "Well, today," he said. "Sweet's going to be a little late."

By the appointed time the rest of our committee had arrived. "It's a mistake," said Jesse Grey, a small, wiry man easily given to contention but in between times quite amiable. "We shouldn't go in there just to talk to an underling. Let's give The Man our piece of paper and leave."

Strickland, tall, thin, self-contained, came up as a policeman, on a wave from the black city planner, opened the barricades for us to enter. Halfway up the steps to City Hall, Strickland motioned for us to stop. "The Reverend Oliver has pulled out," he said calmly. "He doesn't want to see a deputy mayor."

"Well," said Assemblyman Rangel, "is it your sense that by going in, we'll be doing something contrary to what the Reverend Oliver wants?"

"The revolutionary responsibility works both ways," Strickland said firmly. "If Oliver had a question at Forty-ninth Street about meeting with Sweet, he should have raised it then."

We moved on and up. "That's a bad scene," the black city planner said to me with the flicker of a smile, "breaking with your black brother like that."

"Just remember," Jesse Grey grumbled, "I didn't want to go in at all."

We were shown into a large conference room, the Blue

Room, in the West Wing. The city planner stood at the door. Strickland nodded to him in recognition. "Earning money, baby, I see," Strickland said.

"It's the first time I had to earn it this way," the city planner answered.

After we had seated ourselves, the Deputy Mayor, smiling, walked in. As he began to speak, I felt as if I were listening to a tape recorder to which he was synchronized. "May I just preliminarily extend to you the hospitality of City Hall. I shall be glad to meet with you for as long as or short a time as is necessary. I understand the concern that has brought you here and I regret the Mayor is not present. Unfortunately for you, fortunately for me, you have to be satisfied with his deputy, which is me."

"Some of us," Assemblyman Rangel said, "would like to wait for his return."

"I can't give you an undertaking that he will be back," Sweet answered smoothly.

"We did think," Rangel continued, "that the Mayor would welcome our kind of support. We are a broadly representative group that backs his goals of school decentralization."

"I take your presence precisely in that sense."

"It seems to us, however," Strickland spoke, "that if the Mayor's schedule can be arranged to show concern for wounded policemen, it should also be arranged to show concern for the growing polarization in the city about the schools. Mr. Shanker has resources to make his position felt, resources of a size and order that are not available to us and to the children of Ocean Hill–Brownsville. We do feel we have the right to speak to our elected mayor. You, sir, are an appointed official."

"It is perfectly true," Sweet, unruffled, said, "that elected officials should be available to powerful constituencies, and this is one. And no one is more available than the Mayor; but for the Mayor to do his job, he must be able to determine whom he can meet and how he can best arrange his schedule. I can't tell you whether he'll be back tonight because I don't know."

"Nobody has more respect for policemen and for the wounded than I do," Rangel said grandly as Jesse Grey snickered in a back row, "but here we have a beautiful, peaceful demonstration outside—I've never seen one more beautiful—and it's a demonstration supporting the Mayor. *He's* declared the strike illegal. *He's* said the union has gone too far this time. It is insulting to us for him not to be able to arrange his priorities so that he can meet with us too."

Assemblyman Kretchmer, a dapper man in his thirties with a bold mustache, addressed the Deputy Mayor: "Tell us, what applications are you going to make in court? You're now in the third strike. Three strikes and you're out."

"I think," Sweet said, "that the Corporation Counsel has applied for sanctions against Mr. Shanker."

"But what about getting the schools open?" Kretchmer continued. "You're speaking for the Mayor. How are you going to get the schools open tomorrow?"

"The Mayor's efforts today," Sweet said serenely, "have been to contact everyone he can who might have a useful suggestion in that regard."

"Oh God," Jesse Grey groaned.

"The issue before us"—the Deputy Mayor ignored Grey—"is whether the Superintendent of Schools is going to run the schools or whether Mr. Shanker will. The Board of Education is meeting this afternoon. What will come of that I don't know. I have been in meetings with Mr. Shanker all week, and I don't think he will change his mind about the strike."

"So much for the issue before us," Grey said in a mock whisper.

Senator Paterson was annoyed. "What *about* getting the schools open? Why all the hesitation?"

"We might all agree," the Deputy Mayor said unhesitatingly, "that just the physical opening of the schools will go a long way to solving the problem."

"Yes," said Paterson. "Strange things can happen once the schools *are* open."

"I agree, I agree," said the Deputy Mayor.

There was silence as we searched for what had been agreed to. Assemblyman Rangel settled back in his chair. "I assume," he said, "you'd have no objection to our waiting for the Mayor if we are willing to inconvenience ourselves."

"Yes, I do!" For the first time there was an edge to the Deputy Mayor's voice. "I would object because we have not had any sit-ins at City Hall for some time. And we just cannot have any more. If there was a sense of hostility toward the Mayor in this delegation, if there was not a sense of shared objectives, it might be a different situation. But even then—"

"I don't think"—Jesse Grey was smiling—"that we're calling this a sit-in. What we're saying is that we're just resting until the Mayor returns."

"It is not our responsibility"—Strickland looked at Sweet as if the latter were a building—"that the Mayor is not here. This is a question of our expressing solidarity with Ocean Hill–Brownsville, and perhaps the best expression of our concern would be to extend our bodies here to show our solidarity with our brothers in the street."

Extend our bodies? It was apparently, I thought, going to be a lie-in rather than a sit-in. I began to have the distinctly uneasy feeling that before the night was over, I would be arrested. I heard shouts of solidarity in the street outside, but were they for me?

"Let me speak honestly and from the heart," the Deputy Mayor said. "I do have respect for you and the organizations which you represent. The Mayor is deeply committed to a whole host of activities devoted to the strike and ways to solve it. I really do not think you will be doing your cause any good by staying here."

"I would like to caucus the committee," Strickland said, rising. Sweet nodded, and strode out of the room. "I'm for staying," Rangel addressed the caucus. "That legislature I'm going to in January will be the most conservative in years. It's not going to give my community any reason to have faith in constitutional procedures. The only use I can be in that legislature is to dramatize this school situation, and it seems to me I can start doing that right now. Here."

I knew beyond any doubt, and was not cheered by the knowledge, that if the consensus was to stay, I would stay.

"If we stay," said Aryeh Neier of the New York Civil Liberties Union, "it will give Shanker a chance to point to us as another illustration of what he would call the illegality that is synonymous with community control. On the other hand, the Mayor has determined so far not to meet this issue head-on, and maybe we *can* put more pressure on him if this heterogeneous group of responsible citizens does stay."

"I don't see how anyone can call it illegal," said Rangel. "This is not a sit-in."

"Listen," Jesse Grey advised, "I've got some experience at this. I've had my head busted several times here, and I've been arrested here. Sure, it's not a sit-in—until they ask you to leave."

The black city planner came in. "Can I talk to you?" he said to Strickland. They left the room, and Strickland quickly returned alone. "I have some more information to feed to the committee," he told us. "They're all gone out there." He pointed toward the window. "They're marching to Brooklyn on the bridge."

Godspeed, Reverend Oliver, I thought. Would I were with you.

"I don't know about staying," Jerry Kretchmer resumed the debate. "Coming from the West Side, I may lose credibility with my constituency if I stay here and get arrested. I have to figure how I can be most effective."

"Hell," Jesse Grey said cheerfully, "I already lost my

credibility with *my* constituency just by coming in here, just by begging The Man. But I know what you mean. You and Charlie come from different kinds of districts. Look"—Grey stood up and leaned against the wall—"this struggle won't end today, whether we stay or go. The basic thing is we want to stay together even though we may disagree on incidentals. There's nothing wrong in a temporary retreat so that we can regroup our forces. I've made my move for rapprochement by coming in. I ought to be on that bridge right now. I think we should just back out."

Rangel was not persuaded. "Look, the Mayor is concerned that the black community may lose all trust in the system, that they may take things into their own hands. But he's also afraid of his political image and of what he'll lose by bucking Shanker and the unions behind him. I think if we stay, he may benefit by this show of support. And then I have to think of myself too. As an elected official, I don't feel good saying this, but we black legislators are castrated if we go back to our people without doing anything." He turned to Assemblyman Kretchmer. "You're right, Jerry, you go back to different people than I do."

Throughout the caucus, the white ladies from the Public Education Association and the Citizens Committee for Children had been silent but clearly anxious. Finally Mrs. First said, "I do think we've accomplished something by showing broad support."

"Okay," Rangel said. "Not everybody has to stay. If anyone walks out, we say, 'Thanks for hanging on as long as you have.' "

"Yes," Jesse Grey intervened again, "but why break our unity? The task is greater than anything that happens this one evening. We should find another evening and get broader forces for what we decide to do then."

Reverend Donald Harrington spoke. "That's a good idea. We're gathering support all the time, and I think we can run an ad showing how many different organizations *are* behind Ocean Hill–Brownsville. And there are other ways in which we can move. Also I do feel uneasy being here without Reverend Oliver. He's played it beautifully the last few days, putting the heat on Shanker, where it ought to be. We oughtn't to do anything to shift the focus."

At that point, although no vote had been taken, the question had obviously been decided. We all rose, some with more relief than others. "I'll leave the list of demands with The Man," Strickland said to Grey. Grey shrugged.

As I was leaving, Sid Davidoff and Barry Gottehrer, assistants to the Mayor, stopped me. "I expected you to be our guest for tonight," Davidoff said without smiling. I had no answer. "Listen," he went on, "the Mayor's really stringing himself out on this. What do you accomplish by sitting in?"

"We didn't sit in," I said.

"All right," Gottehrer was frowning, "but what about those people marching across the bridge. What do *they* accomplish?"

"I guess they thought it was the right thing to do at that point," I said.

"It doesn't help," Davidoff said gloomily. "It doesn't help. All it'll show is black people stopping traffic. Everybody will forget the nice, peaceful demonstration before they went on that bridge."

"What will help?" I asked. Davidoff shrugged.

Behind us the black city planner had stopped William Strickland. "Strick, what's your phone number?" Strickland gave it to him. "Will you be home later?" Strickland nodded.

I walked down the steps of City Hall with Aryeh Neier. "I was surprised," I told him, "that it turned out to be Jesse Grey counseling against breaking the law."

"It's like he said," Neier answered. "He's been arrested often enough before. He doesn't have to prove himself by staying. As a result, he can have a more realistic view of the situation."

A reporter from the *Times* was getting the names of the members of the committee. He stopped us. I gave him mine. "And whom do you represent?" he asked.

"The unaffiliated."

"What was going on in there?"

"We simply expressed our support of Ocean Hill–Brownsville," I told the press. "In unity."

VII A week and a half later, on a Saturday morning, I was reading the front page of the *Times*. The school strike was still on. A settlement proposed by State Education Commissioner James Allen had been rejected by Albert Shanker. Meanwhile the Patrolmen's Benevolent Association and the Uniformed Firefighters Association were conducting work slowdowns to pressure the city into reopening contract negotiations, and the leaders of the two unions had just defied a State Supreme Court order to cease that strategy. Also on the front page was a story about a city-wide rent revolt being planned for December by an organization of welfare recipients. This rebellion would consist of spending rent money on food, clothing and furniture to point up the inadequacy of the newly instituted flat grants of a hundred dollars a year for clothing and household items. Anticipated were mass evictions and corollary "occupations" of welfare centers and the lobbies of midtown hotels.

The telephone rang, and my wife answered. It was the Mayor. "How are you?" she said, and went on, without pause. "Well, how could you be?" She gave me the phone. The Mayor sounded remarkably brisk in view of what I'd just been reading. "How'd you like to play some touch football?" he asked. "We're having some people over. There'll be hamburgers later."

I hadn't played touch football, or any kind of football, for many years, but as my wife said on the way up to Gracie Mansion, "How can you not go? How often do you get to play touch football with the Mayor in the middle of the worst crisis the city has ever had?"

A large contingent of police was grouped outside the Mansion—the largest I'd ever seen there—in expectation of diverse groups of pickets. Perhaps including, I speculated, some of their colleagues. As we walked past the checkpoint, there was a whistle from within the ranks followed by "Look at the Yippie with the beard!" There was no other beard in view but mine. I turned, but everyone in the ranks was staring straight ahead. I suppose, I thought, I'm another mark against the Mayor. We went through the Mansion to the porch at the rear where Mary Lindsay greeted us. "Glad you could come. John thought of this at two in the morning. 'Let's have a party,' he said."

On the lawn were several members of the Mayor's cabinet, most of the young assistants to the Mayor, others of the more agile members of the administration, and several reporters. The Mayor, in chino pants and a green nylon parka, was tossing a football with zest. On the grass and on the porch were children, wives, and girl friends of the sportsmen. "Doesn't he look great?" A young woman looked at the Mayor. "He's the last Kennedy, even if he's not a Kennedy."

The Mayor came on to the porch. I asked him about chances of ending the teachers' strike. "Shanker thinks he'll win," the Mayor said, "if he can get a special session of the legislature. And he could be right. There's no telling what they'd do. They might kill decentralization entirely. But it has to be made clear to him that there's not going to be a special session."

"Is it clear to you that Rockefeller won't call one?"

The Mayor laughed. "At this point, I don't know." He ran back to the grass, shouting for the ball.

"Well, how come you're not out demonstrating or on

some delegation?" Sid Davidoff had appeared. "Yes, sir, you people took your stand and look where it got us."

"I still think there's a lot more white support for Ocean Hill–Brownsville than the Mayor realizes," I said.

"Oh, sure," Davidoff answered, "there's support all over the city. There are whites everywhere just waiting for the blacks to come out of their holes so they can bop them over the head."

The Mayor summoned us to the field of play. Only a few of us were even moderately proficient. In the awkward majority, I spent most of the next hour as a lineman trying to block Fred Hayes, Director of the Budget, a most determined man. The Mayor was in the backfield of the opposition. On both sides, the plays were daring in conception, but as often happens in the city, the follow-through was fragmented. Most of the passes, for example, were incomplete. The Mayor, however, seemed to be having a particularly invigorating time—running hard, tagging hard. At one point, as we plotted a complex maneuver in our huddle, we suddenly realized the Mayor was among us. "Well," he said with a grin, "I always like to be in on the decision-making," and loped back to his side.

After the Mayor's forces had decisively triumphed, we all went into the ballroom for lunch. It was a cheerfully domestic scene for the headquarters of a city undergoing multiple crises. Children, hotdogs in hand, raced around the room; cabinet members, assistants to the Mayor, and their wives were sprawled on chairs and on the floor. Alone, Police Commissioner Leary was looking out the window at a touch football game in Carl Schurz Park. An aide to the Mayor was talking to a young woman about John Doar, the new president of the Board of Education. Doar had worked in the Justice Department under Robert Kennedy and had specialized in civil-rights cases. "If anybody can be a force for reconciliation, it's Doar," the aide said. "He's so fair, so slow, so straight, so *goyish*."

"Right now," the young woman said, "I'm not so sure that what's needed is another *goyisch* type."

Another of the Mayor's young assistants was disturbed by an imminent complication that might result from the teachers' strike. "If it doesn't get settled soon," he said, "there are going to be awful problems in preparing for Election Day. With the custodians siding with the teachers and keeping most of the schools locked, can we get them all open in time to deliver the voting machines? And if we do get them open, and the strike is still on, voters may have to cross picket lines. And in that case, defeated candidates could charge they lost votes because some of their supporters had been restrained from going in. Not physically, but you know, there are people who won't cross picket lines. It could be a real mess."

"And John Lindsay," a colleague of the assistant said gloomily, "could become the first mayor in the history of the city under whom people were not able to vote. Great."

About to leave, I went over to say good-bye to the Mayor. "Want another beer?" he asked.

I declined, and said, "You looked in good shape out there."

He shook his head. "My H.I. is still up though."

"H.I.?"

"Hostility Index." The Mayor grinned. "I haven't played tennis for a week. I get more aggression out that way than in touch football."

"Rhody McCoy feels the same way," I said. "He plays as often as he can."

"When this is all over," the Mayor leaned against a wall, "we're going to have a game. I hear he's very good."

During that indoor picnic at Gracie Mansion, I had met for the first time a relatively new assistant to the Mayor, Jeff Greenfield. Twenty-five, he had been a legislative aide for the late Senator Robert Kennedy. In Greenfield's brief time with the Lindsay administration, he had already impressed several cabinet members I knew. "He's not only very bright," one of them told me, "but he really does believe the cities are where the action is now. John keeps talking about the new urbanists. Well, Greenfield is a quintessential example of what he means."

In mid-November, I went to City Hall to see Greenfield. The teachers' strike was over, a settlement having been reached before Election Day. The police and firemen had stopped their slowdowns; and the plan for a rent revolt by welfare recipients had been abandoned because the tacticians had decided it wouldn't have sufficiently broad support. But the city was hardly at peace. There were still tensions in the schools; the police and firemen continued to press for new contract negotiations; and other municipal unions were trumpeting alarms in preparation for new rounds of contract renewals. Meanwhile everyone, from residents of ghettos to tenants in luxury apartment houses, appeared to agree that crime was increasing. And *The New York Times* had recently complained that "New York ranks as one of the most polluted cities in the nation, and yet the fight against air pollution, which should have been an all-out war, limps along as a left-footed affair marked mostly by strategic retreats."

Appropriately, as it seemed to me, the skies were gray the morning I went downtown to see Greenfield. Yes, this is where the action is, I thought, if one considered Sisyphus to have been an activist. Early for my appointment, I walked around City Hall. On all four sides, there were stacks of police barricades in readiness. Not for any particular demonstration planned for that day. Just in readiness. I remembered my visits during the first year of the Lindsay administration when most of the time there had been no barricades at all.

Greenfield was on the telephone when I was shown into his office on the first floor of City Hall. Sandy-haired, short, self-assured, crisply informal, Greenfield, smoking a pipe, ended the call and I asked him what his responsibilities were as an assistant to the Mayor. "Research and intergovernmental affairs," he answered. "Doesn't that sound fancy? Actually the two main areas I work in are speeches and legislation."

"Does the Mayor do much rewriting of the speeches you put together?"

"He rewrites," Greenfield said, "more than almost anybody I've ever heard of. He's good on precision. I tend to use vague phrases at times, and those are the ones he'll almost always pick up. 'That's not what we mean,' he'll say."

"What about the way he delivers them?" I asked. "He used to be quite stiff when he read from a text."

"He's getting much less so"—Greenfield lit his pipe— "although he's still best when he ad-libs. Like at the Park Avenue Synagogue a few days ago. The audience was kind of cold at first. He gave a short speech in which he was very candid, very open, talking about what the schools had been doing to the children in the ghettos and going on to explain why there was so strong a feeling in those communities that the schools had to be made accountable. The audience was becoming somewhat warmer. Then in the question period, he was especially effective, and by the end he really had them wrapped up. Remember, Bobby Kennedy wasn't a good speaker either when he had to deal with prepared texts. He really came through in answer to questions which let him get spontaneously into what most interested him. The effects of poverty, for example. Lindsay's the same way. When he's into something he really cares about and can talk without a piece of paper in the way, the caring shows. Before I came here, I didn't think he was capable of expressing that much feeling. I know better now."

I asked Greenfield what his work on legislation consisted of. "Well, for example," he put his feet on his desk and leaned back, "I'm working on federal legislation that would provide underwriting from Washington for the general police

costs of the cities. To a significant extent, crime, after all,
is a national problem, intensified as it is by the migration to
cities caused by national trends in unemployment. I'm hoping
to get the Conference of Mayors and the Urban Coalition
behind this kind of bill as well as a bipartisan group of
legislators from urban centers to introduce it. I don't know
if anything will come of it because it's such a departure
from the usual way of earmarking federal funds. But it's
worth trying.

"My main interests, however, lie in other kinds of legislation." Greenfield was now walking around the room. "Ever
since law school at Yale, I've been trying to get as specific as
I can in devising legislation for community control and decentralization. One of the things that most impressed me
about Kennedy's people was that they did have specific legislative ideas in that direction. Take his plan for tax incentives
to stimulate businesses to go into the ghettos. That's been
attacked, I know, as a cop-out, a sop to business, but the
critics don't mention that the Kennedy bill had provisions
in it for real community involvement in the decision-making
that went along with such corollary ideas as community development corporations.

"What I particularly want to focus on now," Greenfield
continued, "are ways to involve whites in community control. The Wallace vote came from people who are also alienated, from whites who have been deracinated by excessive
centralization. From their perspective, they feel as impotent
in terms of affecting decision-making as the black poor do. I
think you're going to see among people working on urban
affairs a growing understanding of the needs of the white
lower middle class. Look at this city. Community action, as
it's been used in the poverty program, isn't geared to the
needs of white communities. The notion of an Urban Task
Force is suited to neighborhoods like Harlem, East Harlem,
Bedford-Stuyvesant, where there are street organizations and
street spokesmen. White neighborhoods, on the other hand,

are more formally organized. In Flatbush or Midwood, you'll find fifty or sixty organizations, but you don't know which ones to connect with to get anything done. There ought to be ways in which these organizations could be really involved in restoring the sense of a neighborhood as a place in which you participate in its affairs rather than a place where you just take refuge. Sure, there are limitations to what a community can do for itself. As Paul Goodman says, there are some things you can't decentralize. You can't solve air pollution that way. That takes city-wide and regional planning. And the answer to excessive crowding in the subways is to get more cars and build more subways. But there are things people can work on by themselves, if they get the money. I don't understand, for instance, why there couldn't be small federal and city grants of seed money so that local groups could turn grim subways in their neighborhoods into more enjoyable places. And school decentralization can have real meaning for whites too if they can get more involved in the schools and see that a lot more could be done for *their* kids.

"In working out specific legislation of this kind"—Greenfield was back at his desk—"the problem is that you need an awful lot of time. Nothing is easier than to formulate a marvelous plan, but to take hold of a city like this and make your plan realistic, viable and politically possible is an enormous undertaking. I know the Mayor is interested in moving in this direction, but with all the other pressing problems he has, drafting legislation of this sort may not even wind up as a priority of the city. But it's going to be a particular interest of mine because I still insist it can be done."

I asked Greenfield whether his interest in decentralization had been the main reason he had decided to come to work for the Mayor. "Oh, it wasn't as thought out as that," Greenfield said. "When Kennedy was killed, I decided I might write. But I found out I didn't have the discipline to do it full-time. I get more writing done in my spare time now than I did when that was my 'vocation.' I'm finishing a book on popular music, for instance. The other alternative I had was teaching at a law school in Southern California where the climate is nice. But then I got called to talk to the Mayor. He's a guy I'd always admired. A lot of the Kennedy people didn't like him, but I hadn't shared that feeling. Sure, he's different from Kennedy; he has his own assets and liabilities. But *fundamentally,* like Kennedy, the Mayor is willing to put himself on the line for what he feels deeply are the right things to do. Now that is not the most common attribute of American politicians.

"When I talked to him about coming here, it was a time, I felt, of real despair about what was happening to this country. I decided that if he wanted me, I'd give it a whirl. In that first meeting, several weeks after Kennedy was killed, Lindsay spoke very somberly about where the country was going. He impressed me with how concerned he was. He had convictions, and he was committed to act on them. I also found out that the cliche of his being a lightweight—a guy who looked good but didn't have much brains—just didn't apply. Now that cliche is changing to: 'He's very bright but he's not an intellectual.' I hear a lot of that in New York, but those Kennedy-McCarthy primaries, in which I was somewhat biased, changed my impression of the way the intellectual community in this city makes its political judgments of people They didn't care how McCarthy had voted, but he writes poetry. Whoopee! Look, Lindsay has clear ideas and principles, he takes stands on them, and I don't care if he footnotes what he says if that's what is meant by being an intellectual.

"This whole business"—Greenfield was up, pacing again —"of characterizing people in public life is so weird. All those who *know* Lindsay is this or is that. On what do they base their judgments? On interpretations by people who really don't know a hell of a lot themselves. The so-called well-informed intellectuals interested in politics read the news analyses and the political coverage in the *Times*; they read the *New York Review of Books* and maybe *News-*

week and such columnists as Evans and Novak. And on that
basis, they come up with the most facile assumptions. In
Bobby Kennedy—and this is true of Lindsay too—there was
a certain tensile strength and an intellectual core when you
saw him day after day rather than just reading about him.
But the intellectual community didn't know that. You remember Kennedy was supposed to be the kind of person
who was fed ideas and quotations for his speeches. Oh, he
might select from among them but he wasn't a *real* reader.
Well, during the campaign last spring, we were working on
a speech and he said, 'Why not use this line from Agamem-
non?' And he pulled the book out of his pocket. What bugs
me is so many intellectuals simply assumed he wasn't a serious reader of poetry because nobody had told them he was.
Lindsay's the same way. He'll suggest lines from poems he's
been reading. Yet there are people who claim to *know* that
John Kennedy—I mean Lindsay—is not the kind of man who
reads poetry."

Greenfield had returned to his chair, swiveled around a
full circle, and said, "Did you ever realize that out of this
way of 'knowing' things from magazines and political columnists, there are five or six anecdotes about a guy which will
be cited to you again and again as the core of a man. And
all these people think they're informed!"

I asked Greenfield, as one who had been informed by
close working contact, about the differences between the late
Senator and the Mayor. "In a way," he said, "I think Lindsay
is an easier person to talk to than Kennedy was. Kennedy
was withdrawn a lot of the time. There was a sense about
him that kept most people distant. Lindsay's personality is
more easy-going. You see, that too is counter to the con-
ventional wisdom which insists he's stuffy. But they were
alike in having excellent senses of humor, particularly in
private. The Mayor's is very mordant, very irreverent, but I
guess that's a way people in high position have of keeping

their sanity. Maybe he ought to show more of that streak of humor publicly.

"The pressures"—Greenfield filled his pipe—"the pressures on him are incredible. Look at the school thing. He knew from the beginning that however it turned out, his administration would inevitably get the blame. With such deep divisions in the city, neither side is going to get all it wants, and whom do they both find as the target for their frustration? The Mayor, of course. I've been very impressed with how he's handled himself during this whole conflict. Sure, he had his highs and lows, depending on how tough the pressures were from day to day, but he didn't succumb to these pressures. You've got to keep in mind how terribly involved people were emotionally. This wasn't an ordinary labor argument. It was much more intense than 'Why isn't my garbage being picked up?' Most people seemed to be in a state of hysteria. The letters that came in *shrieked!* Obviously it was the most serious thing he's gone through, but he maintained his sense of humor, and he kept trying. It would have been easier for him at various points to just throw up his hands and wait for Allen, the State Commissioner of Education, to take over. But every day, the Mayor was working on specific ways to resolve the dispute. He just kept at it. He wasn't getting enough sleep, he was being attacked from all directions, but he would not let it defeat him *inside.* This is a very strong man."

"How badly do you think he's been damaged politically?" I asked.

Greenfield whooped. "If you're going to ask me about his political future, in view of what's happened this year, and if you think I'll make any prediction, you are out of your skull. By election time next fall, we may have the Second Coming with Christ on the ticket for president of the City Council. Maybe a three-toed Neanderthal will run and win."

Harry O'Donnell, the Mayor's large and outwardly im-
perturbable press secretary at the time, walked in and handed
Greenfield a piece of paper. The young man nodded and
smiled. "Good. I knew if O'Donnell was on it, it would be
done. Harry"—Greenfield pointed in my direction—"I'm
leaking him the information that John's running for controller in 1969."

O'Donnell, without expression, said to me, "Remember
V is the middle initial," and left.

I told Greenfield of the sense I'd felt earlier that morning
that the Mayor, strong as he is, was engaged in the labors of
Sisyphus. "Sure, the city will endure," I said. "But can it be
made a better place to live in? By anybody?"

Greenfield, putting his feet back on his desk, looked out
the window. "In some ways," he began, "I think the press
is right in giving the impression that the city is being continually assaulted by absolutely conflicting interests. But there's
a difference now. As I can figure it out, before Lindsay's guys
came in, New York was run literally without thinking of
what would eventually happen to a city of eight million people if you kept doing things in a jerry-built way. It was as if
they were making a building—putting on parts sideways,
vertically, circularly—without any concern for what it would
eventually look like or how it would work as a whole. They
kept adding wing after wing—in the middle of the air.

"Now I'm not using this as a cop-out, but the Lindsay
administration has come to grips with what amounts to thirty
years of chaos. But it was quiet chaos. The only way to prevent ultimate disintegration was to start really changing
things, even if those changes caused serious discomfort. Lindsay's people are immersed in the difficulties of actual problem-solving. We don't build wings in the middle of the air
any more. The school system, for example, had to be changed,
had to be decentralized. Under Wagner, the ghetto schools
were getting worse and worse. Obviously they're still bad,

but at last a real attempt is being made to finally *do* something about them. And naturally everybody's shrieking.

"For another example, we now have a tough anti-pollution law and the city is taking a lot of flak because its own incinerators won't be upgraded in time for the deadline set by that law. But the point is that something *is* being done about air pollution for the first time. Why wasn't that tough a law passed before? Because there finally is an administration with a sense that problems have to be attacked in the open, even if the administration gets hurt in the process. *That's* the stiff-necked quality about Lindsay I admire. He knew he'd have to take an awful lot of political heat by letting all these problems come out in the open rather than making patch-up, short-term arrangements behind the scenes which would solve nothing basically. The thing is that he and his people are making attempts—even if they're sometimes half-assed—to really come up with solutions.

"And the Mayor is on top of those attempts. A while ago, he was talking to Fred Hayes about getting new kinds of sanitation trucks that can do double the work in half the time. They operate on some kind of suction principle so that they can get underneath parked cars and in other ways pick up a lot more stuff. I was astonished—and somewhat abashed at my own ignorance—to hear the Mayor of a city with as many problems as this one talk so precisely about how the god-damned trucks work. He really is a hard study. He picks up that kind of stuff, retains it, relates it to other problems, and that's how he really does know what's going on.

"But all of that is in the context of the man's genuine sense of public service. That's what some people mean, I suppose, when they call him stuffy. Or what was it they used to call him—'The White Knight'? People are just not accustomed to that kind of mayor. A president can get away with setting moral imperatives, but the mayor is supposed to be the guy who cleans the streets. He said he was elected to change the city, and that's what he went on to do because that's what he *should* be doing. Now, those people who call him stuffy are usually the same people who say that he doesn't basically understand the realities of the city, the conflicting interest groups. Of course he understands them; but he's chosen not to play the old games.

"At the core of what this administration is all about," Greenfield went on, "is a continuing analysis of how to get things working, and people working, with greater efficiency and with a clear sense of direction. A small example. In 1966, much of the equipment in the sanitation department was in bad shape. Trucks were old and kept breaking down. I'm told there were times when only half of them were operating. Okay, it became clear, on analysis, that the way to really improve the functioning of that department was to buy enough new equipment so that repair costs could be sharply cut while more garbage was being collected faster. That's simple planning. Here, look." Greenfield picked up a copy of the city's 1968–9 Executive Budget and pointed to a page. "The replacement of 1,000 collection trucks—over two-thirds of the fleet—over the next year and a half by larger and more efficient models," I read, "will have a lasting effect on the Department's operations. The average age of trucks in the fleet, now eight years, will be reduced to an average of two years by the end of the coming fiscal year. The City intends to maintain a five-year replacement cycle for collection trucks to reduce maintenance and repair costs."

Greenfield leaned back. "As I say, that was a simple solution, but in terms of the city's past, a remarkable one. Similarly, money is being put into buying air-conditioned buses and new subway equipment because in the long run, it makes *sense* to do it that way instead of just stumbling along, patching things up. Obviously there are other problems you can't handle just by placing more funds in the capital budget. But what you can do is face them in such a way that the depth of those problems become clear to every-

body. Sure, the school thing revealed a lot of tensions between blacks and Jews in this city, but it's important that
those tensions finally came to the surface. How are you going
to deal with them until you know how deep they are and
what caused them? And it's now clear to everyone how very
dissatisfied the ghetto communities have been with their
schools. Now *that's* in the open and people are organizing to
change those schools. Lindsay might well have had a much
more peaceful city if he'd been willing to go along with the
way things used to be done, but he's sacrificed the chance for
more resigned tranquillity by insisting on action for change."

"Are you going to stay in urban affairs for the foresee-
able future?" I asked.

"I'm going to stay with Lindsay," Greenfield answered,
"because he's a guy worth walking a long way with. For all
the reasons I've given you, and for one more. He treats his
assistants and subordinates with remarkable consideration,
and that's a rare quality. An awful lot of good political people
don't have it. This man is aware of the feelings of the people
who work for him, and he'll accommodate to them instead of
always demanding that everything be done in only one way—
his. As for myself, I have other interests in addition to urban
affairs, and I have serious doubts about working *within* any
institution at all. But until he chooses otherwise, I'm keeping
on with this man."

VIII Outside Greenfield's office, I saw a pile of
thick, paperbound books, issued by the Bu-
reau of the Budget for the 1969–70 fiscal year and titled
Program/Budget Instruction. In view of what Greenfield had
been saying about analysis and planning being at the core of

the Mayor's approach to city government, I was particularly interested in that section of the introduction devoted to the term, "PPBS," which I'd been hearing with great frequency from assistants to the Mayor and other city officials:

> During the next 18 months, the Bureau of the Budget together with the administrations will undertake to complete the development and installation of a City-wide planning-programming budgeting system (PPBS). The system must meet both general budgetary requirements and the distinct management needs of individual programs and agencies. . . . PPBS is a tool for improving understanding and decision making. It is based on three premises—namely, that:
> The City should identify the objectives of municipal services—i.e., the results it wants to achieve by providing these services
> Different ways (i.e., alternatives) usually exist to achieve these objectives
> The decision maker should be informed about the costs and the effectiveness of the alternatives open to him so that better choices can be made. Thus, PPBS helps to improve decisions on: (1) how to make individual programs operate more effectively and efficiently, and (2) how much emphasis an agency should give to different programs . . .
> Besides aiding the Mayor and the Bureau of the Budget in making budgeting decisions, the PPB system should be useful in agencies in planning and controlling their own operations. It strengthens management by: (1) linking resources and activities to results; (2) framing the choices to be made among program emphasis; (3) providing yardsticks for evaluating performance; and (4) facilitating coordination among agencies operating related programs under separate auspices. Administrations just getting under way will find the PPB effort especially valuable. Furthermore, all agencies will be able to justify their budget requests better to the Bureau of the Budget and the Mayor, since the supporting documentation for budget requests will be developed in the course of analyzing issues and alternatives.

If PPBS had become the core of the Lindsay administration, the man at the core of PPBS was Frederick O'R.

Hayes, whom the Mayor had appointed Director of the Budget in August 1966. Hayes was then Deputy Director for Community Action Programs in the Office of Economic Opportunity and had previously held federal executive positions in the Urban Renewal Administration as well as having worked for eleven years in the United States Bureau of the Budget. When he announced Hayes's appointment, the Mayor had called him "one of the toughest budget men in the United States." In also describing Hayes as "one of a new breed: the urbanists," the Mayor had predicted that "in bringing his tough-minded methods to New York, he will be the key man in putting the city on a new budget planning basis."

"He *is* the key man," Mitchell Ginsberg had told me soon after Hayes had started his third year as the city's Director of the Budget. "He has great influence on the Mayor. If I had to pick one guy who has the largest impact on policy in this city, it would be Hayes. You ought to go see him. You'll learn something. He's as qualified an urbanist as you'll find anywhere."

I took Ginsberg's advice on an afternoon in December 1968. Hayes's office in the Municipal Building near City Hall is large, sparely furnished, and brightened principally by his children's crayon drawings on the wall behind his desk. He is a youthful forty-five, of medium height, wears glasses, speaks quickly and softly, and projects formidable authority. It is the authority of lucid expertise and firmness of direction. The latter quality I had experienced during the touch football game on the lawn of Gracie Mansion.

I was curious as to why he had come to the city after fifteen years in Washington. "My first reaction," Hayes said, "was not to come. John asked me in March of 1966. I thought about it for a week, and turned him down. It probably would have ended there, but I gather he had trouble finding someone, and meanwhile, since I was in O.E.O., I was in frequent contact with the city and so the possibility of my coming was kept half alive. Finally, at the beginning of July, he asked me again and I said I'd come if I could make my wife happy in New York. It's hard to move after fifteen years in a city. Actually though, this was a job I really thought I wanted to try because of the challenge it set. I figured I was as sophisticated as I'd get in terms of working in federal agencies, and now I ought to learn about cities. Another factor that helped me change my mind was the quality of the people Lindsay was getting. In March, the only guy he had in his administration whom I knew and felt to be a pro was Mitch Ginsberg. But by July, he had Jay Nathan in housing, Cyril Tyson in manpower development, and a number of other people I thought were pretty good, some very good. On the lower levels too, some real pros were coming aboard.

"A basic problem here, I found out quickly, is the same one in administration anywhere in the country—adapting old bureaucracies to new problems. It's tough," Hayes said, "getting them up to higher levels of responsiveness, opening them to innovations. That's a primary difficulty everywhere —getting more porosity into our governmental and social institutions. It has been happening in the Federal Budget Bureau, but porosity of any degree is still relatively rare elsewhere in government.

"We've made quite a bit of progress here, I think," Hayes continued in an even, fast flow, "but progress has its problems too. Every time you do something better in an area, you simultaneously discover more problems. For example, you design a new program and it works logically but only if you can find management talent to carry it through. We have some fine men, many from Washington, but we still have only a fraction of the number of really good people we need to run this city right. It's not much trouble getting first-rate youngsters, but it's harder to find the kind of people you need on the senior level—those who are very bright at management and can also relate to other people.

"We've got the Bureau of the Budget itself into shape,

but we're a relatively small operation. The larger problems are with the big city agencies. There's the sheer magnitude of what's needed to make them efficient and then the extraordinary scarcity of personnel with management capacity in American society. Even American businesses have enormous trouble getting people who can run things and run them well. Management is a subtle and difficult skill. The whole pattern in corporations and in much of government has tended to create organization men, people who are knowledgeable in rather specialized activities but who do not have the capacity for real managerial analysis."

Hayes drummed his fingers on the desk. "In fact," he went on, "the training of professionals in nearly every area is just not oriented in this direction. Suppose you're superintendent of a school system with ten thousand students. You want to start team-teaching in two junior highs and one high school. How are you going to design the right program for your particular needs, a program which may well require considerable innovation? How are you going to select your staff in terms of the results you want? What results *do* you want? Have you figured out how to evaluate the cost efficiency of the program? That is, what results would justify this program expenditure? Well, you don't get that kind of training in schools of education. Where is there training to be an educational innovator and analyst? Where is there such training in any field? But admittedly, people do come along who can design good innovative programs. Okay, but knowing how to design a program and running it are two different things.

"And then," Hayes calmly added another dimension of difficulty, "there's a third quality needed which is just as rare. In addition to people who can create innovative programs through real analysis and people who can go on to run those programs, you also need personnel with a capacity for feedback—people with the sensitivity to evaluate what is actually happening as a result of any given program and who can use that information to sharpen or change the structure. That's also what I mean when I say that first-rate personnel is scarce.

"There's another fundamental problem in New York," Hayes said as I wondered how this ceaseless conjugator of problems could maintain such equanimity. "It's a problem that especially strikes management people who come here from a federal agency. They all say they've never seen anything like this city because the availability of information is so primitive. I mean fiscal information. In an ordinary federal agency of no great efficiency—take Housing and Urban Development—on the tenth of the month, you ordinarily expect and get a list of all grants, expenditures, and obligations. By the last I mean money that's been allocated but not yet spent. And perhaps you also get some evaluation of what's going on. In New York however, finding out how much a particular operation is costing becomes a research project. But analysis of costs is a very important tool of management, as is analysis of what it would cost to do some things differently. Again, we *are* making some progress, but we still don't have nearly enough information in a number of areas. There's more information available, for instance, from indifferently run voluntary hospitals than we have yet from our city hospitals. A further complication of that problem is that when centralized activities are taking place in large field operations—hospitals are an example—or when there is a sizable letting of contracts to third parties, as in the poverty operation, you worry not only about insufficient information but also about whether you're able to *deliver* anything at all.

"However," Hayes said, "after two and a half years, I can say that the habit of internal analysis has begun to take root in certain agencies—notably the Police and Fire Departments, housing, environmental purification, and health. They're learning how to analyze program options and how to create supporting information systems while building staffs to handle both functions. I think it's going to work out very well in time."

"What if the Mayor doesn't run for re-election?" I asked. "Or is defeated if he does? Will all this work have been wasted?"

"I suppose," Hayes answered, "there could be a slipping back to a considerable extent. It's hard to say how much, and where. But something has to remain after all that's been started. And I expect that one durable mark we will have made—if there is no second term—is the change that's been established in the way the bureaucracy moves. I can't imagine anyone new coming in who would not want to retain PPBS. That kind of analysis and program planning simply makes complete sense, quite apart from what party you belong to. It seems to me that anyone in charge would want to have the tools to really know what the bureaucracy is doing.

"However, in the event of a new administration, many of our programs under PPBS might not survive unless there were enough people coming in who could handle them. The problem of recruiting managerial personnel of high quality could well be even greater for a different administration than it's been for us. It's easy enough to demonstrate all the advantages in this kind of planning but you also have to generate enough excitement to attract people to work for the city. And that is the most difficult element to arouse. It's in this area that John has had a particularly important impact. I can pull in people from Harvard Business School and guys out of law school who have been on the law review, because they want to be where action, where change, is taking place. But why am I able to do that when for twenty years this city was hardly that successful in attracting people of this quality? The answer is Lindsay. Our interviewers sell John Lindsay. That's what it takes—a man who is a symbol of change, who makes young people of high quality believe there's a reason for them to come here. Okay, maybe a new administration's interviewers will be able to sell someone else. But can you name a person who creates the degree of national interest among the young that John does?

"I don't mean to imply"—Hayes did not wait for an answer—"that John is just some kind of magnetic figurehead. When management people get here, they find out soon enough that he knows what's going on. He's extraordinary in the amount and variety of material he can absorb. For example, this office sent out fairly stiff reading material to the heads of the various administrations in which we explained what PPBS is all about. Because it was so detailed, I had not intended a copy to go to the Mayor but somehow he got hold of one, and as he put it when he saw me around that time, 'I read every damn thing in that.'

"And having absorbed so much material, he proceeds to act on the basis of great confidence in objective analysis of problems. I find this unusual in a politician. Most of those I've known will *say* they're all for objective analysis, but actually they take a taxicab driver's approach to problem-solving. You know, the concept that any intelligent man who keeps his radio on can give you an informed opinion on just about anything. Most politicians actually do operate that way. They don't really want objective analysis; it might interfere with what they *know*. John is quite different. He really believes in it. And he does a lot more homework than many politicians.

"Furthermore," Hayes said, "he's different in other ways. He doesn't go at things in the way Sargent Shriver did, for instance, when he was head of O.E.O. Unlike Shriver, John doesn't assume that most of the staff is incompetent and is trying to put him in an embarrassing situation. John encourages free play of opinion and argument. In fact, he relies on that kind of exchange as a way of finding other and better ways of doing things. He's open, he's not defensive, and so he stimulates the people around him to be frank and open. He doesn't hold back, and he doesn't want them to. If we come in from this office, for example, with a plan to which one of the administrators objects, John will ask that man to find the holes in it and to prove that they are indeed holes. And then we have to support *our* position.

"This free play of ideas along with John's being open and accessible is how we're able to hold the crackerjack young people he's attracted. Some of them are quite fantastic, and we're able to use them directly with the Mayor. They get right into the planning and decision-making. That's an important factor in keeping morale up. I'll admit this causes problems with some of the heads of the administrations. I mean some people in authority who feel, 'I'm not going to be told how to run my operation by some twenty-four-year-old pipsqueak.' Then it's up to me to do some healing work. John, you see, doesn't differentiate by generation or by title. If one of these young people knows what he's talking about, John listens. In fact, I rather think he prefers working with the young people. And it's that quality of responsiveness to *anyone* who has something real to say that characterizes John on the street side of things. He really listens to blacks and Puerto Ricans. This is a guy who is willing—in talking or reading—to take ideas from all kinds of sources. He doesn't limit himself."

Hayes put his feet on the desk, and after a pause, said, "I'll tell you what may be the most crucial quality John has. Crucial for this city. He has an enormous interest in running the city and a great disinterest in politics in the broad sense of the word. Oh, I'm not saying that there aren't times when he has to and does take political considerations into account, but he's really not interested in that aspect of the job. It's action and change, it's making over the city, that absorbs him. I keep contrasting him with Shriver, because Shriver did have a very acute interest in the more traditional ways of politics. You'd be going over a grant with him, and you could see him immediately picturing the size of the headlines in the *Podunk Press* the morning after the announcement. And you could see him anticipating the reactions of those congressmen most concerned. Now that is usually a politician's primary area of interest, but it's not John's."

"In a way though," I asked, "hasn't his disinterest in traditional political tactics been a mistake? I mean particularly with regard to many whites in this city who claim he hasn't shown sufficient interest in them. And they would go on to say that he has been very much the old-style politician in the way he's dealt with black people and Puerto Ricans."

"Yes, I know," Hayes said. "I've had a lot of cab drivers like that. 'All he cares about is the colored.' Well, there's no question that he now does need to open lines to the lower-middle-class and working-class whites. And more than lines. But when he came into office, his first priority, as he had diagnosed it during his campaign for Mayor, was to do something about the huge lack of communication which had developed between the ghettos and City Hall. It's taken him a long time to defuse all that distrust—which, if it had remained unchanged or gotten worse, would have become a very serious factor by now. Moreover, he had to get their support for action and change, and so that was another reason he had to work on ways of getting their confidence. How do you do that? By showing you really care about how blacks and Puerto Ricans feel about things and by finding out what they want.

"But it is true," Hayes said, "that in all the great urban areas, alienation—the lack of even a minimal sense of being part of a community—is a problem that affects all people, not only blacks and Puerto Ricans. On the one hand, the strain of the very environment—from air pollution to noise—intensifies that feeling of being rootless and besieged, creating a beastly situation. And on the other hand, whatever attempts are being made to improve that situation do not give the citizen any sense that he's been consulted. The typical resident of New York is even worse off because we're into more things than any other city in the county. We're trying to make changes in so many different areas simultaneously that the typical citizen is confronted with the incomprehensibility of nearly everything we do. Obviously, this creates problems for a mayor. And certainly John has more problems with the alienation of *whites* than the mayor of any other big city because he has taken particular care to open lines to black and Puerto Rican ghettos. That's why we need more decentralization here, in *all* neighborhoods, so that people can get a feeling of having some control of what happens to them. If there is a second term, that's going to be a primary order of business."

Hayes looked at his watch. "I was thinking about that when I was in London a few months ago. I hadn't realized the degree of decentralization they have there, with the various boroughs fitting into the Greater London Council. We ought to examine that setup closely. It may give us ideas on how to make decentralization work in New York."

"But if significant decentralization does come about," I said, "it will mean allocating part of the budget to various community groups. Won't that make it harder to use PPBS to measure the cost efficiency of the city's expenditures?"

"There's no question it will be harder," Hayes answered, "but it won't be impossible. Take school decentralization. If there are, let's say, thirty different local school boards with some control over what they spend, once they're directly involved, they'll become interested in being able to consider alternatives and to find ways in which to measure the results of the particular courses of action they do choose. No, I don't think PPBS and decentralization are necessarily antithetical. I'm much more concerned with the city as a whole getting the funds it needs to do what has to be done. Whatever is decentralized will have to be adequately funded, as will whatever can't be decentralized."

"The Mayor keeps pointing out," I said, "that as the city's operating costs grow at a rate of thirteen to fifteen per cent a year, revenues increase only three to four per cent. What's the answer to that?"

Hayes leaned way back in his chair and looked at the

ceiling. "Oh, baby, I don't know. Well, I do know, but getting it to happen is something else. The cities, emphatically led by New York, must have a restructuring of their financial responsibilities. This has to happen within five years at the latest. My own view is that we need it in two or three years. By restructuring I mean that cities now are bearing the costs of programs that ought to be much more heavily supported by the state and federal governments. The whole welfare and social service area, for example. And so we need revenue sharing on a large scale. This city now pays some 16 billion dollars a year in personal and corporate income taxes to the federal government. We ought to get more of that back than we do. For the 1968–9 expense budget, federal aid amounts to only 892 million dollars. And in the same fiscal year, we get 1.3 billion dollars in state aid—that's about forty-three cents on the dollar from what we pay to the state in taxes."

"What do you think *will* happen?" I asked.

"Well, we will get more assistance from the state and from the federal government because logically, we have to. The need for it is so evident and so serious. We quite probably won't get enough, but there'll be a sufficient increase so that we can make some progress. But if New York and other cities receive even less than I anticipate, then there'll have to be considerable reductions in city services."

"What about the city getting more power to impose more of its own taxes?" I asked.

Hayes shook his head. "That's not the way out. If you do that on any sizable scale, there are very depressing effects on the residents of the city, and this hardly becomes an attractive place in which to make investments. That's why when someone suggests we ask the state legislature for more taxing power, my answer is that I'm happy not to have those powers. If we had them, we'd be driven to use them. No, the answer for us is a greater share of federal and state tax revenues."

Hayes had slumped deeper into his chair. "There's yet another problem," he said. "The whole labor situation. This city cannot take an indefinite increase in wage raises. It's already having a massive effect on the budget. Labor is our single biggest cost. It'll take up about fifty-seven per cent of this year's 5.9-billion-dollar budget. The climate of wage negotiations is rough, and it's getting rougher. The ultimate solution will have to be some type of juridical determination of salary disputes on the basis of clearly established equity in law. But certainly labor unions right now are far from willing to accept anything like that. So I don't have an immediate solution to the labor dilemma."

As it became darker outside, Hayes seemed to have become gloomier. "Do you have any regrets about having left Washington?" I asked.

He straightened up and grinned. "No, none. Despite all I've just said, there's been a real feeling of growing excitement here, of possibility. And I haven't missed being in Washington, nor am I likely to in the Nixon years. We've made some important starts here. Let me cite just a few. On October 31, the first construction contract for Model Cities housing in New York was signed. It moved faster from concept to contract than any other urban renewal project in the city's history, and in two years we'll have put in ten per cent of the 180,000 housing units designated for the three Model Cities areas in New York. And that's a reflection of the considerable reductions we're also making in the time it takes to get things finished in the whole capital construction area. Then take all the new sanitation trucks. They're going to make a difference. I don't think we're getting the savings yet that we ought to get out of them, but that's stage two. I could go on, but I'll end with school decentralization. We've at least started on that, and it's the most basic move toward decentralization that has been taken in any city in this country. We were confronted with an almost ubiquitous pattern of failure and John decided that the system which had been able to do nothing about that failure had to be broken up. The move had to be made to find things that did work."

Hayes had an appointment, and we left his office together. "Mind you," he said as we took different turns in the corridor, "that too is only a beginning. You still have to find people who can run the schools under decentralization. You can't get away from that—the need for more managerial talent."

It was nearly six o'clock. In the dark, on the sidewalk outside the Municipal Building, I looked at the lights and the flow of traffic on the Brooklyn Bridge. The thrust of the bridge and the speed of the cars set off—as happens to me every once in a great while—an access of affection for and ambivalent awe of this city.

"Hey!" a voice behind me shouted. Alongside one of the entrances to the Municipal Building is a room where city drivers wait for assignments. From there I had been hailed by the urbane visitor at the black city planner's home. "Still writing about the Mayor?" he said. I nodded.

"Do you have any further assessment?" I asked him.

"No immediate comment. I'm watching."

We talked for a while about music—the current state of Count Basie's band—and then he turned to go back. "Keep on keeping on," he said with a last wave.

I X   Several weeks later, I received a call from the Mayor's press office. Months before I had asked to sit in on one of the Mayor's Tuesday morning cabinet sessions. "It's okay for tomorrow," I was told. "Eight o'clock at Gracie Mansion. And they start on time."

"Yes, you might find a Tuesday meeting instructive," a

cabinet member had told me earlier in the year. "That's what the Mayor calls a supercabinet meeting—the heads of the administrations or their deputies, a few other key people, and some staff. I have mixed feelings about them though. I once told the Mayor I could have done without most of them. It was an appraisal which did not meet with his great approval. But they do give us a chance to see each other; otherwise most of us would hardly ever be in contact. And from time to time, I do learn something. By contrast, there are the Friday meetings—administrators, commissioners, deputy commissioners. Sixty to seventy people. Those are held at City Hall, at universities, and at other places around the city. They're supposed to be informational, but most of what comes out I've already read in the *Times*."

At half past seven the next Tuesday, I hailed a cab. When I gave the driver the address, he looked as if I'd named the remotest point in Brooklyn. He was a thin, intense man in his late forties. "I can't stomach that Lindsay," he said. "He's alienated just about every man in every union in this city. Transit workers, police, firemen, sanitation men, teachers, cab drivers—he's alienated them all. I tell you, I wish Al Shanker was running this city. That Lindsay is the biggest goddan phony I ever saw in my life. He couldn't possibly win if he runs again. And if he does, it will only prove that what they say about people is true—they forget from one day to the next."

We rode in silence for a while. "Well, that's not entirely true about him and labor," the driver resumed his commentary. "One day in the paper, I saw a picture of him getting a plaque from a union. I looked at it in stupefaction. What union would do that? Then I looked more closely. The moviemakers' union, for Christ's sake." More silence. "The colored. If you're colored, you're all right with him. If you're white, you got to obey the law. If I have to go to the bathroom and I put on my off-duty light, I'm breaking the law. What we *ought* to do—I mull this over every once in a while

—is do whatever we want. Throw the meter only when we want to. Put on the on-duty light only when we want. *Then,* when we're doing everything illegally, then Lindsay might come out and say we're okay." He turned around, smiling. It was the kind of smile Humphrey Bogart used to direct at Peter Lorre as he disarmed him by bouncing him off the wall.

It was ten to eight when I arrived at Gracie Mansion. I walked downstairs to the pleasant, spacious conference room next to the Mayor's office. Among those already present were Press Secretary Harry O'Donnell; Corporation Counsel J. Lee Rankin; Herbert Haber, Director of the Office of Labor Relations; Sol Hoberman, City Personnel Director; Police Commissioner Howard Leary; Donald Elliott, Chairman of the City Planning Commission; Dr. Bernard Bucove, Health Services Administrator; and August Heckscher, Recreation and Cultural Affairs Administrator.

A young deputy administrator came in, shook hands with a colleague, and said, "My wife grabbed me at the door this morning and showed me the *Times.* 'Here's your name in the paper, you stupid shmuck.' I mean it's not too bad, but they did get the story wrong."

"That's standard," said O'Donnell placidly.

More administrators, commissioners, and other officials were arriving. I saw Mitchell Ginsberg at the door. He, Donald Elliott, Fred Hayes, and J. Lee Rankin had been appointed by the Mayor in early November to make recommendations for a school decentralization bill. I asked him what the prospects for decentralization would be in the state legislature. "We'll get something," he said. "It won't be what we want, but it won't be nothing. And I don't think it will be a step backwards, like splitting the system into five boroughs."

Fioravante G. Perrotta, City Finance Administrator, was now pouring coffee at a table on one side of the room. Harry O'Donnell and I held out our cups as O'Donnell said, "Sometimes we have presentations by systems management outfits, but this is one of the mornings when the cabinet gets up-dated on what's happening."

By two minutes to eight, nearly every chair around the long, rectangular table at the center of the room was filled. I looked toward the door. "Oh, John will be here on time," O'Donnell said.

"Is he getting any more sleep these days?" I asked.

"The usual," O'Donnell answered. "Four to six hours a night. His pre-dawn phone calls are becoming a regular thing. You expect it during something like the school crisis, but now the state is running things out in Ocean Hill–Browns-ville. Still the calls keep coming. John keeps his hand in."

At the table, an administrator was pointing to a story in the *Times*. "That closing paragraph is a bit on the fantasy side," he said. The commissioner next to him nodded in resignation.

Jay Kriegel, whose duties as an assistant to the Mayor include the position of secretary to the cabinet, walked in, carrying a collection of file folders. "Jay works on the agenda for these meetings during the week," O'Donnell explained as he looked around the room to make sure he'd identified all the participants for me. Satisfied that he had, O'Donnell decided on additional briefing. "This place is used a lot dur-ing labor negotiations," he said. "Joint meetings between the two sides are usually held here. There's nothing more boring than those negotiations. They quibble over the damndest little things. Contract talks have certainly gotten a lot more complicated in recent years. Television has become a basic tool of labor negotiations. It's like John says. There's a con-siderable amount of what he calls 'necessary rhetoric' that goes on when the cameras are on the negotiators, and then they come in here and try to get down to reality. But even here it's like a set script. They have to go to the brink because the way the rank and file is now, the leaders can't settle two weeks before the contract runs out. If they did, the young Turks would be yelling. 'Why didn't you keep at it? If the city gave you this much, they'd have given you more.' And even when they finally do settle at the edge of the deadline, you can't be sure any more that the script is over. The rank and file is getting into the habit of repudiating its leaders."

At five past eight, the Mayor arrived. He strode quickly to the head of the table, nodding greetings, and sat down. The casual conversations around the table stopped. O'Donnell and I were sitting to the side, against a wall. "I'm not telling you this as a press secretary," he whispered to me, "but as me. This guy's got balls. He knows what he wants to do, he wants to do what's right, and he stays with it." I was surprised at the explicitness and warmth of the endorsement because O'Donnell customarily is the soul of dispassion.

The Mayor began the meeting by bringing the cabinet up to date on the situation in Ocean Hill–Brownsville. The current crisis concerned a union teacher there against whom there was a considerable amount of ill-feeling among his non-union colleagues and some of the parents. The local governing board, itself technically under suspension, was insisting that he be suspended. Tensions in the district were mounting again. "I've met that gentleman," one of the administrators said acidly. "From my point of view, he shouldn't be in that school district. He's a thoroughly disagreeable character. There's solid, substantial evidence that he's one guy who's been out to force a confrontation from the beginning of that experience."

"Well," the Mayor said, "they're working on it—the State Commissioner of Education, his trustee out there, and the three-man Israelson committee that was part of the settlement to handle complaints on both sides. Where it's going to come out, I don't know."

The Mayor nodded toward Donald Elliott, who reported on the need for more construction money in the capital budget for the coming year. "There was relatively little construction last year," he said, "but now a lot of things are ready to go—hospitals, schools, upgrading of the city's in-

cinerators. Getting the amount of money we need may lead
to an argument with the Controller but we've got to have
it. And we need to figure out new sources of revenue while
measuring the extent of our requirements by looking ahead
two years." He asked the administrators and commissioners
at the table to examine the draft of the capital budget which
he had helped prepare. "Then if any of you have questions
or problems about your particular areas," Elliott said, "you
can go into them with the staff privately.

"Tomorrow," Elliott continued, "we're going to announce a proposed amendment to the zoning laws as they
affect the elderly." The Mayor, a sheaf of papers in front of
him, was listening intently. "The change," Elliott said, "will
allow for thirty-five per cent more rooms in buildings for the
elderly to be built in certain residential districts. There may
be some opposition, but I expect there'll be general rejoicing
from the various councils of the elderly."

A cabinet member asked for a fuller explanation. "Well,"
said Elliott, "if you follow the rules under existing zoning
for the number of apartments in each building, housing for
the elderly contains about thirty-five per cent fewer residents
than housing designed for younger families. They don't have
children, and many of them live alone. But under present
mortgaging costs, that makes it economically difficult for non-
profit housing organizations to build new housing for them.
You not only have thirty-five per cent fewer people in each
building, but since the incomes of the elderly are often low,
they can't afford the same rents as other families. But if you
have thirty-five per cent more rooms in buildings for them,
then it becomes more feasible economically. You see? We're
also going to propose a two-thirds reduction in the require-
ment for provision of parking space since not as many elderly
people own cars. That also helps make construction more
economical."

"What you're talking about," said the cabinet member,
"is higher density housing for the old."

"Yes," Elliott looked at him, "that's what I'm talking about."

The chairman of the City Planning Commission proceeded to problems connected with new housing construction under the Model Cities bill. "Let me first report on the Bronx," Elliott said. "There I think we can be quite optimistic. There are encouraging signs that vest-pocket housing programs in that area will now really be moved. It took some force or compromise, depending on how you look at it, to get agreement among the various community groups. But in East New York, there's a snag, the genesis of which, as usual, is shrouded by different people complaining about other people. There have been a lot of meetings, a lot of conflicts, and there's nothing to be done right now except to hold it up."

The Mayor was disturbed. "The worst evil," he said to Elliott, "is to get so snagged up that the units won't be moved at all."

"We'll move those units," Elliott answered with a firmness which indicated he had his own ultimate deadline for the resolution of conflicts in that part of the city.

"There's a further issue that's important to us all," Elliott continued. "How can we get local contractors and local people into those jobs? The problem is that local contractors often are not competent enough technically or administratively to handle jobs on this large a scale. And unless we have real competence, we can't bring all this in within cost. To get many of the existing local contractors to qualify, we'd have to break the work down into very small units, and that just won't do economically. However, we *are* going to bring them in and give them experience, but we'll pay for that separately so that the economic balance isn't disturbed. Meanwhile, however, we're having real trouble getting competitive bids from the experienced contractors who *can* do the jobs. They're leery about getting into Model Cities work. They're afraid of vandalism and of the problems that might come with community participation in the planning of these projects. And since there's a lot of construction work in town —despite the screams of the building trades unions—the contractors clearly aren't hungry. It is, then, a considerable problems."

It was a little after eight thirty as Budget Director Fred Hayes came quietly into the room and took a chair against the wall in back of the Mayor. The latter turned around. "Good afternoon," he said coolly to Mr. Hayes. "You've just lost a hundred million dollars." The Budget Director was not amused, but the Mayor, as he turned back to the table, was having difficulty suppressing a smile.

"Keep me informed about that problem," the Mayor said to Elliott. "The worst alternative is doing nothing."

Dr. Bernard Bucove, Health Services Administrator, was next on the agenda. He reported on the city's continuing experience in the use of methadone to rehabilitate heroin addicts. Methadone, itself a narcotic, blocks the effects of heroin so that all desire for the latter drug disappears. Methadone is inexpensive, produces no "high" of its own, and dosages of it can be stabilized. Most of the patients in the methadone program for the past two years have been able successfully to return to work or school after an initial six-week hospital stay and subsequent supervision. "We're in phase two of the program," Dr. Bucove said. "We're moving the treatment out into the health districts from the hospitals in a limited way, and Beth Israel is experimenting with a more ambitious ambulatory plan. If all this works out, we can use the hospitals more as a back-up, shorten the whole treatment process, and cut the costs. As you're aware," he told the Mayor, "we're still having problems with the Federal Bureau of Narcotics. Even though the people in the program can now resume productive lives, the bureau is still concerned that methadone is a narcotic."

"Yes"—the Mayor frowned—"I know of the difficulties with the bureau. Okay, keep me informed."

The Mayor turned to Constantine Sidamon-Eristoff, Commissioner of Highways, for a report on the dedication a few days before of Co-Op City, a huge complex in the Bronx being built by the United Housing Foundation. On completion in early 1971, the development will contain slightly over fifteen thousand units of low- and middle-income housing. There had been constant conflict between the builders and the city, the former claiming that the city was being exceedingly slow in providing such essential municipal services as streets, schools, and additional public transportation. The city, on the other hand, had insisted with some success on higher standards of design and on more environmental planning than had been the custom in previous large-scale projects put up by the United Housing Federation.

"I was the only city representative at that dedication," Sidamon-Eristoff said rather wistfully. "It was not a pleasant experience. You can look forward," he directed himself to the Mayor, "to a series of attacks for political reasons from that quarter."

The Mayor laughed. "That's no surprise, Connie."

"Hell," said a cabinet member, "they've had some kind of ceremony there once a year for the past three years, and each time they've found a way to attack the city."

"It was a miserable example of bad planning, Co-Op City," the Mayor shook his head. "They know we know it and they know we say so. We've picked up more pieces, despite their mistakes, than anybody thought we could. Anyway, Connie, in that particular neighborhood now, after the school strike, no city official could expect anything but a cold reception."

There was a break in the cabinet meeting as an aide came in with a message for the Mayor. One of the administrators started talking about the strike underway by members of District Council 50 of the State, County and Municipal Employes at a number of state mental hospitals. The strike, called in protest against Governor Rockefeller's negotiations with a rival union, had already resulted in nearly five thousand patients having been sent home or transferred to other hospitals. It was the first serious labor dispute under the Taylor Law in which the Governor had become involved as a target rather than as a dispenser of advice.

"Of course," the Mayor looked up, "we'd be glad to assist the Governor in this state-wide strike in the mental hospitals if he'd only come and ask us to help him after he's exhausted all his powers." The Mayor's face was mock-solemn, his tone sardonic. Everybody laughed. "By the way, Connie"—he looked at Sidamon-Eristoff—"you shouldn't have been all that taken aback by the hostility in the Bronx. Still, I'm very glad you went to the dedication in so innocent a frame of mind." More laughter, except from Mr. Sidamon-Eristoff.

Amid the levity, a cabinet member said, "By the way, did you hear about Robert Moses's humane solution for the Bedford-Stuyvesant ghetto in his speech at the dedication? Eradicate it, he said, and move fifty thousand people to Breezy Point at the west end of the Rockaway Peninsula. He has a similarly sensitive, resourceful approach to Central Harlem. Demolish that slum and put the people into Battery Park City downtown. Just like that. Destroy, relocate, and you solve all your problems."

"It's too bad," a colleague said tartly, "that Mt. Morris Park is too rocky. Otherwise we could put a few thousand there too. But there's still Central Park."

The Mayor clearly was impatient at the time being wasted. "Okay, march forward. Connie, the Long Island Rail Road strike this morning, what effect is it having?" (Employees of the railroad were protesting new time schedules introduced by the management.)

"At this point," the Commissioner of Highways answered, "all roads going into the city are completely clogged. I've ordered a stop to all but emergency construction in the streets and have so informed the utility companies."

The Mayor nodded. "Now about Richmond Parkway," he said. (The long-standing controversy over the parkway to be built on Staten Island concerned the Mayor's insistence on a route that would entirely avoid the Staten Island Greenbelt, one of the last unspoiled natural areas in the city. Since 1966, the Mayor had been pressing for what had come to be known as Alternate Route 4. Other proposed routes would have taken at least six hundred acres from the Greenbelt.)

"It looks like we've won." Sidamon-Eristoff smiled. "The Tri-State Transportation Commission is going to modify its plan and put in Alternate Route 4. We've saved the Greenbelt thanks to the strong lobbying efforts of Don Elliott."

The Mayor smiled. "That's not where the real power play took place," he caid cryptically.

"The next stage," Sidamon-Eristoff went on, "will be the hearing on Staten Island at which, under federal regulations, all suggested alternate routes must be discussed."

"The sooner you get that done, the better," the Mayor said.

"We need the state to get up more money for brochures, maps, throwaways," Sidamon-Eristoff emphasized. "But the state still says it needs some form of Board of Estimate procedure to do that. We've told them it's not necessary under the law and that the Mayor doesn't want to set a precedent, but it remains an issue. We're also going to have to get the absolute support of all the conservation groups at the public hearing. That hearing is going to be a hell of a donnybrook. We're going to have to give enough advance notice so that there'll be time to muster support."

The Mayor drummed a pencil on the table. "You know, there's more interest in and support for saving the Greenbelt nationally than there is locally. The Sierra Club and other conservation groups in a lot of places around the country consider what we've been able to do so far a real achievement."

"The trouble with these public hearings," Sidamon-Eristoff looked somewhat worried, "is that it's the antis who always show up. You don't get a broad-based constituency. But it does give the antis a chance to blow off steam, and after you hold the hearings, things quiet down. We've had a lot less flak after the hearings on the Lower Manhattan Expressway."

"The Lower Manhattan tunnel," the Mayor said drily.

Sidamon-Eristoff grinned. "Okay, the Lower Manhattan Depressway. And that, by the way, is slowly percolating along."

The Mayor asked for a report on the progress being made toward bringing the meat industry into the city's Hunt's Point Food Processing Center in the Bronx.

"We had a meeting yesterday," said Patrick Crossman, the Commissioner of Ports and Terminals, "with the Controller and with Edward Ellman, the chairman of the Hunt's Point Cooperative Market. The difficulty has been getting cold-storage facilities included in our plans for the Market. I think we're okay now. Procaccino is going to introduce at the Board of Estimate an amendment to the lease with the co-op which will include the right to build a cold-storage plant. I don't think our commitments are terrible. We've gotten things from them, and they've gotten things from us."

The Mayor asked Crossman to get him more details on the capacity of the cold-storage plant. "Mitch"—the Mayor turned to the Human Resources Administrator—"do you want to talk about your new appointee?"

"We have established," Mitchell Ginsberg began, "what we euphemistically call the Office of Review. And we've hired a good man, Don Mathis, who used to be with the O.E.O., to head it. The Office will try to uncover any misrepresentations and frauds. And it'll examine administrative policies. How efficient are they? Are they being complied with? It will also investigate complaints and it'll act as an early warning system, looking into difficult areas before they get worse."

"Has your new man been cleared by Fraiman?" asked Housing and Development Administrator Jay Nathan. Eyes turned to Arnold Fraiman, Commissioner of Investigation. [He has since been elected to the State Supreme Court.]

"Oh, yes," Ginsberg answered.

"We've not only cleared him," Fraiman said matter-of-factly, "we've arrested him." There was general laughter.

"Lee"—the Mayor looked at the Corporation Counsel—"will you go into that court decision on car rentals?"

"We've been having a problem with car-rental agencies," Rankin said, "as to their responsibility for the unpaid traffic tickets of their clients. The City Council unanimously passed a bill allocating that responsibility to the rental agencies, but they took it to court. Now we've won a valuable decision in the State Supreme Court which upholds the City Council's bill. Originally we had tried to work out a much more limited program with the rental agencies but they thought they had enough power in Albany so that they needn't compromise at all. It was at that point the City Council got very exercised on its own and worked with us."

"This decision," the Mayor added, "is very important for traffic enforcement. It will help morale. The traffic-enforcement people won't feel they're passing out tickets in vain."

"But can we really collect from the rental agencies?" asked Police Commissioner Leary.

"Oh yes," the Mayor said. "Now that we've got this decision. A lot of those unpaid tickets were given to out-of-towners who figured that since they were renting, what the hell? Now we don't lose that money. There's something else about tickets, by the way. I've gotten a tentative okay from

Cassese of the P.B.A. to give a thousand sanitation officers ticketing powers for cars that break the alternate side of the street parking regulations. This will grant sanitation officers *only* the power to ticket *only* those cars that are in the way illegally as the sweepers go through."

"Can this include the power to ticket cars that are parked alongside hydrants?" asked Fire Commissioner Robert Lowery.

"You already have that," the Mayor said. "Your people can give those tickets."

"I meant giving the sanitation men power to ticket for that violation too."

"Here we go," Jay Kriegel, sitting alongside the Mayor, murmured.

"One step at a time," the Mayor ended that discussion. "Later today," he directed himself to the Police Commissioner, "I'm going to visit a synagogue in the Bronx that was burned out last night. I'll be getting back to you on it later, Howard. And Bob"—he turned to the Fire Commissioner—"there was that other synagogue fire the day before yesterday. Can you crank up the Chief Fire Marshal's report on that?"

"I want to announce," Jay Nathan declared, "one victory of good over evil. Rankin's Raiders over one Mitchell-Lama delinquent."

The Mayor looked at the Corporation Counsel, who explained that there were fourteen cases involving sponsors of projects built under the Mitchell-Lama program who were behind in city tax payments. (The program, established in 1955, assists the development of limited profit, middle-income housing through low-interest, long-term mortgage loans from the city, along with considerable realty-tax abatement. The owners of the projects are responsible for the payment of taxes.) "The city holds these mortgages," Rankin said, "and last week we started action against the fourteen to force payment. A man from my office met with one group of sponsors and its leader became quite vituperative, so our man started to walk out, making clear that we fully intended to go ahead with the foreclosure proceeding. There was a quick apology, and at nine a.m. the next morning, we had a check for the entire balance due. That makes one down, thirteen to go. The court had already appointed a receiver, however, and this group of sponsors would now prefer that the receiver not get a fee. We told them," Rankin smiled slightly, "that no Supreme Court justice appoints someone he knows without expecting that the man get paid. It's going to be expensive for these people to have to pay that four hundred thousand dollars with a fee added, and I hope it will be educational for them."

At that point, the Mayor ended the supercabinet meeting. It was five minutes past nine. On the way out of the conference room, I asked the Mayor if he had come any closer to deciding whether or not to run for re-election. He was assembling his papers, looked up, and said, "No, I haven't made a decision." He smiled. "I would say at the moment that all the pressures these last weeks would shift the balance to my running again. There's so much more to be done. You could get a brief idea this morning of how much. And, anything else I can think of in comparison to this job would be dull."

X   I did not see the Mayor again until early February. In the time between, there were more strikes, including one by fuel deliverers and oil-burner servicemen that left thousands of New Yorkers, many of them victims of the Hong Kong flu, without heat and in late December, led the Board of Health to declare the City to be in "a state of imminent peril." Meanwhile, among the many organiza-

tions of diversely concerned citizens petitioning the Mayor
about other perils, a group of taxi driver-owners were protesting the city's lenient treatment, in their view, of un-
licensed "gypsy" cab drivers (the latter service ghetto neighborhoods into which few licensed drivers will go). During
one of the meetings, there were such suggestions for civic
reform as "Let's shoot Lindsay!" and "Let's burn down City
Hall!" I was watching these deliberations on television at a
bar; and when a tribune of licensed drivers threatened a
strike, a young, neatly dressed man next to me, wearing
a large orange-and-white "Dump Lindsay" button on his
jacket, said feelingly, "Let the bastards go out on strike. You
can never get them anyway." He went on, however, to share
their views, if not their prescriptions for the Mayor. "He
doesn't know what the hell he's doing," he said.

In the mail that week, I received a letter from a black
member of the governing board of the I.S. 201 Complex—
an experimental school district in East Harlem. In it he
accused the Mayor of being a "racist" for not having supported the local board in its long-drawn battle with the
United Federation of Teachers. There was also a note that
week from a white teacher who had opposed the U.F.T.'s
strikes during the fall but was now fearful of what she
claimed to be a rise in anti-Semitism among Negroes in the
city. She blamed this in part on the Mayor for not caring
enough about what happened to Jews.

All of these problems did nothing to make the Mayor
more popular, but his esteem among the citizens may have
reached its lowest point in mid-February, when a fifteen-inch
snowstorm paralyzed sizable sections of the city—particularly
in Queens and Staten Island—for several days. Matthew J.
Troy, Jr., a Democratic City Councilman from Queens, urged
Governor Rockefeller to bring in the National Guard to clear
the streets and also asked the Governor to suspend the Mayor
"pending an investigation of his handling of this crisis." Dr.
Ralph J. Bunche, the United Nations Under-Secretary-Gen-

eral, was unable to get from his home, in Queens, to the U.N. during this period, and he sent the Mayor a telegram saying, "I may as well be in the Alps. This is a shameful performance by the great City of New York." When the Mayor himself ventured into Queens, a number of citizens berated him on the streets.

"You should be ashamed of yourself!" a woman yelled at the Mayor as he passed, staring straight ahead.

"Face the facts, playboy!" another woman shouted at his back.

Eventually, the streets were cleared, and the city moved on to other exacerbations. Before and during the snow crisis, the increasing tension that followed the school conflict remained a source of concern, and the Mayor was appearing frequently at meetings in synagogues and Jewish centers throughout the city, at which he kept stating emphatically that his administration would see to it that action was taken against both anti-Semitism and racism in the schools. "We have come through a difficult time in New York," he said at the Forest Hills Jewish Center, in Queens, in late January, "and the danger of further tension still exists. But my own belief is that the spirit of this city is going to win out and that the worst of these dangers is going to be overcome by the best of our instincts."

During the question period that evening, the Mayor was pressed hard by opponents of school decentralization who insisted it would create more racial and religious division. "The school system needs to be changed," the Mayor persisted, "and we have to divorce decentralization from this poison of racial and religious fear. We have to put aside the easy catchwords and the tempting stereotypes. We must start talking about what we want for our schools—about who shall spend funds, who shall establish studies, what mechanisms will protect professional rights, how parents can specifically help the schools in their neighborhoods."

His questioners were unpersuaded, and finally the Mayor said flatly, "I have to stand for what I think is right."

Another source of trouble for the Mayor was a series of articles in *The New York Times* which began in mid-January by stating: "Multiple investigations of the city's 122-million-dollar-a-year anti-poverty program are disclosing chronic corruption and administrative chaos that have already cheated New York's poor of uncounted millions of dollars."

The articles resulted in the swift formation of a number of investigating committees and teams—from Congress, from federal agencies, and from the City Council. During this period of siege for the Lindsay Administration and particularly for Human Resources Administrator Mitchell Ginsberg, I spoke to one of the Mayor's closest advisers, a man who had come into office with the Mayor. "John won't say this publicly," the adviser told me, "but what disturbs him most about this attack on H.R.A. is that Ginsberg is getting blame he doesn't deserve. But to say that, John would also have to point out that the weaknesses in budgetary and other controls in H.R.A were *inherited* by Ginsberg who has been steadily and exhaustingly setting up the kinds of controls that operation has clearly needed from the beginning.

"This was a classic example," the adviser went on, "of what can go wrong in hiring top people. John was assured by everyone he asked—in the federal government, at the foundations—that Ginsberg's predecessor, Mitch Sviridoff, was a superb administrator. It turned out that he was a first-class mediator and a very resourceful designer of plans. He knew, in concept, what had to be done; and if he accomplished nothing else, Sviridoff was important to John because his being in the administration persuaded Fred Hayes and Ginsberg to join. But Sviridoff was a poor administrator. He was able to set up programs, but he couldn't run them well. Keeping in mind what Ginsberg had to start with, and adding the chronic unreliability of Washington in meeting its funding deadlines, it's remarkable that H.R.A. is in any shape at all. Yet it has been getting itself together; administratively, it's much stronger now than it was last year."

Soon after that conversation, I spoke to the Mayor, at Gracie Mansion, about the beleaguered Human Resources Administrator. It was a clear, cold Friday afternoon in early February, and the Mayor was in a reflective, somewhat subdued mood. "Mitchell Ginsberg told me last fall," I said, "that if H.R.A. became discredited with the public, he'd resign. Has that time come, do you think?"

There was no hesitation in the Mayor's answer. "Having Mitch is one of the great accomplishments of this administration. Yes, he's told me many times that if it became politically necessary for me to dump him, I ought to go ahead and do it. My answer to him was—and remains—'When you go, I'll go.' "

"The attacks on H.R.A.," I said, "go beyond Ginsberg. They've led to a revival of the criticism about your whole reorganization plan." I showed the Mayor a statement in the most recent issue of *City Club Comments,* a publication of the City Club of New York: "The Reorganization Plan which provided for ten or more consolidated super agencies was primarily a plausible campaign gimmick calculated to convince the people that the candidate was a master of the mechanics of public administration. . . . Possibly a better plan for administering the city would have kept the department setup pretty much as it was, consolidating where the need developed."

The Mayor shook his head. "They just don't know what's been happening. I can assure you that without the reorganization, and without the chance it gives us to make PPBS work, we never would have gotten Fred Hayes to stay or a lot of other new, top-quality fellows we've attracted from the federal system. And people with years of experience in New York City government have also felt the change strongly.

Take Maurice Feldman [the Commissioner of Water Resources under the new Environmental Protection Admin-
istration]. He's been with the city for thirty-two years,
bouncing around in various engineering and administrative
positions in sanitation and public works. Feldman's one of
the best men we have, and he was very skeptical when I
started the reorganization plan. A couple of weeks ago, at
a Friday-morning cabinet meeting, we were discussing exactly what you're talking about—the extension of the attack
on H.R.A. to the whole concept of the ten superadministra-
tions. Well, Maurice got up and gave an improvisatory talk.
He said, 'I've been in environmental work all my life, and
I've never seen anything like what's been happening here
now that the problems of streets, water, air and noise are all
consolidated into a single budget with a professional team.
I've gotten more satisfaction from my work during the last
six months than in the whole thirty-odd years before.' You
ought to talk to Feldman."

(Later that week, I called the Commissioner of Water
Resources, and he added: "In retrospect, I don't know why
I was so skeptical, except that so many grand plans just
remain plans. But now, we actually are free of all those
separate, multitudinous departments and all those councils
which used to be set up under deputy mayors on a temporary
basis with no real power. It's been an extraordinary breakthrough. The problems are no longer disjointed; you can
get at solving them within one administration. You don't
have to deal with separate fiefdoms, and you can follow
through on each one in a logical order of responsibility. It's
already become easier to recruit first-rate people because they
can see they're not going to be caught up in the usual
bureaucratic undergrowth.")

In the Mayor's office, as he began to describe other
changes the reorganization plan had brought about, I asked
him about the continuing charge that he himself was a poor
administrator. "That seems to be one of the main criticisms

your opponents will be directing against you if you run again," I said. "And then there are those who say that it's not even possible to tell if you are a good administrator or not. Last Sunday, for instance, the *Times* quoted a man they described as a close friend of yours: 'You just have to look at John's private schedule to know he doesn't have time to run the city.' "

"It's simply not true," the Mayor shook his head again. "Either count. The second is really a somewhat more subtle way of phrasing the first charge. People keep assuming things, but they don't know. I spend a substantial amount of my time on administration, on overseeing what's going on. For example, once every two weeks, I spend two to three hours at a clip with the Policy Planning Council. It consists of the two deputy mayors, Don Elliott, Fred Hayes, and the Planning Council's staff. We have an agenda and we go right into the heart of each administration. Who's there? What's he doing? How is the budget being managed? What's the output for what we've put into a particular program? And then there are the weekly supercabinet meetings. You've seen what happens there—plain, hardboiled administrative work. And that's just the amount of time I spend at these meetings. Other administrative matters come up every day."

"There's another theme the opposition has been developing," I said. "The claim that quite apart from whether you're a good administrator or not, you've given priority to the needs and concerns of blacks and Peurto Ricans."

The Mayor nodded, affirmatively this time. "Yes, the white middle class and working class do feel neglected. And I'm trying to remedy that. One way is by going out and talking to them at neighborhood meetings and by using more of my television time to communicate my interest in what's bothering them. The other way, quite concretely, shows up in what's being done for the middle class and the working class in our new capital budget. We're putting a billion dollars into mass transit during the next ten years.

There'll be another six hundred million coming from the state, but all the planning is being done here. The 1968–9 capital budget provides for a substantial start on that. And more schools are going to be constructed, not only in ghetto areas. Also in the capital budget is over a million dollars to keep the Grand Concourse section of the Bronx from deteriorating into a slum."

(The Concourse Action Program, to which the Mayor referred, is unusually structured, I later learned from a member of the City Planning Commission. Appropriations for it are coordinated into a single line in the budget, allocating funds specifically to that area for more police and sanitation department equipment, the construction of a shoppers' garage, the planting of trees and remodeling of parks, the installation of new street lights, the purchase of a bookmobile, and a number of other projects. Since all the money is in this one budget line—the first such line ever written into the New York City Budget—the appropriations for the Grand Concourse can't be sliced away by separate departments suddenly finding more urgent priorities elsewhere in the city, as might occur if the funds were in the customary way divided among the budgets of the various departments involved.)

"And that Grand Concourse plan," the Mayor added, "was developed through real community participation in deciding what was needed and how the different elements should be designed. There were many, many meetings between the staff of the Bronx office of the Department of City Planning and neighborhood people. Obviously this has to happen more often in middle-class areas. That's why we've added urban task forces to work outside as well as inside the ghettos. The first was a Flushing-Bayside force in Queens, and we've recently set up two in Crown Heights and East Flatbush in Brooklyn. There'll be others. We've got to give these people too a sense of having the power to make the city government respond to what they need. The task forces have been coordinating city services in the ghettos with direct lines from the community to city officials. Now we're going to try to do this throughout the city.

"In making the decision as to whether you're going to try to stay on so that these and other programs work out the way you want them to," I said, "what are the most powerful factors *against* your running again?"

"I'm glad you didn't ask me if I had made the decision yet," the Mayor smiled. "Because I haven't. I would say the strongest reason for me not to run is the way my wife and family feel. They're pretty negative. You know, it's a serious question as to whether one human being can hold a city together for more than one term without exhausting himself completely. Another reason not to run would be my agreement with Henry Stimson's approach to public life. As I mentioned to you years ago, Stimson would go in, leave, and come back—the idea being that in the time away, he was able to read, reflect, get recharged. And a third factor on the side of not running is that despite my reputation as an urbanist and a walker of city streets, the public area in which I've most enjoyed working has been international affairs. The time, for example, I spent on the NATO Parliamentarians' Conference and the work on foreign affairs legislation. That gave me the most *personal* satisfaction."

"What, then, might lead you to overcome these arguments against running for re-election?"

The Mayor paused. "Well, there is the question of how one keeps one's voice alive if he's not in office. Secondly, I obviously do have a very great interest in urban problems. There's certainly an enormous amount of frustration that comes of staying in that battle, but there are also rewards. There's going to be a hell of a lot of unfolding in this city in the next few years. We've spent most of our time so far organizing the whole show to get it on the proper track. Now that we're going to have so many things to show for what we've done, I would regret not being here as they emerge. I'd hate to have someone else take the credit at the ribbon-cutting—for the new subways, the new schools, the new convention hall, the new passenger-liner terminal on the West Side, the completion of the Lower Manhattan and Jamaica developments, the flowering of the Model Cities programs." He stopped and grinned. "I know, you can be in the business for twenty years and still feel that way. No, that won't be the determining factor if I run again. I can survive missing the ribbon-cutting.

"If I run again," he said slowly, "the primary reason will be that I'm still an idealist on the possibility of holding the center on the urban scene. It was sad when Ivan Allen of Atlanta, a very good man, announced last year that he was going to bail out. He said that all the problems were being dumped on the doorstep of City Hall but without the money to solve them. And so Allen decided there was no future in being a mayor." He drummed his fingers on the desk. "Well, I do think there is a future in being a mayor." He looked at me. "That doesn't mean I've decided to run again, mind you."

It seemed to me that he had.

The Mayor and the City: The Asphalt Road and a Thousand Lost Golf Balls

One person who discovered Lindsay's convictions the hard way was a truck driver, who had parked his trailer truck on a Midtown thoroughfare on an icy winter night shortly after Lindsay was inaugurated.

The driver, weary from battling his way through heavy traffic, took a cautious exploratory sip of coffee, reached into a zippered jacket pocket and pulled out a pack of cigarettes. He lit up the last smoke and scaled the flip-top box out of the window.

In the blink of an eye, the box came sailing back through the window and landed in the driver's lap. Along with the missile came a message—"Hey, what do you think this is, a junkyard? Keep your junk off my streets!"

The driver found himself staring into the cold blue eyes of Lindsay, who was on one of his frequent walking tours of the city. The trucker meekly put the box back into his pocket and drove away.

New York Daily News, March 20, 1969

I On March 18, 1969, John Lindsay announced that he would run for a second term. As John Lindsay, he had no other choice. Less for political than for moral reasons. Politically, to be sure, a decision to withdraw would have been interpreted—in the nation as well as in the city—as resulting from the Mayor's fear of defeat. But politically, he might well have survived that imputation of timorousness. The memories of the electorate are rather short; and it would be far from impossible—given circumstances unpredictable in 1969—for Lindsay to emerge as a national candidate at some point in the 1970's. The political history of Richard Nixon, after all, gives hope to all who feel a continuing call to govern their fellow men.

It was the moral element in the decision that convinced me Lindsay would choose to run. He sees himself, as has been indicated throughout this book, as fundamentally a moral man. For him to stop after one term—in a city seething partly as a result of his thrust to change it—would be moral cowardice in his view. And in mine too, for that matter. So I was not surprised.

On that morning in March, Lindsay, looking back, said, "It has not been easy; change is never easy. But I believe the tide of spiritual and physical decay has been turned. We have faced up squarely to hard issues and have asked the city and its people to do the same."

Had the tide been turned? In *A City Destroying Itself*, published in September 1965, Richard Whalen had written: "Quite obviously, the mounting disorder of the nation's largest city is unique in the sense that its scope cannot be duplicated elsewhere. Every large U.S. city is different, and each will succeed or fail as an environment in its own terms. But the uniqueness of New York is not absolute. Although this world metropolis has seemed alien and unrepresentative to the rest of the country since the days when Squire Tom Jefferson denounced it as 'a cloacina of all the depravities of human nature,' New York is destroying itself under the impact of forces that are being felt in every city. New York represents the fullest expression—for good or ill—of our urban culture. It is the macrocosm of every city's problems and aspirations. It matters, therefore, to Americans everywhere what New York is—and what it is not."

Four years later, toward the end of John Lindsay's first term as Mayor of "the fullest expression—for good or ill—of our urban culture," visitors were still seeing the city much as Jefferson did. "When I come to New York," Canadian film director Allan King witnesses, "it always takes me two or three days to inure myself to the bitterness on the faces of all those people living in that enormous garbage can between Manhattan and Kennedy Airport. It just eats people alive!" And S. J. Perelman of Bucks County, Pennsylvania, describes how he prepares himself for his monthly visit to the city: "I confine myself for two days to a closet without any air holes and I turn on the radio full blast." Once in the city, looking at "ten million damply moist faces showing mingled hostility and depression," Mr. Perelman observes of the ordinary New York citizen that "he is constantly on trial for something the nature of which he doesn't understand."

In the summer of 1965, there had been large posters in every subway station—a picture of a smiling, striding John Lindsay in shirt sleeves and over it a quotation from a New York *Post* column by Murray Kempton: HE IS FRESH AND EVERYONE ELSE IS TIRED. In the 1969 mayoralty campaign, these posters would have value only for a collector of ferocious graffiti.

New York had become a place where, the *Wall Street Journal* noted, "if the welfare recipients all left and set up their own city, it would be the eighth largest city in the U.S. It also would be one of the fastest growing. . . . If the present trend should continue, half the people in New York would be on welfare in 1980."

Meanwhile, the Bureau of Labor Statistics was informing the citizenry that an annual income of $9,997 was now required for a family of four to maintain a moderate standard of living in New York. Unfortunately, more than seventy per cent of New Yorkers were earning less than $7,000 a year. And twenty-five per cent of New York families survived somehow on less than $4,000 a year.

As for housing, at least 800,000 dwelling units—a quarter of the total in the city—were listed as substandard. And in all neighborhoods, crime and fear of crime had become endemic. "The situation is so bad," a citizen of Harlem said in the winter of 1969, "that even the hustler is subject to being mugged." In a not-untypical case, a woman moved out of a regularly burglarized building on Central Park West to a new apartment house near Sutton Place at twice the rent with half the space she'd lived in previously. She then discovered that the percentage of burglaries was the same in her new as in her old neighborhood. More and more New Yorkers, a *New York Times* survey indicated. "live ever-larger portions of their lives behind locked doors. Feeling themselves besieged by an army of muggers and thieves, they are changing their habits and styles of life, refusing to go out after dark, peering anxiously through peepholes before opening their doors, sidestepping strangers on the street, riding elevators only in the company of trusted neighbors or friends and spending large sums to secure their homes with locks, bolts, alarms and gates."

Health services were such that in September 1968 Dr. Edmund O'Rourke, then the city's Health Commissioner, protesting a federal cut in funds for Medicaid, declared that twenty per cent of the deaths in the city were unnecessary. Providing an index of the ultimate pathology of poverty, the

Commissioner added that "the death rate is four to ten times higher in Harlem than in Forest Hills." Even those outside the ghettos did not achieve immunity from inadequate hospital facilities. As of the spring of 1969, a man with pneumonia had to wait five to eight days for a bed at New York Hospital, one of the city's superior health facilities. "A man in imminent danger of losing his life," the *Times* noted, "usually can get a bed somewhere, but often it is in a second- or third-best hospital instead of the well-equipped, well-staffed one where he could have the best chance to survive."

Survival was increasingly becoming a concern of the young in the city. My thirteen- and eleven-year-old daughters, living on Riverside Drive in the Nineties, consider each block they are able to get through without incident to be an achievement. It is not that they have been in actual danger more than a few times, but danger and the streets have become synonymous to them. And to their friends. There are other kinds of danger. Dr. Lewis M. Fraad, a New York pediatrician, told the *Wall Street Journal* in the fourth year of the Lindsay administration, "Our wards are full of kids with broken legs and smashed-in heads because we've got too many cars driving through our streets." Dr. Fraad, the report went on, "says he wouldn't advise anyone to bring up a child here if it could be avoided. He ticks off case after case of children who have died or been crippled because the city is so densely populated it is hard to keep track of the youngsters."

There is a quite different kind of danger for a large number of the young in New York. Having survived, what will their expectations be? A report in February 1969 by the New York State Commissioner of Education disclosed: "There are 275 school buildings in the state in which over half of the pupils are educationally disadvantaged. Of these buildings, 195, or 71 per cent, are New York City public schools." The report added that in the average public school in New York City, 44 per cent of the pupils were "educationally disadvantaged." Put another way, less than 5 per cent of the youngsters in predominantly black and Puerto Rican schools in the city go on to college by contrast with 60 per cent of the young in largely white schools.

And the members of this generation of the black and Puerto Rican young are bitterly conscious of the difference in options they have as the "educationally disadvantaged." But they and their parents don't use that term. They blame the schools, the principals, the teachers for not educating them, for not believing them to be educable. And in various ways, they rebel.

The city, then, appeared still to be destroying itself. Or as one of the administrator's chief urban designers said rather euphemistically early in 1969, "We've got to face the fact that New York is a very hostile environment right now, more hostile than it has ever been."

Not absolutely more hostile than it has ever been. The streets were more dangerous in the 1850's; there were, after all, the Draft Riots of 1863; and in 1906, Byron Rufus Newton wrote of the city as a "raving, rotting . . . squirming herd . . . a wilderness of human flesh." But by 1969, there was certainly more overt hostility in the city than had been evident four years before—and more sustained hostility than had been manifest in all the years of Robert Wagner's terms and those of his Democratic predecessors.

Those eager to succeed John Lindsay as mayor of the exacerbated city—and there were a considerable number in the spring of 1969—ascribed the rising hostility to the manifold failures of Lindsay and his administration. Polls indicated the majority of the citizenry agreed. "Well," the Mayor said when I asked him about the polls shortly before he announced that he would run again, "there just *have* to be times when the mayor is the most unpopular man in town if he's committed to doing more than just trying to survive politically. And if I don't survive politically, at least I'll know I haven't been only a caretaker of afflictions. Damn it, you can't say this administration has been passive."

The question was whether the Mayor's activity and commitment had resulted in anything more substantial than his unpopularity. Positively substantial. There were many— of all races, parties, and frustrations—who would have agreed with Nora Sayre's indictment ("Breakdown of Metropolis," *New Statesman,* February 14, 1969): ". . . It's become sadly apparent that New York has sagged under Lindsay and his staff."

Yet most of those who felt Lindsay to be a failure would also have agreed with Nora Sayre's contention that "few doubt the sincerity of Lindsay's idealism or his desire for decency. Even his sternest critics agree that his instincts are nearly always good—although he rarely knows how to translate them into tangibles."

The Puritan was at bay because, his numerous and diverse critics insisted, a desire for decency was not enough. Lindsay was naïve. Lindsay was a poor administrator. Lindsay had given in to "the colored." When he spoke before a Jewish audience on the Lower East Side the week he declared for re-election, a voice roared from the back of the hall, "What's happening with all the violence in the schools, Mr. Lindsay? Mr. Quisling? You gave the city to them, quisling Lindsay!" (Many of the politicians in opposition to him did not identify "them" as black but stirred fear a bit more fastidiously by saying instead that Lindsay had yielded to "extremists.") Lindsay, moreover, was still too much of a patrician to deal with the representatives of the working man without provoking crises. Lindsay had been far too permissive about welfare. "I'll vote for a man who'll reinstitute those midnight raids," a young secretary told me. "How else can we keep welfare under control?"

And some of "them" also felt that a desire for decency was far from enough. "I don't give a damn about his instincts," an organizer of welfare clients instructed me early in the year. "After four years of Lindsay, a welfare family gets only 33 cents a meal a person." "Give in to *us!*" a black teacher said contemptuously. "It's the whites he's given in to!"

"I do feel sorry for Lindsay," a former assistant to Robert Wagner was saying in the spring of 1969. "No matter who had been mayor these past four years, it was just no longer possible to have the appearance of a peaceful city. Wagner too would have been under siege. Maybe not from labor, but certainly from the blacks. There are too many people in this damn place with too many problems and there are not enough resources to cope with them. Big John made his move at the wrong time. He should have stayed where he was safe—and away."

While the Mayor chose to try for four more years of acute vulnerability, there were those who spoke as if the city were a terminal case. Architect Percival Goodman, for example—"Size can mean healthy growth or cancer. In New York, it's become cancer."

The Mayor agreed with Goodman on the name of the disease, but added, as an achievement of his administration, "The cancer has been brought to the surface. Not all cancers, once exposed, are fatal." And the Mayor *is* entitled to a considerable degree of credit for the surfacing of civic malignancies. Even Nora Sayre ended her broadside against Lindsay by emphasizing: "Despite much of his record he did perform one particular service: that of making the office of Mayor important in the national consciousness as it hadn't been for years. And we still hope that his demands for federal aid may yet awaken Washington—on behalf of all cities in the United States."

"It's bizarre," the Mayor has pointed out, "how long it took for people to recognize what was happening in the cities. Somehow people assumed that the American city would work by itself—that it would keep providing enough police protection and run the schools and build housing.

People just *assumed* it would happen and it didn't—and for years hardly anyone paid any attention. Also, for a long time, it way easy for politicians on other levels—in the state and federal governments, in Congress—to cop out. They knew that in the last analysis, if there were a particular crisis, the people would storm City Hall because that's the nearest and most immediately visible target. When I was in Congress, I kept running into that kind of thinking. I'm not saying it was articulated explicitly, but the feeling was that the mayors were the ones who would have to man the barricades. But now, finally, there's the real beginning of a *national* awareness that these massive and acutely infectious problems cannot be solved by the cities alone. From this point on, that awareness has to become sufficiently politicalized to make the federal government mount the equivalent of the effort that was made to win World War II. Or, put another way, the cancer will be arrested and then cured only by funding and implementing a huge Manhattan Project. If we were able to do it to bring the atom bomb into being, why can't we do it for the cities—and for the states and localities?"

The Mayor, however, could not at all agree with Nora Sayre and others of his critics that he has done little more than help awaken the national consciousness to the plagues of the cities. In a *State of the City* message on January 11, 1969, he claimed, "We have done more than any Administration in the history of New York City—and we have not done enough—to meet the needs of the citizenry."

There have been substantial accomplishments. Instead of merely waiting for a Manhattan Project for the cities, Lindsay did—with much difficulty—institute a city income tax along with an earnings tax on commuters. And, structurally, the rest of the city tax system has been reorganized to minimize nuisance taxes and to place greater emphasis—within the city's powers—on connecting taxation with the ability to pay. "Three years ago," Lindsay pointed out in that

1969 *State of the City* message, "New York was bankrupt. Its financial reserves were exhausted. It was—literally—on the verge of financial disaster. . . . This has been stopped. For three years, the city has balanced its budget without borrowing to pay the costs of running the government—the first time this has happened since the La Guardia administration." On the other hand, although the city's expense budget —about $6.2 billion for fiscal 1969—already exceeded that of any of the fifty states, "never has there been such a gap between the money the city has to spend, and the money it needs to provide services New Yorkers need."

Lindsay also cited, among the tangible achievements of his term, the reorganization of city agencies. He has not yet by any means won the definitive battle against the often glacially moving bureaucracy, encapsulated by anachronistic civil service regulations. But I would agree with Fred Hayes that the reorganization plan is a decisive means to improvement, particularly with the corollary infusion of PPBS (the planning-programming-budgeting system). It is at last beginning to be possible to see where money is going, how effectively it is being used, and what better alternatives there might be to current practices.

Also listed by the Mayor were a one-billion-dollar commitment to mass transit over the next ten years; demanding and getting the redesign of highways to save recreational and neighborhood space in New York; and the start of a concentrated attack on air pollution. Of the latter, he said: "We have at times fallen behind our own demands and found ourselves unable to implement our own regulations. Yet we *have* begun shutting down more than 1,000 public and private incinerators; the city and its largest utility [Con Edison] are burning cleaner fuel. And New Yorkers are now breathing air which is 25 per cent cleaner than it was three years ago." Actually, Lindsay, as he later acknowledged, was referring to the alleged reduction by 25 per cent of air pollution caused by sulfur dioxide—the most noxious of the pollutants. That figure has been disputed, but there certainly is more awareness by the city of the need to combat pollution, and increasingly sophisticated techniques are being used by the Environmental Protection Administration. Merrill Eisenbud, head of that administration, claims the city will have clean air by 1971 or 1972. It would appear to be a highly fanciful prediction, but clearly a start has been made to cope with that particular blight.

In the *State of the City* review, the Mayor added that six thousand more policemen were on the streets and the city now had "the fastest police communication system in the nation." This, however, is hardly enough to reverse the rate of crime, nor would the "revolution in police science" which Lindsay called for in the same statement. Crime will diminish when and if more people have a stronger sense that there is a legitimate place *in* society for them. And crime will diminish when and if there is a much greater sense of communality in the city. Communality all around. As Daniel Patrick Moynihan points out, "The millionaire who owns a plant and pours soot into the air does so because he doesn't know who you are and doesn't feel he has to act as if it matters to him. He doesn't have a sense of community. He's no different from the half-crazy kid snatching purses in the ghetto."

II   Obviously Moynihan is correct in his assessment of the soot-pouring millionaire, but the rest of his equation reveals his failure to understand that the kid snatching purses in the ghetto is quite sane, though predatorily so. He has been "educated" for economic obsolescence, and is reacting accordingly. At the root of the kind of crime that concerns patrolmen is a sense of powerlessness that the plant-owning millionaire hardly shares. And it is this particular sense of powerlessness which may yet explode the cities.

A basic measure of John Lindsay's value as a mayor—in New York and nationally—has been the degree to which he understands, viscerally as well as intellectually, what it is like to live in permanent exile in the underclass. There are, of course, limitations to his understanding, as there are to mine and to that of anyone else only passing through. But Lindsay, more than most whites and certainly more than most government officials, has no difficulty retaining his sense of rage that ghettos not only exist but are growing bigger and spreading more widely.

In the summer of 1968, appearing in Washington before the National Association of Counties, he spoke primarily of where New York City was failing—which is not the customary focus of a politician *in* office. He was talking about Brownsville in central Brooklyn. "We think there are about 100,000 people there. Nobody really knows, because with all our census tracts and computers, more than 20 per cent of the people we think may be there have dropped out of official sight. They hold no permanent job, live in no permanent home, receive no permanent public or private aid. We simply do not know where they are. But we do know about those we can find: their average annual income is little more than half the city average—an average which includes such depressed neighborhoods as Harlem and Bedford–Stuyvesant. Not a single census tract in Brownsville approaches a middle-class income figure. Of almost 50,000 households, about 4 per cent are standard. The rest are below that minimal index of adequacy.

"There are other statistical indexes, and, in each, Brownsville ranks very high," the Mayor continued mordantly. "More infants die there than anywhere else in New York. More of its young people are delinquent. More of its citizens are the victims of crime. By every number we have to measure the suffering of a community—narcotics addiction, welfare dependency, sickness and malnutrition—Brownsville is a leader. But Brownsville is more than numbers. It is streets lined with rubble and homes without water. It is a newsman writing, 'Animals in a zoo live better than this. Zoos are heated and kept clean.' It is a local pastor bitterly observing, 'If there is a Hell, the people of Brownsville will take it in stride.' "

Lindsay went on to assure his listeners that they were not immune—there are extensions of this Hell everywhere. "It reaches into smaller cities, now finding for the first time the meaning of substandard housing and insufficient municipal services. It reaches into the suburban communities. For example, in two neighboring suburban counties of New York, the welfare and crime rates are increasing at a faster rate than the central city's. Everyone in this room must confront the agonizing consequences of pervasive poverty in America. There is no escape from this dilemma—nor from our own responsibility. To flee the big cities is futile, as shown by the report of the National Advisory Committee on Civil Disorders. The Commission found that fully one fourth of the urban disorders during the summer of 1967 took place in communities with populations under 50,000."

His audience was polite but not visibly moved. The Mayor kept at them: "The heart of the matter, I believe, is understanding. And this means a willingness to put aside easy answers which confirm our own prejudices and justify our own indifference. For let us make no mistake about it. White America is increasingly fearful of its black communities—fearful of crime, fearful of riots, fearful of a threat to its own comfort. Too many of us do not see the lawlessness which condemns a man to poverty because he is black; which makes of his color a badge of oppression; which subjects him to illegal and unfit homes and schools and goods. And too many of us do not understand the sense of powerlessness in the ghetto, the sense that decisions are in the hands of immense governments and institutions distant from their communities and their concerns. Those in the ghetto do not help write the rules. They are often not part of the public process."

And in this area, the opening of the public process to the poor, there has been the beginning of a breakthrough in New York City in John Lindsay's first term. Through the poverty program, flawed as it is, and particularly with regard to making ghetto schools accountable to their communities, he did recognize the need for power to be redistributed. Not much real power had been redistributed by 1969, and the Mayor himself had not always been as clear and forceful an educator of the city's whites on this issue as he could and should have been. But a start had been made.

He did say publicly during the school strikes in the fall of 1968 that "many established groups, and many whites, deep down, don't want to see that kind of change and don't want to see that kind of gain on the part of disadvantaged people. They resent it very deeply although they'd be the first to complain if you had violence—violence brought about over the absence or impossibility of any change at all." The revelation of the depth of that resentment in New York City, the Mayor said some months later, was rather ironic "since everywhere else in the country, New York is supposed to be so liberal a city, even a cauldron of radicalism. The school battle showed us who we actually were."

By the time of that battle, it was no surprise to the Mayor when William Booth, Chairman of the city's Human Rights Commission, walked into a high school as three hundred white picketing members of the "liberal" United Federation of Teachers howled "Black bastard!" Even less surprising to him was the reception he himself received in the spring of 1969 in Bay Ridge, Brooklyn, when he started to campaign for re-election. It is a conservative neighborhood, and while the Mayor was speaking at a Republican meeting, picketers outside tried to smash the windows. When he was finished, the Mayor refused to leave, as he had come, by the back door. And as he walked out the front entrance, he was heralded with cries of "Nigger lover!" "Pinko" and—a dominant motif of the demonstrators—"Traitor, traitor, traitor!"

And by their criteria, he was a traitor—a race traitor. And to the majority of the city's teachers, many of whom had voted for him in 1965, the Mayor had turned out to be a traitor to "liberalism," to that quality of white liberalism which finds it easy and vaguely noble to march in Selma with Martin Luther King—as Albert Shanker, head of the United Federation of Teachers, had done—but reacts to black insistence on becoming part of the public process at home as "Nazism."

The conflict over the schools in particular bears closer analysis because in this confrontation—the most serious and divisive in his term—the Mayor was at his best and at his worst. He understood from the beginning that this was not a labor dispute. "It has to do," he pointed out during that turbulent fall, "with social change and therefore with vested interests in power. For a long period of time, you've had two powerful groups that have been very deeply involved with their own involvement with each other. One was the United Federation of Teachers; the other was the school system— the Board of Education and the Superintendent's office. Those two great power groupings became so deeply involved over the years in their own context with each other that they lost sight of the parents and the children. And as these two groups engaged each other in various confrontations—mainly peaceful bargaining sessions—the bureaucracy grew and grew. And pretty soon it became a single bureaucracy— management and labor all intertwined together. Meanwhile, left out of that contest were those who had no power base, the parents and the children. Especially, black and Puerto Rican parents and their children."

It was because the Mayor recognized what had happened and strongly felt the need for basic change that he became a catalytic force in beginning the movement toward breaking up that intertwined bureaucracy. As he spoke to Joe Flaherty of the *Village Voice* in March 1969 about the resultant strikes and their bitter aftermath, he emphasized, "Of course, I'm sorry it got ugly and out of hand, but you can't tolerate a system that keeps 50 per cent of our ghetto children illiterate, with another 80 per cent never finishing high school. It was a bitch, but I don't regret it. The school system just had to be revised and reconstructed."

The battle would have been ugly in any case—given the racism in this "liberal" city, given many teachers' fears of becoming accountable to local communities, and given the union's determination to keep its city-wide power. But the Mayor made two serious errors. From the time the initial experimental school districts were set up, he could have made certain that the then Board of Education provided clear guidelines so that the local governing boards knew exactly what powers they had and what powers they did not have. He failed to do this. Then, during the strikes, he could and should have consistently made clear to the city as a whole exactly what the issues were. Why black and Puerto Rican parents were so desperate to change the schools. And the difference between a union's legitimate insistence that its members' due-process rights be protected and a union's transmogrification of that "due process" issue as a device to destroy the experimental school districts. Instead, as I have indicated, during that period he was too often the politician and too seldom the Puritan. And it is when he tries to be a politician—in the traditional pejorative connotation of that word—that he is most unconvincing and, in view of his basic instincts, most disappointing. The Ocean Hill–Brownsville governing board was not without fault, but the weight of justice was on its side. The Mayor knew this, but from time to time during the conflict, he temporized for fear of losing white "liberal" votes.

The post-strike furor about "black anti-Semitism" in the

city was in large part a result of the tensions and fears caused by the strike, and the Mayor bears culpability for not having emphasized the extent to which the existence of black anti-Semitism had been exaggerated. The key report allegedly documenting "a crisis of anti-Semitism" in the city was a survey by the Anti-Defamation League of B'nai Brith released in January 1969. It was given unmerited prominence on the front page of *The New York Times* and served to further escalate fear among many New York Jews; but this flimsy report was based on only forty instances of anti-Semitic utterance or incident over two and a half years—and thirteen of those were ascribed to anonymous persons standing in the street. The Mayor, however, acted as if there were a crisis. He not only spoke in terms of crisis but he also removed William Booth as Chairman of the Human Rights Commission.

Booth had been attacked by some Jewish groups for having been "insensitive" to anti-Semitism. The charge was never proved, the evidence was to the contrary, and Booth, in fact, had been an exceptionally committed chairman of that commission—the best by far it had ever had. But in response to pressure, and acting as a politician, Lindsay "promoted" Booth to the Criminal Court bench. Booth had indeed wanted a judgeship eventually, but not under these circumstances. He left his position involuntarily, his reputation for fairness injured. He was a Lindsay sacrifice.

But for most of his term, Lindsay did not act as a politician in that sense. He did provide ways—entry points, he would say—for blacks and Puerto Ricans to participate in decision-making. Only fragments of power, as I've noted, had been redistributed by 1969, but a process had begun which subsequent mayors would find exceedingly difficult to reverse. In the schools. In community planning for Model Cities areas. And in the city departments most directly involved with the poor. By 1969, of those working throughout the city in the poverty program, 50.7 per cent were black and

26.8 per cent were Puerto Rican. Moreover, 71.4 per cent had no education past high school and 38.4 per cent had never finished high school. There was inefficiency and some corruption—bringing the poor "into the mainstream of American life" means just that. But the city's commitment had been made clear, and by the end of the first term, the poverty services—still inadequately funded—were markedly less inefficient and much stronger safeguards against corruption, spurred in part by press exposures, had been established.

But 70 per cent of the city's population is white, and the Lindsay administration was indeed late in beginning to make them feel more a part of the public process. Yet the Mayor was correct in making his first priority those whom the rest of the city would much prefer to ignore. One of his political opponents, City Councilman Robert Low, has stated accurately—by way of indictment—that for most of his term, Lindsay "concentrated his attention in slum areas and on raising standards for minority groups without making the middle class feel he offers compensatory programs for them." Considering the resources the Mayor had, I do not see that he had any choice—any moral choice. Politically, that choice was damaging. Not only because many whites felt left out but also because many utterly failed to understand, let alone agree with, the Mayor's sense of urgency about the ghettos. As an elderly black woman from Brownsville has said with remarkable understatement, "I might be speaking out of turn but you know that white people don't really care about us."

Much of the white hostility to the Mayor by the last year of his term unquestionably had an intensified, special racial intensity, underlining thereby how many whites in New York—and if in New York, how many more elsewhere! —are still unwilling to acknowledge that, as the Kerner Report stated, "white society is deeply implicated in the ghetto. White institutions created it, white institutions maintain it, and white society condones it." John Lindsay, whatever the other failures of his administration, cannot be accused of "condoning" the conditions in the ghettos. Nor can he be fairly charged with limiting his concern to rhetoric or with simply trying to "cool" the ghettos. No one is "cool" in New York after four years of Lindsay—and that too is to the Mayor's credit.

A paragraph from an early draft of a long-range *Plan for New York City,* prepared over the past four years by the City Planning Department, underlines the moral etiology of urban decay: "The plight of New York City is not unique. All the nation's large cities are faced with a crisis. It has developed from the callous disinterest of . . . mostly white middle-income citizens in the widening gap between their lives and the desperate condition of the growing group of urban poor, mostly black and Spanish-speaking."

Many whites in New York City may still be callous, but few are able any longer to ignore the consequences of that "widening gap" after four years of Lindsay. He could not have presented—let alone maintained—the illusion of tranquillity in any case. But for four years, he kept making it necessary for the city to confront itself, acting on his conviction that "the cities are not only governable but can be civilized." And the process of civilizing—of humanizing—the callous white majority is not without danger to those who try.

Early in 1969, when hostility to Lindsay was particularly high among large numbers of whites in the city, Stephen Smith, brother-in-law of the Kennedys, was asked whether he intended to enter the Democratic primary for the mayoralty. His public answer was: "Why would anyone want to be Mayor? The city has an obsolete plant with no money in the till." Privately, he told a labor union official, "I think that perhaps I could be a better administrator than Lindsay has been, and I do think I'd have a good chance of beating him. But if he is defeated, he'll go down for all the wrong reasons.

Too many people will vote against him on basis of their worst instincts. I don't want any part of that."

III John Lindsay's education as Mayor of New York has made it clear to him that the fundamental question is not whether the cities are governable but whether they are going to get the funds they need to radically attack the decay of their institutions and the intensifying urban plagues bred by that decay. He also knows, as he keeps saying in speeches, that "merely spending money is not enough. Suppose we had what we need. But if that money is used to build high-rise slums which destroy neighborhoods; if that money is used to inflate a degrading, inadequate welfare system; if that money builds more highways which cut the heart out of urban neighborhoods and further congest city streets; if that money is used to finance schools which do not teach children—then that money will have been wasted. The point is not to finance conditions of servitude. The point is to use that money to *change* those conditions, by changing the responsible institutions."

But as of the fourth year of his term, the primary problem was still money itself. "What New York needs to live is about $50 billion in federal funds," the Mayor said with the vehemence of accelerating frustration in that interview with Joe Flaherty. "This nation doesn't give a damn about its cities. You talk to Senators and Congressmen and they look back at you like little children, blankly staring and shaking their heads. We could use $10 billion for mass transit alone. Three years ago, when I quoted $50 billion over ten years as a remedy while testifying before a Congressional committee, they looked at me like I was crazy. You have to feel for the city in your gut. You have to live here. The rest of the country just isn't interested."

The Mayor, like many other urbanists, keeps under- lining the chasm between the cities' needs and its resources in an attempt to somehow awaken the country and more particularly, the Congress. "It's all been turned around," he was talking about resources one afternoon at Gracie Mansion. "In 1934, two-thirds of all taxes were collected by the states and localities, and one-third by the federal govern- ment. Today the federal government collects two-thirds of all tax revenues and the states and local governments collect the rest. Sure, federal expenses have risen enormously dur- ing that period, but I bet you didn't know this." He found a sheet of paper in a file and read: "In the years since 1946, annual expenditures of *state and local* governments have risen by almost 600 per cent—from $14 to $95 billion a year. During the same period, federal expenditures increased by only 107 per cent.

"Okay," he continued, " 'only' is a hell of a lot of money. But look where we are. This city's yearly expenditures are going up by 15 to 20 per cent. Yet, even with inflation, city tax revenues are increasing by no more than 8 per cent. Like every city government in the country, we're caught in a financial squeeze. What the hell are we supposed to do?"

The Mayor is certain about what *ought* to be done. "To start with," he said, "there has to be federal assumption of the costs of all direct welfare assistance. Granted, federal welfare standards should reflect obvious variances in the cost of living around the country while at the same time elim- inating gross disparities among State welfare payments. This state's average monthly payment for dependent children is $50, for example, but Mississippi's is $8. The country, after all, has already agreed in principle that some sort of federal aid, in rather large amounts, is necessary to maintain and improve the education of its children. Now we have to agree that welfare too is a national problem—one that can only be solved by federal action, federal programs and federal money on a massive scale.

"What also needs to be done," he said, "is for Congress to set aside an amount equal to a given percentage of the federal income tax base for annual grants to the states and to local governments." Autobiographically mindful of the often differing priorities, political as well as financial, between governors and mayors, he added: "Grants should be given directly to urban local governments as well as to the states. And they should be open-ended. The way it is now, the inadequate federal aid we get comes in tied to specific proposals. Obviously that doesn't give us much latitude in applying funds where they're most needed. The new and much larger aid should be in the form of block grants to be allocated by the receiving government as it sees fit. I've told this to the new administration."

"And their reaction?" I asked.

The Mayor looked glum. "We have to keep putting the pressure on," he said. "And on Congress. If anything like this is going to happen, the more than two-thirds of the electorate that lives in and around cities is going to have to make itself heard. And as I've said before, my hope is that as the average age of the American voter keeps going down, we may finally have enough people in the electorate who understand what Congress ought to do and who will politicalize that understanding."

And so the Mayor continues to speak at colleges, spreading the urban gospel. In March 1969, he told students at the Polytechnic Institute of Brooklyn: "Since World War II, we have spent more than a trillion dollars on defense and defense-related spending. Because of the pervasive atmosphere of the Cold War, defense spending became an unchallenged good in itself. The same Congressmen who would laugh a rat control bill off the floor, or who could spend hours debating the spending of $100,000 for a hunger study, would pass a $70 billion defense appropriation without a murmur, without debate, almost without a quorum—as I often saw on the floor of the House of Representatives. In fact, so ingrained was that habit of approving all money for defense, regardless of the merits, that on occasion key domestic programs were labeled 'defense' to win political support."

The Mayor looked at his audience, and went on sardonically, "The key federal law providing loans to college students is the National *Defense* Education Act. The $60 billion spent on highways is for a national defense highway system. I sometimes think that the fastest way to get funds for the cities is to introduce a national defense middle and low-income housing bill.

"It's especially critical for you to understand," the Mayor told the students, "exactly what has been going on in this country. An almost unimaginable amount of money has been spent by the Defense Department in contracting out to private enterprise for weapons development. From nuclear aircraft to the M-16, from the Nike to the Polaris, government and private industry have forged a partnership which is practically a fourth branch of government.

"Let me be more specific. Since 1950, the Defense Department has granted more than $550 billion in prime military contracts—a figure which rivals the amount spent by *all* state and local governments in that time. That stark figure has determined for us the use of scientific and technological skills in recent decades. What's happened is that the overwhelming bulk of technical skills has been put at the service of the defense aerospace effort, because that's where the resources are. When the federal government spends a trillion dollars in a generation—when it channels incentives such as cost-plus contracts, scholarships, and employment—when it makes defense spending all but invulnerable to political challenge—then it determines the kind of work that science and technology will be doing."

The Mayor went on to focus on what he called the resultant "schizophrenia in this nation, which demands strict accounting of funds spent on domestic needs, while somehow exempting the incredible, indefensible wastefulness of defense spending. For instance, a great deal has been heard about mismanagement in this city's Human Resources Administration. Clearly, any misuse of funds is a serious thing. Taxpayers have a right to be angry at any loss of public money. But where is the outcry over the billions of dollars in unfinished or abandoned exercises of defense? Where was the outcry when for years former Senator Paul Douglas attacked military procurement policies, showing that the Defense Department was paying five, ten, twenty, forty times as much for goods than they had to? Where was the outcry when a former Budget Bureau official disclosed that, in the last decade, $25 billion worth of contracts had either been cancelled, phased out, or found to be 75 per cent unreliable? Where were the disclosures of defense boondoggles that drained billions of dollars in resources from our cities and farms, our schools and hospitals? Where were the headlines over the Sugar Grove radio telescope, cancelled after $50 million? The nuclear aircraft, after spending more than $1 billion? The nuclear-propelled space booster, cancelled after costing $2 billion?"

The Mayor stopped, and then, speaking with particular emphasis, said to the students: "We are talking about enough money to provide critical yet missing services in this city and every other major city. We are talking about money to build and rehabilitate housing, money to train and hire police, money to improve mass transit, money to clear wasteland and clean the air and water. And yet this obsession with defense continues. Right now, when big cities across the country are facing their worst financial crisis, when Philadelphia doesn't have enough cash to buy supplies for its police, when Detroit and Chicago are contemplating shorter school years, when this city may have to cut vital services, the national government is urging that we spend $6 billion on an antiballistic missile system—a system which may well buy us not one whit of security and which may ultimately cost us $50 billion or, as Senator Stuart Symington has suggested, *$400 billion.*

"We have got to reorder our priorities. And we have to use our technology for human ends. We know that computer technology could revolutionize our hospitals, leaving doctors and nurses free from clerical and routine diagnostic duties. We know that, with research and development incentives, technology could lower the spiraling cost of urban housing—a cost which now cripples our efforts to provide decent housing for low- and middle-income families. We know that advanced technology can help lower crime, by dispatching police on a more rational basis, and by speeding communications. We know that engineering breakthroughs can vastly improve mass transit and our efforts at environmental protection, now set back by tools which simply cannot meet the need for drastic action.

"This is where we are," the Mayor ended. "We know we can use the knowledge you are gathering, the skills you're learning, the techniques you're perfecting. Yet we lack the funds. Not because they don't exist, but because they're spent so disproportionately in other areas. But what area is of greater priority than our beleaguered cities?"

I told the Mayor later that I'd thought it a particularly useful speech. "Well," he said, "you have to keep on. Damn it, if the country doesn't turn itself around, at the rate we're going, T. S. Eliot will have written our epitaph. You remember?

> 'They were a decent, Godless people;
> Their only monument, the asphalt
> road and a thousand lost golf balls.'

You know, I wonder more and more, what kind of a people are we?"

IV My own assessment of John Lindsay as Mayor parallels that of a young lawyer, quoted in the *Wall Street Journal:* "Lindsay hasn't lived up to anyone's expectations, but he's done better than anyone expected."

Considering the disintegrating city he inherited; the chronic inadequacy of federal and state resources at his disposal; and the time required for him to fully understand what the questions were—before going after answers—he has substantially illuminated the possibilities, as well as the problems, of making the cities both governable and accountable to those under siege in them.

There were failures. Some of them in personnel—as in the case of former Water Commissioner James Marcus, jailed halfway through Lindsay's term after having been convicted on charges of corruption. And it is certainly arguable that more could have been accomplished in housing and health services, among other areas. (Although I am not persuaded—in view of the city's money problems—that significantly more could have been achieved under the most efficient of administrators.) Also, as *The New York Times* observed on the morning after the Mayor declared his intention to run again, ". . . the city remains dirty, it gives much and gets little from its overfat municipal unions, and many of its facilities are still running downhill."

I would qualify the last point by denying that the pay scales of the municipal unions are "overfat" after four years of Lindsay. In a city where, according to the United States Bureau of Labor Statistics in March 1969, an annual income of $6,021 was needed to maintain a family of four on a low level of living—and $9,977, as I've noted, on a moderate level—the gains the unions have won are hardly exorbitant.

But the *Times* is right in that there has hardly been a notable rise in efficiency and, let us say, commitment along with the increased wages and benefits. However, even within the strictures of still far-too-rigid civil service regulations, the growing and deepening use of the program-planning-budgeting system can bring more efficiency in the years ahead among middle- and low-level bureaucracy.

An inchoate city government—as was Robert Wagner's before Lindsay's—protects fastnesses of power responsible only to itself. Under Lindsay, by contrast, a start has been made toward functional reorganization that is moving toward making all levels of officialdom accountable as well as providing fewer places in which municipal hobbits can hide. "Reorganization was political idiocy in the short run," Housing and Development Administrator Jason Nathan has pointed out. "Anybody who knows anything would know it would be a real crunch. But if you have enough guts, reorganization gets at the goddam cancer."

And as the *Times* also said in that post-declaration editorial, "urban planning has become a priority matter, not a neglected afterthought" under Lindsay. It has been planning, moreover, that involves—more than in any other city—those for whom the planning is being done. These are very small starts in restructuring decision-making power; but in Model Cities planning, in the poverty program, in the schools, and even, slightly, in middle-class neighborhoods, the city administration is beginning to resemble Kafka's Castle less.

"The city is designed to shrink people," emphasizes Leonard Fein, associate director of the M.I.T.–Harvard Joint Center for Urban Affairs, "so one doesn't feel plugged in, connected, part of a family. At least then, let's resurrect the neighborhood, the community within the city. That's what decentralization is all about. It's not about schools. It's about neighborhoods and plugging people in. I think John Lindsay knows that."

In addition to the Mayor's thrust toward reorganization

and decentralization, it is also of significance that after four years, Lindsay has retained the respect of a considerable percentage of the young. Not only in New York but also, as I've discovered at many college campuses in the past two years, throughout the country. As I noted in the prologue to this book, some of the young, to be sure, consider him irrelevant. They are convinced that only a total, radical restructuring of all institutions can possibly reverse the dehumanization of the cities and the country. But many others do continue to regard Lindsay as one of the few political figures who may —just may—offer hope for change within what they consider real possibility. "Sure, I'd like to see a revolution in values and in the sharing of power," a young Lindsay volunteer told me in the spring of 1969, "but this isn't Batista Cuba or Algeria under the French. Not yet anyway. You've got to work with where people are, and we're not even in a pre-revolutionary stage. What counts right here, right now, is decolonizing places like Bedford–Stuyvesant and Harlem. What counts is liberating the schools. And quite apart from moral imperatives, this city can't be anything but a dangerous place to be in until those changes happen. Lindsay being mayor makes a difference as to whether they'll happen fast enough and deep enough."

And in continuing to speak directly to the young, the Mayor is saying things which can hardly bring him many votes. Not until the 1970's anyway. In 1969, an election year for him, when most of his Republican and Democratic opponents were emphasizing—with varying ways of euphemism —"law and order," Lindsay spoke before the student body at Brooklyn College in February about growing dissent on campus. Students are asking questions, he said, that make crucial sense. "What does it mean, they ask, to cherish a university devoted to knowledge and free inquiry when significant parts of a school's budget comes from government defense contracts? What does it mean to preach open pursuit of knowledge if a university harbors secret, classified research centers? What does it mean to teach what must be done to end racial prejudice and reform institutional discrimination if the school itself will not change itself to grapple with the crisis in black education? What does it mean to tell us of the duties of citizenship and democracy if students are shut out of decision-making on the campus, and are regarded not as people to be taught, but as so many units to be processed? What does it mean to preach the sanctity of free speech and then shut down plays, confiscate campus newspapers, and suspend students for expressing themselves in unorthodox ways? What does it mean, in other words, to tell us to accept and preserve a civilization's values when that society does not live by those values—and in fact repudiates them in the way it treats the people who live in it?"

The Mayor was not just telling students what they wanted to hear. At Brooklyn College, as earlier at Columbia and on other campuses, he also reminded them that there is a fundamental conflict in values for those who would humanize society by brutalizing their opponents. "How are the values of the single human spirit advanced by shouting down a speaker or resorting to outright violence even if his policies are in basic disagreement with deeply held beliefs? I think we should recognize that those techniques are nothing more than the tactics of suppression. We should recognize that they promise not an end to manipulation and rigidity, but only another-color robe for the executioner to wear. But the questions being asked by students, I repeat, are hard and telling. And in part it has been the refusal to face up to these questions that has led us to much of the upheaval which now threatens so many campuses."

There remains a basic decency in the man and a considerable understanding of what has gone wrong with this country, and has been going wrong for a long time. I cited his persistent concern with civil liberties during his years in Congress. He was also outraged at the Kennedy administration's morally as well as militarily disastrous venture into the Bay of Pigs—on the day it happened, not in rueful retrospect. Lindsay was one of the first congressmen to openly and harshly criticize the war in Vietnam. And now he is able to understand—and be understood—by many, not all, of those now in domestic resistance to morally illegitimate authority.

That understanding has its boundaries. John Lindsay is essentially a liberal. Some of the reforms to which he is committed go beyond what has become the traditional canon of liberalism in this century—his concern with decentralization, for example. But he has based his political life on a belief that reason can prevail, even over "power brokers," and that the processes of democracy can still be made viable. Unfortunately the burden of proof is on him. And it may be that in the next decade, more of the young and of the underclass will feel it necessary to commit civil disobedience even more often and otherwise engage in forms of confrontation politics which are alien to Lindsay's convictions. Conceivably, if he remains in political life, as is highly probable, the 1970's could be an even more difficult time for him than his first term as Mayor of New York. Reformers by then may be under fierce siege from all sides as they try to hold a diminishing center.

So far, however, the Mayor has remained almost intact under the sizable pressures he has already undergone from many different directions during his grueling post-congressional political education in the past four years. I say "almost" because he has, it seems to me, become somewhat less of a civil libertarian. Congressman Lindsay would have immediately and repeatedly attacked Mayor Lindsay for having refused Shea Stadium to George Wallace. Congressman Lindsay would have been appalled at the emergency measures for "riots and other disorders" that Mayor Lindsay had promulgated and made into law in the spring of 1968. Those measures severely restrict civil liberties by the imposition of curfews and the closing off of "disturbed" areas with accompanying harsh penalties for infractions of these emergency laws. Certainly provisions have to be made for times of riot, but under these new bills, the Mayor is permitted to impose these restrictions on the free movement and free assembly of New Yorkers whenever he has "reason to believe there exists a clear and present danger of a riot or other public disorder." As the New York Civil Liberties Union pointed out in a futile protest, "This condition does not pretend to be objective. It does not even require that a clear and present danger actually exist; it merely requires that the mayor *believe* it exists. He doesn't have to be right; he only has to be sincere. Such a provision truly substitutes the rule of men for the rule of law."

I made my own protest to the Mayor at the time. "We had to be ready," he explained. "Besides, I'm not about to be arbitrary or irrational in applying the law."

"But *you* are not about to be mayor forever," I said. He ended the discussion at that point. I was troubled, and I remain troubled. I also think that Congressman Lindsay would have attacked the removal by "promotion" of William Booth without due process. This diminishment of Booth's reputation is the Mayor's culpability and, I believe, a grave one.

But that's politics, right? Yet not characteristic of Lindsay, as the other instances of his retrogression as a civil libertarian are not characteristic. He is still least himself when he is most "political." He is still most himself when he ends a speech in the winter of 1968 by saying—sounding like the boy at St. Paul's, the president of the class reviewing the year—"What is significant, I think, is that we have tried to do the right thing, and that may be of more lasting value to this city than any of the accomplishments and plans I have reviewed tonight." Or, as Murray Kempton wrote after the Mayor had declared for a second term, "There are small ways in which every Mayor in my lifetime has been his better; but in the large ones, he is our best since La Guardia, just because he has been our least accommodating."

V   He is grayer, thinner, and harder than when he began his term. He is much more self-assured; he enjoys the exercise of authority but not at all his continuing education in the limits of that authority. He has learned that he can take much more pressure, criticism, and face-to-face abuse than he could have imagined when he was the resplendent Congressman from the Seventeenth who did not have to remove the snow, clean the air, pick up the garbage, and deal with the combustible consequences of a state legislature which, in alliance with the Governor, reduced welfare payments in the fourth year of the Mayor's term so that as of July 1, 1969, a family of six on welfare in liberal New York City is allotted 66 cents a day each for food unless the city finds money to add a little more. He is indeed learning, some would say, what kind of people we are.

I remember Leslie Booth, a City Hall secretary, saying at the start of the term: "The pity of big-time politics is what will happen to a nice guy like this? It seems to me the nice guys get so hurt they have to toughen up to survive." And the Mayor has become tougher, but without losing his capacity for rage at the kind of men who can legislate a cut to 66 cents a day in food for other men. And he has not lost the essence of his politics—that seemingly rational but essentially apocalyptic belief in the perfectibility of man, though perhaps not including upstate Republican legislators who do "feel for the city in their gut," but whose feeling is hatred and fear.

There was something else, as I wrote earlier, that Miss Booth said at the beginning: "A young man like Lindsay really needs to bump into a big storm. So far he's always been rolling along, the fair-haired boy who could do no wrong. I feel somebody like him in public life has to stub his toe sometime, and maybe it's better if it happens early in a career. I'd hate to have it happen at the brink—just before he might get into the White House, for example."

The rarity for Lindsay in the past four years has been a period without storms. The day before he declared for a second term was St. Patrick's Day. "Are you really going to be part of the march?" a reporter asked him. "I mean, you're hardly the most popular man in town."

The Mayor laughed. "The first one I marched in as Mayor was right after the transit strike— and there are a lot of Irish in that union. I was booed without let-up all the way. And I've been booed a lot since. I expect I'll survive." And he marched—to considerably less vocal castigation than in 1966.

As a public man, the Mayor has more than survived. And his wife has persistently fought the private battle, as she describes it, "of the eight million vs. our four children. Sometimes I have to simply insist, 'This is it. No more telephone calls. Give one-half hour of concentration to them.'" Although Mary Lindsay understood that her husband had to run again, the Mayor's family would have been greatly relieved had he chosen not to try for four more years of further testing—of himself and of the city. On the day of his declaration, he said, "My wife, Mary, and our four children join me in this decision." One of his daughters turned to her sister and whispered, "We do?"

He had to try to continue, both because of his temperament and also because he had found his vocation. For now. After an apprenticeship in Congress, he was—as he likes to say—exactly where the action is. He may prefer foreign affairs and may yet get a chance to exercise that preference, but it is as an urbanist that John Lindsay has become a national figure and a national force.

As Fred Hayes said, the city's recruitment interviewers "sell John Lindsay. That's what it takes—a man who is a symbol of change, who makes people of high quality believe there's a reason for them to come here. Okay, maybe a new administration's interviewers will be able to sell someone else. But can you name a person who creates the degree of national interest among the young in urban problems that John does?"

By the end of his first term, while commissioners and other high-echelon officials had come and gone, most of the young in key roles in the administration had stayed, and had been joined by others. It was as if they were all engaged —with the Mayor—in a continuous seminar on possibility. Except that their assignment was loomingly real—the biggest and most complex city in the country. It was they who were particularly delighted when the Mayor said he would keep on keeping on. Or try for the chance to. "Hell," said Jeff Greenfield, "look at what's been going on in the city for the last four years. Subtract whatever failures and blame you want to allocate to Lindsay, but damn it, we have started to move."

And as for the man himself, I cannot imagine ever having a bronzed figure of John V. Lindsay, holding on to a ship's wheel, standing on a radio in my living room. In so far as I am drawn to iconography, which is not very far, my choices would be A. J. Muste or Eldridge Cleaver. But Lindsay has come through so far—as a man in politics who still finds it natural, not in the least embarrassing, to talk about "doing the right thing" and who then actually tries to do it.

Personally, he is not a riven man, whirling in ambiguities, but nonetheless, as Murray Kempton observes, "he engages you in his fate. . . . There are good plain reasons for liking John Lindsay and not bad plain reasons for disliking him; and everyone responds to one set of reasons or the other with no great effort. Lyndon Johnson was that sort of man too, but, after a while, it was hard to care how his novel came out; Lindsay, like the Kennedys, compels you to read on."

And reading on may continue to tell us more about what kind of a people we are. He is not a comfortable man, and he does not make others comfortable. For many, he has a disturbing idea of what a life is about, of what this country should be about. He would, I think, agree with Thoreau that "what a man thinks of himself, that is which determines, or rather indicates his fate."

This is also likely to be true of a city, and of a nation.

Epilogue

On Tuesday, June 17, 1969, John Lindsay experienced the first political defeat of his career. John Marchi, a Republican State Senator from Staten Island, running with the support of the Conservative Party, defeated the Mayor in the Republican primary by 6,332 votes out of a total Republican vote of a little over 200,000. (Two thirds of the city's registered Republicans did not go to the polls.) In the Democratic primary, another "law-and-order" candidate, City Controller Mario Procaccino, overcame four variously liberal rivals—Herman Badillo, former Mayor Robert Wagner, Congressman James Scheuer, and author Norman Mailer.

Lindsay's loss raised again the question of his future as a Republican—let alone his future in politics. Of the five boroughs of the city, only the Republicans in Manhattan gave him a majority. A measure of the personal rebuke to the Mayor by his fellow Republicans was the fact that his two running mates—former Chief Police Inspector Sanford Garelik and City Finance Administrator Fioravante Perrotta—won in the Republican primary over the rest of Marchi's ticket. Throughout the city, moreover, Lindsay lost in working-class and middle-class neighborhoods. Republicans with incomes of over $15,000 a year did support the Mayor by a margin of 7 to 3, but they constituted only 20 per cent of those who voted in the primary.

Following Lindsay's defeat, President Nixon, Vice-President Agnew, National Republican Chairman Rogers C. B.

Morton, and New York State Republican Chairman Charles T. Lanigan declared that, as Republicans, they would support Marchi. Nelson Rockefeller, although a financial contributor to Lindsay's primary campaign, had pledged that he would back whoever won the Republican primary. There were, on the other hand, individual Republican officeholders —in the city, state, and country—who concurred with Senator Mark Hatfield of Oregon: "I'm for John Lindsay regardless of what party ticket he runs on—I'm for Lindsay the man."

But with regard to organized backing, Lindsay once again was going to have to build his own—from volunteers. His chances for re-election were based on how strong a coalition he could assemble of black and Puerto Rican voters, liberal Democrats, independents, and that minority within a minority—those Republicans in the city who do not consider him a traitor to the Grand Old Party. Lindsay already had the nomination of the Liberal Party; and the day after his defeat in the Republican primary, he announced that he would "create a new urban party" to provide him with a second line on the ballot in November.

The New York Times gave the Mayor "a fighting chance," noting that "he must now run without the organizational support of the Republican Party and he must overcome the formidable arithmetic of voter registration that shows Democrats outnumbering Republicans by a three-to-one margin."

Lindsay had hardly had that much organizational support from the Republican Party before, but not since his entry into politics—as a rebel against the party's choice for congressman in the Seventeenth Congressional District—had he been so thoroughly on his own.

Two days after Lindsay's defeat in the Republican primary, I saw the Mayor's new press secretary, Tom Morgan, who had previously been a free-lance journalist and novelist. We were watching the Mayor take part in a poetry reading at Bryant Park, behind the main branch of the New York

Public Library at Fifth Avenue and Forty-second Street. His appearance—part of a series of readings under the auspices of the City's Department of Cultural Affairs—had been arranged before the primary.

I asked Morgan if he had recovered yet from primary night. "Recovered?" He smiled. "I think it's worked out marvelously. Now we're the only liberals in the race. After all, this is still predominantly a liberal town. Two thirds of the Democratic vote went *against* Procaccino. Where are they going to go, if not to John? Also, less than a million people voted in the primaries. When the rest come out in November, I can't see our losing unless the liberal Democrats run their own man. And I don't think they'll do that. Sure, they might be able to knock John off that way, but what kind of a city will they have left?

"Another thing," Morgan continued, "this defeat has humanized John in relation to the electorate. By God, he's capable of losing. He's not Superman any more. They're no longer going to expect him to be able to clean the streets and do everything else all by himself. And once he was proved vulnerable, he came back fighting on the very night he lost. Did you notice that he didn't even congratulate Marchi? He started in on him and Procaccino right away. He got off the floor swinging. It's a great way to go into the final campaign."

Meanwhile the Mayor was reading poems about the city, poems he had chosen by Hart Crane, Langston Hughes, Ogden Nash, e. e. cummings, Archibald MacLeish, and Stephen Vincent Benét. When he finished, Lindsay was immediately surrounded by well-wishers, shaking his hand, pledging support.

"You've got to keep up the fight," said a young black woman who stepped in front of the Mayor.

"I intend to." He smiled.

"I tell you"—Morgan was at my side—"this thing has really been a shock to a lot of people. Now they really know what's at stake."

I followed the Mayor out of the park and into Forty-first Street, where his car was waiting. He sat in front with a detective and I moved into the back seat with Morgan. Just as the car was starting, a tense man in his early thirties leaned into the front window and said to the Mayor, "Why don't you take your defeat like a man?"

The Mayor roared with laughter as the car moved away. "Now how are you supposed to answer that?"

Seconds later, we were stopped by a red light. Another citizen recognized the Mayor, came over, and said, "I sent you some material on low blood sugar. You ought to look at it. This is a serious problem. It has a lot to do with delinquency in the ghettos."

The Mayor looked puzzled, and then smiled. "Oh, I thought you were saying that *I* had low blood sugar."

When the car was in motion again, I asked the Mayor how he had taken the first political defeat of his career.

"It's curious," he said. "I was more detached about this election than any other I've been in. I'm getting that way more and more about politics. You've got to be scientific and look at things more objectively." He was now smiling slightly, and I suspected a put-on.

"But if you stay detached, how are you going to infuse any passion into the campaign?"

He laughed. "I expect I'll get enough blood running in me so there'll be enough passion."

Earlier that day, I told Lindsay, Paul O'Dwyer, a leading liberal Democrat, had said to me that he might be disposed to support the Mayor in November provided the Mayor fully realized that his primary defeat had actually liberated him. "I'll probably do it anyway," O'Dwyer had gone on, "because the alternatives to Lindsay are too dangerous to the city. But he ought to realize that he's free now of the biggest hindrance to his own development—the Republican Party, or at least the most reactionary wing of it."

"Well," the Mayor said after a pause, "I never felt I

had any obligations to that wing. Look, I don't take the position that I'm abandoning the Republican Party. Sure, we're forming this new party to get another line on the ballot, and I can't predict how durable that coalition will be— whether it'll last beyond this election. If it has a sizable vote in November, it may carry a message that will be significant in the future. But I'm still an enrolled Republican and I intend to stay that way although the city administration will continue to be a Fusion one. And when the election is over, I hope to bring the Republican Party back into the progressive channels in which it ought to be."

I asked Lindsay's reaction to the theory that his first political defeat had brought him down to a more human scale and would thereby make him more attractive to the electorate.

The Mayor was wryly amused. "It's an interesting theory, but when you get into a battle, you're usually in it to win. I'm not going to pretend I didn't want to win the primary. For a Republican who is a Fusion candidate in New York, it's best to keep all the marbles you can. It's difficult to win in a city that is so strongly Democratic. *Very* difficult."

"But now that you *have* lost the primary," I asked, "how can you possibly expect to turn the Republican Party here into the channels in which you want it to go?"

"By winning," Lindsay said instantly. "The party is still reacting to a different way of doing things in this city. My job as mayor has been to challenge people, including Republicans. Shake them up, change things. And no established groups like that. They'll always fight you unless you lie down and play dead. Okay, now I've lost a round, but I've hardly given up."

"Do you agree with those who feel that the odds now are actually in your favor for November because the lines are so clearly drawn?"

The Mayor shrugged. "Who knows? It depends on so many factors. It depends on how people behave in the city during the summer and in the fall. I would think the outcome will be uncertain until the very end. I felt that way before the primary; I feel that way now."

"Did you ever seriously think of not running for re-election?" I asked. "It seemed to me your mind was made up all along."

"No," the Mayor said, "it wasn't. While deciding, I was listening to a wide spectrum of opinion, and if the weight of that opinion had come down strongly against my running again, I might well have taken that route."

"Even if that meant leaving unfinished so much of what you've started?"

"Yes," Lindsay answered, "and I'll tell you why. For everyone involved, a campaign in a city like this is a killer. It's murderous in terms of energy, time, money—and nervous systems. And you can't go into it alone. I had to find out—and it's a hard thing to do—if there were enough people I respected who were committed to go through all of that with me. Then I had to decide if it was worth putting them through that ordeal. Well, I came to the conclusion that there are enough people willing to go through the meat-grinder with me. And once I did decide to run, there were no longer any doubts. Now, the way it's worked out, with Marchi and Procaccino on the other side, I'm glad I'm in it. This city has got to be kept moving into change. It has to be guided. No city—not this one, nor any other—can survive unless it is willing to face up to hard reality, and do something about it."

By now, we were crossing Lexington Avenue on the upper East Side. "Will you look at what came out of that taxi?" the Mayor said.

A young lady, with long black hair and an admirable figure, was crossing the street. "What are we doing here, talking politics?" the Mayor said, laughing. The car moved on toward Gracie Mansion.

"Well"—the Mayor leaned back—"let us continue to proceed to find out what kind of a city this is."

A NOTE ON THE TYPE

THIS BOOK was set on the Linotype in Baskerville. The punches for this face were cut under the supervision of George W. Jones, the eminent English printer and the designer of Granjon and Estienne. Linotype Baskerville is a facsimile cutting from type cast from the original matrices of a face designed by John Baskerville, a writing master of Birmingham, for his own private press. The original face was the forerunner of the "modern" group of type faces, known today as Scotch, Bodoni, etc. After his death in 1775, Baskerville's punches and matrices were sold in France and were used to produce the sumptuous Kehl edition of Voltaire's works.

This book was composed, printed, and bound by The Colonial Press Inc., Clinton, Mass. Typography and binding design by Anthea Lingeman.